Spurgeon's Sermons

on

LEVITICUS

(Sermons on the Whole Bible)

Charles H. Spurgeon

BIBLIOGRAPHIC INFORMATION

Charles H. Spurgeon (1834–1892), affectionately known by many as "the Prince of Preachers," addressed more than 10 million people during his ministry, baptized thousands of converts, and wrote so extensively and persuasively that his sermons have sold more than 50 million copies worldwide. Spurgeon's sermons were initially published in 1855 in a multi-volume series known as *The New Park Street Pulpit.*

an Ichthus Publications *edition*

CONTENTS

1 Putting the Hand upon the Head of the Sacrifice ❃ *Leviticus 1:4-5 //* 5

2 Slaying the Sacrifice ❃ *Leviticus 1:5 //* 26

3 Salt or Sacrifice ❃ *Leviticus 2:13 //* 46

4 The Sin Offering ❃ *Leviticus 4:3 //* 59

5 The Sprinkling of the Blood of the Sacrifice ❃ *Leviticus 4:6 //* 79

6 Blood Even on the Golden Altar ❃ *Leviticus 4:7 //* 99

7 The Sin Offering for the Common People ❃ *Leviticus 4:27-31 //* 120

8 Laying the Hand on the Sacrifice ❃ *Leviticus 4:29 //* 140

9 Sins of Ignorance ❃ *Leviticus 5:17-18 //* 156

10 The Clean and the Unclean ❃ *Leviticus 11:2-3 //* 177

11 The Cleansing of the Leper ❃ *Leviticus 13:12-13 //* 196

12 The Annual Atonement ❃ *Leviticus 16:30 //* 215

13 The Day of Atonement ❃ *Leviticus 16:34 //* 234

14 The Day of Atonement ❃ *Leviticus 16:34 //* 252

15 A Plain Man's Sermon ❃ *Leviticus 22:21 //* 267

1

Putting the Hand upon the
Head of the Sacrifice

"And he shall put his hand upon the head of the burnt offering; and it shall be accepted for him to make atonement for him. And he shall kill the bullock before the LORD." (Leviticus 1:4-5)

N O DOUBT THERE ARE CLEAR distinctions in the teaching of the burnt offering, the meat offering, the peace offering and the sin offering. In those various sacrifices we have views of our Lord's atoning work taken from different standpoints. On another occasion it will be profitable to note these delightful lessons and lay them to heart, but at this time I am not about to enter into such matters. These instructive distinctions are the special property of those who by reason of years have had their senses exercised and, therefore, can discern not only the great work of our Lord, but the details of it. I am not sufficiently strong in mind at this time to bring forth "butter in a lordly dish" for men of robust constitution, but I must be content to serve the little ones with a cup of milk. I cannot carry the great cluster from Eshcol and, therefore, I will bring you a few grapes in my trembling hands.

I desire to preach, this morning, so that I may fulfill the prayer of a little boy who, one Saturday evening before he went to bed, said in his prayers, "Lord, grant that our minister may say something tomorrow that I may understand." I am very sorry that such a prayer should ever be necessary, but I am afraid it is not only necessary for children, but sometimes for grownup people to pray, "Lord, help our minister to say something that we can understand and that is worth understanding." Some of my Brothers appear to dwell on high Olympus among the clouds—it were better if they lived on Calvary. Little dew comes from the dark mountains of intellectual dreaminess—far more refreshing drops are found upon Mount Hermon of the Gospel!

I feel like Dr. Guthrie when he desired those around him to sing him a child's hymn—I would like to be a little child in preaching to you. Simple things are the most sublime and, to a sick man, the most sweet. I wish to be plain as a pike- staff in setting forth the way of expiation by the death of Jesus. I also have a reason for preaching foundation Truth of God today which, to myself is serious, though you may smile at it. It is this—if I have but few shots to fire, I should like each time to hit the center of the target, that is to say, if I may only speak to you once, today, after having been laid aside for three weeks, I desire to speak only upon topics which touch the vitals of godliness. I would plunge into the heart of the matter and deal with the essence and soul of true religion!

There are some things that may be or may not be and yet no great evil will come either way. But there are other things that must be, or all goes wrong! Of these "must-be's" I would now speak. Some things are important for the well-being of Christians, but certain other things are absolutely essential to the very being of Christians—and it is upon these urgent necessaries that I shall now speak—namely, concerning the precious blood of the Lord Jesus Christ and our faith in it. These two things are of the highest importance and they cannot too often be brought before our minds. Two matters were essential in the sacrifices of the Ceremonial Law and you have them both in our text—"He shall put his hand upon the head of the burnt offering," and, "he shall kill the bullock before the Lord." The appropriation by the offerer and the death of the offering are most fitly joined together and must, neither of them, be overlooked. For our immediate objective, there was no need to have taken our present text, for there are many others of the same effect. Look at Leviticus 3:2, "And he shall lay his hand upon the head of his offering, and kill it at the door of the tabernacle." Glance at the 8th verse: "And he shall lay his hand upon the head of his offering, and kill it before the tabernacle." Turn to chapter 4, verse 4, the second clause of the verse: "He shall lay his hand upon the bullock's head, and kill the bullock before the Lord."

Also at the 15th verse: "And the elders of the congregation shall lay their hands upon the head of the bullock before the Lord: and the bullock shall be killed before the Lord." To the same effect is the 24th verse: "And he shall lay his hand upon the head of the goat, and kill it in the place where they kill the burnt offering." All through the Book of Leviticus, the laying on of the hand and the killing of the victim are mentioned in immediate connection. These are, each of them, so important and so full of meaning that we must have a sermon upon each of them. Let us, on the present occasion, look at *the leading act of the offerer*—"He shall lay his hand upon the head of the burnt offering." All that goes before is important, but this is the real sacrificial act so far as the offerer is concerned.

Before he reached this point, the person who presented the offering had to make a selection of the animal to be brought before the Lord. It must be of a certain age and it must be without blemish—and for this latter reason a careful examination had to be made—for the Lord would not accept a sacrifice that was lame, or broken, or bruised, or deficient in any of its parts or in any way blemished. He required an offering "without spot." Now I invite all those who seek reconciliation with God to look about them and consider whether the Lord Jesus Christ is such an atoning Sacrifice as they need and as God will accept.

If you know of any other atonement for sin, examine it well, and I am persuaded that you will find many a fault and flaw in it. But concerning the Lamb of God, I have no question—you may search, but you shall find no blemish in Him. If there were any fault in Him, either of excess or deficiency, you might well refuse Him! But since there is nothing of the kind, I pray you joyfully accept Him at once. Come, now, and look at the Lord Jesus Christ—both at His Godhead and His Manhood; at His life and His death, His acts and His sufferings—and see if there is any iniquity in Him. He knew no sin—He had no acquaintance or dealing with it! "He was holy, harmless, undefiled."

After you have well examined His blessed Person and His spotless Character, if you arrive at the conclusion that He is a fit and acceptable Sacrifice for you to present before the Lord, then I long that you may take the much more practical step and accept the Lord Jesus to be your Representative, your Sin Offering, your Burnt Offering, your Substitute and your Sacrifice. I long that every unsaved person here may, at once, receive the Lord Jesus as his Atonement, for this is the main part of that which the sinner must do in order to be cleansed from sin and accepted by God! Happily you have not to find a sacrifice as the Jew had to supply a bullock—God has provided Himself with a perfect Sacrifice! That which you have to bring to God, God first brings to you!

Happily, there is no need for you to repeat the examination through which the Lord Jesus passed both at the hands of men, of devils and of God, when He was tested and tried and examined, and even the Prince of this world found nothing of his own in Him! You have to attend to this one thing, namely, the laying of your hands upon the Sacrifice provided for you. To the Jew it was a sacrifice to be slain. To you it is a sacrifice already offered—and this you are to accept and recognize as your own. It is not a hard duty! You sang of it just now—

> "My faith does lay her hand
> On that dear head of Yours.
> While like a penitent I stand,
> And there confess my sin."

If you have already attended to this, do so again this morning! If you have never done so, I pray from my inmost soul that you may immediately do that which was meant by laying the hand upon the victim's head.

I. To our work, then, at once. What did that mean? It meant four things and the first was,

Confession. He that laid his hand upon the head of the offering made confession of sin. I do not care what offering it was that was brought by a believing Israelite—there was always a mention of sin in it, either implied or expressed. "But," says one, "the burnt offering was a sweet-savor offering! How could there be any reference to iniquity therein?" I know that the burnt offering was a sacrifice of sweet smell and that it sets forth our Lord as accepted of the Father. But let me ask you, why did the Israelite bring a sweet-savor offering? It was because he felt that in and of himself, he was not a sweet savor unto God, for if he had been so, he would not have needed to have brought another sweet savor!

When I accept the Lord Jesus to be my righteousness, it is a confession of sin, for I should not need His righteousness if I had any of my own. The very fact of presenting a sacrifice at all contains within it a confession of the need of a sacrifice, which is the confession of personal shortcomings and a need of personal acceptableness. This is true of the burnt offering, but in other sacrifices—especially in the trespass offering—where the hands were laid upon the victim's head, the offerer was charged to "confess that he has sinned in that thing" wherein he had trespassed. There was a detailed confession of sin joined with the laying on of hands in the case of the scapegoat. Let us read the passage in Leviticus 16:21, "And Aaron shall lay both his hands upon the head of the live goat and confess over him all the iniquities of the children of Israel, and all their transgressions in all their sins, putting them upon the head of the goat, and shall send him away by the hand of a fit man into the wilderness."

See, then, that if you would have Him to be your Atonement, whom God has appointed to be His Sacrifice, you must come to Him confessing your sin! Your touch of Jesus must be the touch of one who is consciously guilty. He belongs not to you unless you are a sinner. Ah, Lord, confession of sin is no hard duty to some of us, for we can do no other than acknowledge and bemoan our guilt! Here we stand before You, self-condemned—and with aching hearts we each one cry, "Have mercy upon me, O God, according to Your loving kindness." Do any of you refuse to make confession of guilt? Then, do not think it hard if, since according to your own proud notions you are not sinners, the Lord should provide you no Savior! Should medicine be prepared for those who are not sick? Why should the righteous be invited to partake of pardon? Why should a righteousness be provided for the innocent?

You are the rich and you are sent away empty—the hungry shall be filled with good things. Go away, you that say, "I am clean; I am not defiled." I tell you that you have no part in the great Sacrifice for sin! For the blackest sinner out of Hell that will confess his sin, there is mercy—but there is none for you—your pride excludes you from pity! It bars the gate of hope against you. You sprinkle the blood of the lamb upon the threshold and trample on it in your arrogant self-conceit by making yourself out to have no need of its cleansing power! O self-righteous man, you make God out to be a fool since He gave His only-begotten Son to die, when, according to you there was no necessity for His death! In your case, at any rate, there is no need of a sacrifice by blood, no need of an Atonement through the Son of God laying down His life for men. By your refusal to trust in the Lord Jesus you charge God with folly and, therefore, into His holy place, where His glory shines forth in its excellence, you can never come!

Many of us come most readily, at this time, and lay our hand upon the head of the appointed Sacrifice, even our Lord Jesus Christ, because we have sin to confess and we feel that we need a Savior, even a Savior for the guilty! We are unworthy and undeserving. We dare not say otherwise! The stones of the street would cry out against us if we should say that we have no sin! The beams of every chamber in our house would upbraid us if we dared to assert that we are without transgressions! Our true place is that of sinners—we plead guilty to the dread indictment of God's holy Law and, therefore, we are glad to lay our hand upon the head of the sinner's Savior and Sacrifice.

In this act there was also a confession of self-impotence. The Believer who brought the bullock did as good as say, "I cannot, of myself, keep the Law of God, or make atonement for my past breaches of the Commandments. Neither can I hope, through future obedience, to become acceptable with God. Therefore I bring this sacrifice because I, myself, cannot become acceptable without it." This is a Truth of God which you and I must also confess if we would be partakers of Christ and become "accepted in the Beloved." Oh, Brothers and Sisters, what can we do without Christ? I like what was said by a child in Sunday school, when the teacher said, "You have been reading that Christ is precious: what does that mean?" The children were quiet a little while, till, at last, one boy replied, "Father said the other day that Mother was precious, for 'whatever would we do without her?'"

This is a capital explanation of the word, "precious." You and I can truly say of the Lord Jesus Christ that He is precious to us, for what would we do, what could we do without Him? We come and take Him, now, to be ours because if He is not ours, we are utterly undone! I, for one, am lost forever if Jesus cannot save. There is, in us, no merit and no strength—but in the Lord Jesus Christ we find both righteousness and strength—and we accept Him, this day, for that reason. Because we are so deeply conscious of our own self-impotence, we lean hard upon His All-Sufficiency. If you could read the text in the Hebrew, you would find it runs thus—"He shall put his hand upon the head of the burnt offering, and it shall be accepted for him to make a cover for him"—to make atonement for him. The word is *copher* in the Hebrew—a cover.

Why, then, do we hide behind the Lord Jesus? Because we feel our need of something to cover us and to act is an interposition between us and the righteous Judge of all the earth! If the Holy One of Israel shall look upon us as we are, He would be displeased. But when He sees us in Christ Jesus, He is well pleased for His Righteousness' sake. When the Lord looks this way, we hide behind the veil, and the eyes of the Lord behold the exceeding glories of the veil, to wit, the Person of His own dear Son! And He is so pleased with the cover that He refuses to remember the defilement and deformity of those whom it covers! God will never strike a soul through the veil of His Son's Sacrifice. He accepts us because He cannot but accept His Son, who has become our covering!

With regard to God, when I am a conscious sinner, I long to hide away from Him and lo, the Lord Jesus is our shield and hiding place—the cover, the Sacred Atonement within which we conceal ourselves from Justice. Even the all-seeing eyes of God see no sin in a sinner that is hidden in Christ! Oh, what a blessing it is, dear Friends, when our sense of self-impotence is so great that we have no desire to make a show of ourselves, but, on the contrary, long to be out of sight and, therefore, we enter into Christ to be hidden in Him, covered in the Sacrifice which God has prepared! That is the second confession, and thus we have a confession of sin and of need of covering.

There was a further confession of the desert of punishment. When a man brought his bullock, or his goat, or his lamb, he put his hand on it and as he knew that the poor creature must die, he thus acknowledged that he, himself, deserved death. The victim fell in the dust, struggling, bleeding, dying. The offerer confessed that this was what he deserved. He acknowledged that death from the Almighty hand was due to him. And oh, when a man comes to that—when he acknowledges that God will be justified when He speaks in anger, and clear when He judges and pronounces sentence in justice—when he confesses that he cannot deliver himself, but has so sinned as to deserve to be cursed of God and judged to feel the horrors of the second death, then is he brought into a condition in which the great Sacrifice will be precious to him! Then will he lean hard upon Christ and, with broken heart, acknowledge that the chastisement which fell upon Jesus was such as he deserved and he will be amazed that he has not been called upon to bear it!

For my own part, I deserve eternal damnation, but I trust in the Lord Jesus and believe that He was punished in my place. "The chastisement of our peace was upon Him, and with His stripes we are healed." If you can thus confess sin and bare your neck to punishment—and then lay hold upon the Lord Jesus—you are a saved man! Can your heart truly confess, "I am guilty. I cannot save myself. I deserve to be cast into the deepest Hell, but I now take Jesus to stand in my place?" Then be of good cheer, "Your faith has saved you: go in peace!" May the Spirit of God bless this first point!

II. Secondly, the laying on of hands meant *acceptance*. The offerer, by laying his hand upon the victim's head, signified that he acknowledged the offering to be for himself. He accepted, first of all, the principle and the plan. Far too many kick against the idea of our being saved by substitution or representation. Why do they rebel against it? For my part, if God will but graciously save me in any way, I will be far enough from raising any objection! Why should I complain of that which is to deliver me from destruction? If the Lord does not object to the way, why should I? Moreover, as to this salvation by the merit of another, I remember that my first ruin did not come by myself.

I am not speaking to excuse my personal sin, but yet it is true that I was ruined before I committed any actual sin by the disobedience of the first father of the race who was my representative. How this was just, I do not know, but I am sure it must be right, or God would not so reveal it. In Adam we fell—"By one man's disobedience many were made sinners" (Rom. 5:19). If, then, the Fall began by the sin of another, why should not our rising be caused by the righteousness and the atonement of another? What says the Apostle? "For if through the offense of one, many are dead, much more the Grace of God, and the gift by Grace, which is by one Man, Jesus Christ, has abounded unto many."

At any rate, it is not for you and for me to raise objections against ourselves, but to feel that if God sees that this is a proper way of salvation, He knows best and we cheerfully accept what He approves! Who is there among you that will not do so? God grant that no one may hold out against a method of Grace so simple, so sure, so available! But then, remember. After you have accepted the plan and the way, you must not stop there, but you must go on to accept the Sacred Person whom God provides. It would have been a very foolish thing if the offerer had stood at the altar and said, "Good Lord, I accept the plan of sacrifice—be it burnt offering or sin offering—I agree thereto." He did much more than that! He accepted that very bullock as his offering and, in token thereof, placed his hand upon it!

I pray you beware of resting satisfied with understanding and approving the plan of salvation. I heard of one who anxiously desired to be the means of the conversion of a young man and one said to him, "You may go to him and talk to him, but you will get him no further, for he is exceedingly well acquainted with the plan of salvation." When the friend began to speak with the young man, he received for an answer, "I am much obliged to you, but I do not know that you can tell me much, for I have long known and admired the plan of salvation by the Substitutionary Sacrifice of Christ." Alas, he was resting in the plan, but he had not believed in the Person! The plan of salvation is most blessed, but it can avail us nothing unless we believe! What is the comfort of a plan of a house if you do not enter the house, itself? What is the good of a plan of clothing if you have not a rag to cover you?

Have you never heard of the Arab chief at Cairo who was very ill and went to the missionary, and the missionary said he could give him a prescription? He did so and a week later, he found the Arab none the better. "Did you take my prescription?" he asked. "Yes, I ate every morsel of the paper." He dreamed that he was going to be cured by the plan of the medicine! He should have gone to the chemist and had the prescription filled—and then it might have worked him some good. So is it with salvation—it is not the plan—it is the carrying out of that plan by the Lord Jesus in His death on our behalf! The offerer laid his hands, literally, upon the bullock. He found something substantial there, something which he could handle and touch. Even so do we lean upon the real and true work of Jesus, the most substantial thing under Heaven!

Brothers and Sisters, we come to the Lord Jesus by faith and say, "God has provided an Atonement, here, and I accept it. I believe it to be a fact accomplished on the Cross that sin was put away by Christ and, therefore, I rest on Him." Yes, you must get beyond the acceptance of plans and doctrines to a resting in the Divine Person and finished work of the blessed Lord Jesus Christ—and a casting of yourself entirely upon Him.

III. But thirdly, this laying of the hand upon the sacrifice meant not only acceptance, but also *transference*. The offerer had confessed his sin and had accepted the victim presented to be his sacrifice and now he mentally realizes that his guilt is, by Divine appointment, to pass over from himself to the sacrifice. Of course this was only done in type and figure at the door of the Tabernacle. But in our case, the Lord Jesus Christ, as a matter of literal fact, has borne the sin of His people. "The Lord has made to meet on Him the iniquity of us all." "Who His own self bore our sins in His own body on the tree." "Christ was once offered to bear the sins of many."

But do we, by faith, pass our sins from ourselves to Christ? I answer, No. In some senses, no. But by faith he that accepts Christ as his Savior agrees with what the Lord did ages ago, for we read in the Book of Isaiah the Prophet, "The Lord has laid on Him the iniquity of us all." That was Jehovah's own act in the ages past—and it was complete when Jesus stood as the great Sin-Bearer and redeemed us from the curse of the Law, being made a curse for us. All the transgressions of His people were laid on Him when He poured out His soul unto death and, "was numbered with the transgressors, and bore the sin of many."

Then and there He expiated all the guilt of all His people, for He, "finished transgression, made an end of sin and brought in everlasting righteousness." By His death He cast the whole tremendous load of human guilt, which was laid upon Him, into the depth of the sea, never to be found again! When we believe in Him, we agree to what the Lord has done and we may sing—

> "I lay my sins on Jesus
> The spotless Lamb of God.
> He bears them all and frees us
> From the accursed load."

There are two ruling religions around us in this day, and they mainly differ in tense. The general religion of mankind is *"do,"* but the religion of a true Christian is, *"done."* "It is finished" is the Believer's conquering word! Christ has made Atonement and we accept it as done. So in that respect we lay our sins on Jesus, the holy Lamb of God, because we set our humble seal to that grand transaction which was the confirming of the Covenant of old. The laying of the hand upon the head of the sacrifice meant a transference of guilt to the victim and, furthermore, a confidence in the efficacy of the sacrifice then and there presented.

The believing Jew said, "This bullock represents to me the sacrifice which God has provided and I rejoice in it because it is the symbol of a sacrifice which does, in very deed, take away sin." Brothers and Sisters, there are a great number of people who believe in the Lord Jesus Christ, after a fashion, but it is not in deed and in truth, for they do not believe in the actual pardon of their own sin! They hope that they may one day be forgiven, but they have no confidence that the Lord Jesus has already put away their sin by His death. "I am a great sinner," says one, "therefore, I cannot be saved." Man alive, did Christ die for those who are not sinners?! What was the need of a Savior except for sinners? Has Jesus actually borne sin, or has He not? If He has borne our sin, it is gone! If He has not borne it, our sin will never depart.

What does the Scripture say? "He has made Him to be sin for us, who knew no sin; that we might be made the righteousness of God in Him." If, then, Christ took the sinner's sin, it remains not upon the sinner that believes! Assuredly, you, my Hearer, if you are a Believer, cannot have sin if Jesus has taken it away! You are made clean in the sight of God because your uncleanness has been washed away in the blood of the Great Sacrifice! Can't you see this way of salvation? If you see it, will you not accept it now? Do you not already feel a joy springing up within your soul that there should be such a blessed way of deliverance?

At any rate, I tell you where I stand today—I stand guilty and without a hope in anything I have ever done or ever hope to do! But I believe that the Lord Jesus Christ bore my sin in His own body on the Cross and I am, at this moment, putting my hands on Him in the sense in which the Hebrew has it, leaning all my weight upon Him! If Jesus cannot save me, I must be damned, for I cannot help Him, neither can I see anyone else who can do so much as a hand's turn in that direction! If there is not virtue enough in the blood of Jesus to cleanse me from all sin, then I must die in my sins! And if there is not sufficient merit in His Righteousness to save me apart from any righteousness of my own, then I am a castaway, a spirit shipwrecked on the ironbound coast of despair! But I have no fears, for I know whom I have believed, and I am persuaded that He is able to keep that which I have committed unto Him until that day!

Now I pray you, dear people of God, to lean on Jesus and keep on leaning on Him. Oh, that you who as yet do not know Jesus may be brought to touch Him by faith and to lean upon Him by full reliance! In times of sharp pain, or great depression of spirit, or in seasons when death is near, you are forced to look around you to see where your foundation is, and what it is and, believe me, there is no groundwork that can bear the weight of a guilty conscience and a trembling, tortured body, except this foundation—"the precious blood of Christ cleanses us from all sin." Jesus is the Atonement—He is the Covering—the Refuge! In fact, He is our All in All!

IV. Once more, this laying of the hand upon the head of the victim meant *identification*. The worshipper who laid his hand on the bullock said, "Be pleased, O great Lord, to identify me with this bullock, and this bullock with me. There has been a transferring of my sin, now I beseech You let me be judged as being in the victim, and represented thereby." Now consider that which happened to the sacrifice. The knife was unsheathed and the victim was slain! He was not merely bound, but killed—and the man stood there and said, "That is me, that is the fate which I deserve." The poor creature struggled, it wallowed in the sand in its dying agonies—and if the worshipper was a right-minded person and not a mere formalist—he stood with tears in his eyes and felt in his heart, "That death is mine."

I beseech you, when you think of our blessed Lord, to identify yourselves with Him! See the bloody sweat trickling down His face? That is for you. He groans, He cries! For you. Your sins deserved that you should sweat great drops of blood, but Jesus sweats, instead. The Lord is taken prisoner and scourged. Look how the red streams of gore flow down those blessed shoulders! He bears the chastisement of our peace. He is nailed to the Cross and we are crucified with Him. By-and-by He dies. And we die in Him—"We thus judge that if One died for all, then all died." Believer, you died there in Christ! When your Substitute rendered to the Law of God, the penalty which it demanded, you virtually rendered it! "The soul that sins, it shall die," and you have died, Believer! You have paid the debt in the Person of the Lord Jesus Christ whom, by the laying on of your hands, you have accepted to be your Substitute!

You know that story—it is a capital one, well worth telling a thousand times! In the great French War a person was drawn for a conscript but as he could not leave his family, he paid a very heavy sum for a substitute. That substitute went to the war and was killed. After a time, Napoleon called out the rest of the conscription and the man was summoned because he had been formerly drawn, but he refused to serve. He said, "No, by my substitute I have served, and I am dead and buried— I cannot be made to serve again." It is said that the question was carried up to the highest court and laid before the Emperor, himself, and the Emperor decided that the man's claim of exemption was a just one. He had fulfilled the conscription by a substitute and that substitute had served for life. Therefore he could not be called upon to do more and, therefore, the person for whom he was the substitute could not further be summoned under that conscription.

This sets forth our joy and glory! We are identified with Christ; we are crucified with Him; buried with Him and in Him raised to newness of life! "I am crucified with Christ, nevertheless I live." "You are dead, and your life is hid with Christ in God." It ought to be remembered that we were identified with Christ in His passing under the wrath of God as a Sin Offering. If you read in this Book, you will find that the sin offering was burnt outside the camp as an unclean thing—and so you and I were put outside the camp long years ago as an unclean thing! That is over, now, and we are, at this hour, no more cast out from the sight of God than Jesus is! The burnt offering was consumed upon the altar as a sweet savor unto God and in this, also, we are identified with Christ. We are now a sweet savor unto God in Christ Jesus our Lord. We are accepted in the Beloved. We are joined unto the Lord and there is no separating our interests from His, nor His from ours.

Who shall separate us from the Christ of God forever and ever? That is what the laying on of hands upon the beast meant. I trust, dear Friends, you have known all this for years and, if not, may you know it now. If the Lord will enable me, I intend to enter into the second part of my text next Lord's-Day morning, and for this time it will suffice for me to drive this one nail home. Oh, that the Spirit of God would fasten it in a sure place in your hearts! My soul's yearning desire is that each one of you may come, at once, and lay your hands on Christ by confession, acceptance, transference and identification. Nothing short of such an act will suffice to give you salvation!

Now, suppose that the Jew, who went up to the tabernacle and to the altar, when he got there, had been content to talk about the sacrifice without personally placing his hand on it? To talk of it would be a very proper thing to do, but suppose that he had spent all his time in merely discoursing about the plan of a sacrifice, the providing of a substitute, the shedding of blood, the clearance of the sinner through sacrificial death? It would have been a delightful theme, but what would have come of it? Suppose he had talked on and on and had gone back home without joining in the offering? He would have found no ease to his conscience—he would, in fact, have done nothing by going to the house of the Lord! I am afraid that this is what many of you have done so far. You are pleased to hear the Gospel. You take pleasure in the Doctrine of Substitution and you know true doctrine from the current falsehoods of the hour—for all of which I am very glad—but yet you are not saved because you have not taken Christ to be your own Savior!

You are like persons who might say, "We are hungry and we admit that bread is a very proper food for men, besides which we know what sort of food makes bone, and what makes muscle, and what makes flesh." They keep on talking all day long about the various qualities of food—do they feel refreshed? No. Is their hunger gone? No! I should suppose that if they are at all healthy, their appetite is increased, and the more they talk about food the more hungry they become. Why, some of you here have been talking about the Bread of Heaven for years—and yet I am afraid you are no more hungry than you used to be! Go beyond talking about Christ and learn to feed upon Christ! Come, now, let us have done with talk and come to deeds of faith. Lay hold on Jesus, who is set before you in the Gospel! Otherwise, Friend, I fear you will perish in the midst of plenty, and die unpardoned, with mercy at your gate.

Suppose, again, that the Israelite, instead of talking with his friends, had thought it wise to consult with one of the priests. "Might I speak with you, Sir, a little? Have you a little room somewhere at the back where you could talk with me and pray with me?" "Yes," says the priest, "what ails you?" "My sin lies heavy upon me." The priest replies, "You know that there is a sacrifice for sin—a sin offering lies at the door and God will accept it at your hands." But he says, "I beg you to explain this matter more fully to me." The priest answers, "I will explain it as well as I can, but the whole of my explanation will end in this one thing—bring a sacrifice and over its head confess your sin—and let an atonement be made. The sin offering is what God has ordained and, therefore, God will receive it. Attend to His ordinance and live. There is no other way. Fetch your offering. I will kill it for you and lay it on the altar and present it to God."

Do you say to him, "I will call again tomorrow, and have a little more talk with you"? Do you again and again cry, "Tomorrow"? Do you go again and again into the Inquiry Room? O Sir, what will become of you? You will perish in your sin, for God has not appointed salvation by Inquiry Rooms and talks with ministers, but by your laying your own hand upon the Sacrifice which He has appointed! If you will have Christ, you shall be saved! If you will not have Him, you must perish! All the talking to you in the world cannot help you one jot if you refuse your Savior! Sitting in your pew this morning, without speaking to me or any living man or woman, I exhort you to believe in Jesus! Stretch out your withered hand, God helping you, and lay it on the head of Christ, and say, "I believe in the merit of His precious blood. I look to the Lamb of God that takes away the sin of the world." Why, Man, you are saved as sure as you are alive, for he that lays the hand of faith upon this Sacrifice is saved thereby!

But I see another Israelite and he stands by his offering and begins to weep and groan, and bewail himself. I am not sorry to see him weep, for I trust he is sincerely confessing his guilt. But why does he not place his hand on the sacrifice? He cries and he sighs, for he is such a sinner! But he does not touch the offering. The victim is presented and, in order that it may be of any use to him, he must lay his hand upon it. But this vital act he neglects and even refuses to perform. "Ah," he says, "I am in such trouble, I am in such deep distress," and he begins explaining a difficulty. You hunt that difficulty down, but there he stands, still groaning and moaning, and producing another difficulty and yet another, world without end! The sacrifice is slain, but he has no part in it, for he has not laid his hand upon it—and he goes away with all the burden of his guilt upon him, though the sacrificial blood has reddened the ground on which he stood.

That is what some of you do. You go about lamenting your sin, when your chief lament should be that you have not believed on the Son of God! If you looked to Jesus, you might dry your eyes and bid all hopeless sorrows cease, for He gives remission of sins to all penitents. Your tears can never remove your sins—tears, though flowing like a river—can never wash away the stain of guilt. Your faith must lay her hand on the head of the Lord's Sacrifice, for there and there, only is there hope for the guilty!

"But surely," says one, "that cannot be everything." I tell you it is so much everything that—

> "Could tears forever flow,
>   Could your zeal no respite know,
>   All for sin could not atone,

Christ must save, and Christ, alone."

Jesus will only save those who accept Him and desire to be identified with Him. I would to God that you would delay no longer, but come at once and freely accept what God has provided! I know the devil will tempt you to look for this and to look for that, but I pray you look at nothing but the Sacrifice that is before you. Lean on Jesus with all your weight! Observe that the Israelite had to put his hand upon a victim which was not slain as yet, but was killed afterwards. This was to remind him that the Messiah was not yet come. But you, Beloved, have to trust in a Christ who has come, who has lived, who has died, who has finished the work of salvation, who has gone up into Glory and who always lives to make intercession for transgressors! Will you trust Him or will you not?

I cannot waste words. I must come to the point. John Bunyan says that one Sunday when he was playing the game of tip-cat on Elstow Green, as he was about to strike the cat with the stick, he seemed to hear a voice saying to him, "Will you leave your sins and go to Heaven, or will you keep your sins and go to Hell?" This morning the voice from Heaven sounds forth this question—Will you trust in Christ and go to Heaven, or will you keep apart from Him and go to Hell?—for there you must go unless Jesus becomes your Mediator and your atoning Sacrifice. Will you have Christ or not?

I hear you say, "But"—O that I could thrust your "buts" aside! Will you have Christ or not? "Oh, but"—No, your "buts" ought to be thrown into limbo, for I fear they will be your ruin. Will you trust Christ or not? If your answer is, "I trust Him with all my heart," then you are saved! I say not you shall be saved, but you are saved! "He that believes in Him has everlasting life." You know how our dear friend, Mr. Hill, put it, the other night, at the Prayer Meeting? "He that believes in Him has everlasting life." "H-A-S"—that spells—"Got it." Very good spelling, too!

24

If you believe in the Lord Jesus Christ, you have eternal life in present possession! Go your way and sing for joy of heart, because the Lord has loved you! Mind you, keep on singing until you join the choristers before the eternal Throne of God!

May the Lord save every person that shall hear or read this sermon, for Jesus' sake! Amen.

2

Slaying the Sacrifice

"And he shall kill the bullock before the LORD." (Leviticus 1:5)

Y OU REMEMBER THAT LAST Lord's Day we spoke of two things vitally essential to a true sacrifice and the first upon which we then enlarged was the laying on of the hands of the offerer upon the victim, by which he accepted it as his sacrifice, and made a typical transfer of his sin from himself to the victim. Now, the second essential thing, of which we are to speak this morning, is this—that the victim, thus bearing the guilt of the offerer, must be killed—its blood must be shed before the Lord. Nothing short of its death by violence would render it an atonement for the offerer—"he shall kill the bullock."

You will find this order continually repeated whenever a sacrifice is spoken of. As I said on the last occasion, I feel great satisfaction, in this time of my weakness, in being permitted to speak to you about essential things. It was always a stigma upon the character of Caligula that he gathered his warriors, fitted out his ships and, when the people of Rome looked for some great addition to the empire by the vast naval expedition, he simply anchored his vessels near the beach and bade his legions advance upon the shore and gather shells and pebbles—and carry them home as trophies of their undisputed conquest. He trifled where he should have struggled. He spent time and labor upon matters of no importance and neglected the weighty business of his kingdom.

We shall not do so today—we have nothing to do with shells and stones! We have to do with matters worth more than gold or pearls— things essential to eternal life and vital to the salvation of the souls of men! Neither have I, this morning, a controversial topic upon which to debate before you. However important controversy may sometimes be, we are glad to be away from its strife and to consider a doctrine around which true Believers gather in hearty unity—a doctrine which must be taken for granted in the Christian Church! A doctrine which lies at the very root of the Truth of God and in the very heart of true religion!

Without controversy, great is this mystery of godliness, that Christ, manifest in the flesh, must die for sin, or otherwise sin cannot be put away. You remember what the Greek said when he heard an old philosopher with hoary head and gray beard disputing upon how to live. "Goodness!" he said, "if at his age he is disputing upon that subject, when will he be able to practice his conclusions should he arrive at one?" Truly, I may say to you to whom I have so long ministered—if we are forever to be learning and never coming to a knowledge of the Truth of God, what will become of us? If we are to have nothing but questionable matters laid before us, when shall the time come for the actual possession and enjoyment of the blessings of the Gospel?

At this hour my theme is such that I speak to you without diffidence or hesitation. In this case, "we believe and are sure." Concerning our Lord Jesus Christ, the great Sacrifice for sin, it was essential that He should die, for only through the blood which He shed on Calvary for human guilt can there be preached among men the remission of sins—

"What can wash away my stain?
    Nothing but the blood of Jesus!
What can make me whole again?
    Nothing but the blood of Jesus!
This is all my hope and peace—
    Nothing but the blood of Jesus!
This is all my righteousness—
    Nothing but the blood of Jesus!"

May the Holy Spirit lay home the blood of Atonement to our consciences at this time to the glory of God and our own peace!

I. Concerning the killing and slaying of the offering, our first point is that it was *absolutely essential*. The pouring out of the blood of the victim was of the very essence of the type. The death of Christ by blood-shedding was absolutely necessary to make Him an acceptable Sacrifice for sin. "It behooved Christ to suffer." He could only enter into the Presence of God with His own blood. He could not be the grain of wheat which brings forth much fruit unless He should die. Remember that although there were important matters about the victim, yet nothing would have mattered if it had not been slain.

The Israelite brought an unblemished bullock, but the fact of its being unblemished did not make it an atonement for sin. No doubt many faultless bullocks and lambs still fed in the plains of Sharon. If the most perfect animal had gone away from the altar, alive, it would have effected nothing whatever by way of atonement. It must be unblemished in order to be an offering at all, but still, its perfections did not make it a sacrifice until it was killed. No matter what could be said of that bullock—it may have been the most laborious animal throughout all Israel; it may have dragged the plow to and fro, or even drawn the wagon loaded with the harvest—but that was nothing to make it a sacrifice for sin. It must die and its blood must be sprinkled upon the altar, or else the offerer has brought no acceptable oblation. All its life and its labor would not satisfy.

Nor would it be enough to bring the bullock there and dedicate it to God. Some animals which had been dedicated to the Divine service were used in the drawing of the wagons which carried the sacred furniture through the wilderness, but they were not sacrifices, for all that, neither did they avail for the bearing away of sin. It was indispensably necessary that the bullock should be without blemish—it was necessary that it should be voluntarily dedicated to God—but if it had not been killed, there would have been no presentation of an offering according to the Divine Law, nor any easing of the conscience of the Israelite. And even so, Jesus must die—His perfect Nature, His arduous labor, His blameless life, His perfect consecration could avail us nothing without the shedding of His blood for many, for the remission of sin. So far from His death being a mere adjunct and conclusion of His life, it is the most important matter connected with Him! It stands in the fore- ground. It is the head and front of His redeeming work! We justly value Him for His example and for His living intercession—but in the business of Atonement, it is beyond all things necessary that we view Him as the Lamb slain!

Now notice that this was expressly declared by God in the Jewish Law book in express words. Kindly turn in this Book of Leviticus to the 17th chapter, and there read in the 11th verse, "For the life of the flesh is in the blood: and I have given it to you upon the altar to make an atonement for your souls; for it is the blood that makes an atonement for the soul." It is not the burning of the victim, it is not the flaying of it, nor the washing of it—it is the shedding of its blood—that is to say, the taking of its life, which makes it an atonement for sin. I need not quote another Old Testament text, because this is so completely to the point and so fully covers the whole of the ground. The atonement is not the animal itself, but the blood of the animal, which blood represents its life.

As to the entire Scriptures, they teem with statements of this Truth. I will only call to your recollection a few prominent passages, to collect them all would be impossible. When a child gathers flowers in the spring meadows when they are all golden with the kingcups, he fills his hands once, but he is almost persuaded to throw away what he has gathered that he may pluck yet more from the inexhaustible store around him! So do I feel that what I now bring before you might fitly be exchanged for another selection, yes, for many such, if time did not fail us. In the Old Testament, one of the most instructive types of redemption ever given is that of the Passover lamb. When God was about to smite Egypt He promised to spare His people—and in order to their safety He bade each family take a lamb, kill it and sprinkle the blood upon the lintel and the two side posts of their door.

Then they were to stay within the house till morning and the destroying angel would not touch so much as one of them. What is expressly said by God Himself about this passing-over? Hear the words and wonderingly drink in their teaching! "And when I see the blood, I will pass over you." There was never a fuller type of the redemption of Christ, I hardly think one so full, as that of the passing-over of Israel through the blood of the paschal lamb! But the essence of that passing-over is displayed to us in this sentence—"When I see the blood, I will pass over you." God's eyes resting upon the evidence of a life having been taken instead of the sinner's life, is the reason why He passes over the sinner so that he does not die!

When Isaiah, the great evangelical Prophet, spoke concerning Him upon whom the Lord laid our iniquity, he mentions His death as the main cause of His glorious reward! The last verse of the 53rd chapter of Isaiah is the culminating point of the whole, and it runs thus—"Therefore will I divide Him a portion with the great, and He shall divide the spoil with the strong; because He has poured out His soul unto death." It is a wonderful expression—it shows that Christ must die, or else He could not achieve the victory for us, nor share the spoil. He must pour out His Soul. He must relinquish life, must pour it out lavishly, as though He possessed much of it! He must make it flow like water gushing in a river from the smitten rock. This He must do voluntarily and without stint—"pouring out His soul unto death"—till none remained and the bottom of the vessel was reached in death.

It is clear that if He had not done this, He had done nothing, for the victory comes to Him because of this—not because He kept His soul free from spot, not because He preached righteousness in the great congregation! Not because of anything else which Jesus did was He rewarded—the victorious deed was that, "He poured out His soul unto death." This is the verdict, not only of the Holy Spirit in the Inspired Prophecy, but also of all that dwell with God above, for they sing with sweet accord before the Throne of God—"A new song, saying, You are worthy to take the book, and to open the seals thereof: for You were slain, and have redeemed us to God by Your blood out of every kindred, and tongue, and people, and nation."

In the New Testament the passages abound which set forth the doctrine upon which we are now speaking. Look at that passage in Hebrews 9:12. There we are told expressly, "Without shedding of blood there is no remission." There is no remission by the life of Christ, no remission by the teaching of Christ, no remission by our repentance, no remission by our faith—apart from the shedding of the blood of Christ, by whom, alone, sin is put away! This is negative; but in this case the negative is as strong as the most positive statement could be, for if without shedding of blood there is no remission of sin, then we see how all-important that blood-shedding becomes! If you desire a positive statement, a sentence rises to our lips at once—"The blood of Jesus Christ His Son cleanses us from all sin."

31

Observe, not the life, not the Incarnation, not the Resurrection, not the Second Coming of the Lord Jesus, but His blood, His death, the giving up of His life is that which cleanses us from all sin! This is that purging with hyssop of which David speaks when he laments his sin and yet looks to be made whiter than snow by the free pardon of his God. This Truth is the subject of all true Gospel preaching! Do you not know how Paul puts it—"The preaching of the Cross is to them that perish, foolishness; but unto us which are saved, it is the power of God." "For," he says, "the Jews require a sign, and the Greeks seek after wisdom: but we preach Christ Crucified." It is not Christ in any other position, but Christ as Crucified! Christ as made a curse for us upon the tree—that is the first and most prominent fact that we are called to preach among the sons of men! "In whom we have redemption through His blood, the forgiveness of sins, according to the riches of His Grace."

Take away this substitutionary death of our Lord and you have taken all away! Without the death of Jesus there remains nothing for us but death! Forget the Crucified One and you have forgotten the only name by which we can be saved! Oh, that all of you would trust in Him. "Whom God has set forth to be a propitiation through faith in His blood, to declare His righteousness for the remission of sins that are past, through the forbearance of God." My Brothers and Sisters, this is the cause of the saints being in Heaven! In the first chapter of the Book of the Revelation, verse 5, we have the doxology, which begins, "Unto Him that loved us, and washed us from our sins in His own blood." Thus say all the glorified! Further on we are told concerning the saints, "They have washed their robes, and made them white in the blood of the Lamb. Therefore are they before the throne of God, and serve Him day and night in His temple: and He that sits on the throne shall dwell among them."

This is the true reading of the 14th verse of the last chapter of the Book of Revelation, "Blessed are they that wash their robes, that they may have the right to the tree of life, and may enter in by the gates into the city." Thus the passport to Glory is the precious blood of Jesus! Access to God, either on earth or in Heaven, is only by the blood of the Son of God! Now and then we meet with some squeamish person who says, "I cannot bear the mention of the word, blood." Such individuals will be horrified this morning—and it is intended that they should be! Sin is such a horrible thing that God has appointed blood to wash it away, that the very horror which the thought of it causes may give you some notion of the terrible nature of sin as God judges it! It is not without a dreadful blood-shedding that your dreadful guilt could by any possibility be cleansed!

Sin-bearing and suffering for sin can never be pleasant things—neither should the type which sets it forth be pleasing to the observer. On great days of sacrifice, the courts of the tabernacle must have seemed like a shambles, and fitly so, that all might be struck with the deadly nature of sin. If it is so, that the blood of Jesus is mentioned in the songs of Heaven, let it not be forgotten in the hymns of earth—

"To Him that loved the souls of men,
And washed us in His blood,
To royal honors raised our head,
And made us priests to God.

To Him let every tongue be praise,
And every heart be love!
All grateful honors paid on earth,
And nobler songs above!"

The Church militant is called upon continually to commemorate the blood-shedding. So often as we gather to the Communion Table we may ask the question, "The cup of blessing which we bless—is it not the communion of the blood of Christ?"

At the sacred table we show the death of our Lord until He comes. He says to us in express words, "This is My blood of the new testament, which is shed for many for the remission of sins." He bids you remember the blood as you drink of the fruit of the vine, saying, "This cup is the new testament in My blood." Take the blood away and the communion of the Lord's Supper has gone—there remains nothing but the Popish "mass" which is so blasphemously called an un-bloody sacrifice for the quick and the dead! Forget not that every person gathering to that table of communion is, if he is what he professes to be, a consecrated man and how comes he to be so but for this reason—"You are not your own, for you are bought with a price?"

We are redeemed unto God by the blood of Jesus. "You were not redeemed with corruptible things, as silver and gold, but with the precious blood of Christ, as of a lamb without blemish and without spot." It is the blood that makes you what you are—and the blood that permits you to enjoy what God has prepared for you—so that in every way you see the absolute essentiality of the death of the great Sacrifice. Here let us further consider that death is the result and penalty of sin—"The soul that sins, it shall die." "Sin, when it is finished, brings forth death." "The wages of sin is death." It was right that the Substitute should bear a similar chastisement to that which would have fallen upon the sinner. Our Savior did not endure annihilation, for that is not the meaning of death—neither the first nor the second death should be so explained.

Jesus was not annihilated, but He bore the pain, the loss, the ruin, the separation, the overwhelming which is intended by death. He was even forsaken of God, so that He cried out, "My God, My God, why have

34

You forsaken Me?" The penalty was death and, therefore, Jesus was exceedingly sorrowful even unto death. He laid down His life for us and became obedient to death, even the death of the Cross. The Law of God demanded death and death has fallen upon our great Covenant Head. "In due time Christ died for the ungodly." There is great comfort to my soul in this, for if the Lord Jesus has paid the capital sentence, nothing remains unpaid! "He that is dead is freed from sin." That is to say, if the law has killed the man, it can ask no more of him—he must be free from further charge of guilt.

When the criminal has died, he has suffered the last sentence of the law, and is now beyond its jurisdiction. Our Lord Jesus has died—the Just for the unjust, and as that which He has borne is nothing less than death, it must cover all that is due to sin—

> "He bore on the Tree the sentence for me,
> And now both the Surety and sinner are free."

Since Jesus has died unto sin once, He dies no more. Death has no more dominion over Him. He has borne the last and most far-reaching penalty of the Law of God and there can be nothing left upon the score. His Atonement was a complete redemption. If you were in debt and were bound to pay so much every month, you would be very grateful to a friend who should step in and pay several installments for you. But if one of more liberal spirit discharged the whole amount, your gratitude would be deep and overflowing!

Let us rejoice that the Lord Jesus Christ has evidently, by His substitutionary Sacrifice, put away not a part and a portion of our sin, but the whole of it! By bearing death, itself, He has removed all our legal obligations and has placed us beyond the reach of further demands. "Christ has redeemed us from the curse of the Law, being made a curse for us." Now we may sing to Him who has removed our transgressions from us as far as the east is from the west.

This death of Christ was also absolutely necessary for the clearing of the troubled conscience. An awakened conscience will never be quieted with anything less than the blood of the Lamb—it rests at the sight of the great Sacrifice, but nowhere else. A conscience smarting under a sense of sin is an unequalled fountain of misery. Let Conscience once begin to scourge the sinner and he will find it to be the most terribly tormentor out of Hell! I do not know whether the Prophet Isaiah was really sawn asunder by Manasseh, but we know that some of the saints suffered that torture. Yet, surely, a saw that should gradually cut a man in half from head to foot is a faint picture of what your conscience can do when it begins to operate upon the mind with all its cutting force!

What a Divine Atonement that must be which calms the storms of an accusing conscience and gives the soul a lasting peace! Some may trifle with their consciences, but where God is at work, men dare not attempt it. The most important thing in the world to a sensible man is the condition of his conscience—if that is restless, he is in an evil case. Thomas Fuller, in his quaint way, tells us that he, one day, asked a neighboring minister to preach for him, when he called upon a short visit. "No," said the other, "I cannot, for I am not prepared." "But," said Fuller, "though you are unprepared, I am sure you will preach well enough to satisfy my people." His friend answered, "That may be true, but I could not preach well enough to satisfy my own conscience."

There's the rub with a true man. We cannot live well enough to satisfy our conscience and we cannot pray well enough to satisfy our conscience! A really tender conscience is as greedy as the horseleech which cries, "Give! Give!"—it asks for perfection and, as we cannot render it by reason of sin—Conscience will never cease its outcries till it is quieted with the precious blood of Jesus Christ! Once let us see Jesus offered up upon the Cross for sin and our heart feels that it is enough! When God is well pleased, we may well be satisfied and get on our way enjoying peace with God from that time and forever. Thus much, then, upon our first point—for many reasons it was absolutely essential that our great Sacrifice should die.

II. Secondly, we will, with great delight, meditate upon the fact that the death of Christ is *effectually prevalent*. Other offerings, though duly slain, did nothing thoroughly, did nothing lastingly, did nothing really, by way of expiation, for the Scripture says, "It is not possible that the blood of bulls and of goats should take away sins." The true purification is only found in the death of the Son of God! When our Lord was fastened to the Cross and cried, "It is finished," and gave up the ghost, He had finished transgression, made an end of sin and brought in everlasting righteousness. By offering one Sacrifice for sins, forever, the work was done, the accusing record was altogether blotted out!

Why was there such cleansing power in the Redeemer's blood? I answer, for several reasons. First, because of the glory of His Person. Just think who He was! He was none other than the, "Light of light, very God of very God." He counted it not robbery to be equal with God, yet He took upon Himself our nature, and was born of a virgin. His holy Soul dwelt in a perfectly pure Body and to this, the Godhead was united. "For in Him dwells all the fullness of the Godhead bodily." Now, for this glorious, this sinless, this Divine Person, to die, is an amazing thing! For the Lord of angels, Creator of all things, sustaining all things by the power of His Word—for Him, I say, to bow His head to death as a vindication of the Law is an inconceivably majestic recompense to the honor of eternal justice!

Never could justice be more gloriously exalted in the presence of intelligent beings than by the Lord of All submitting Himself to its requirements! There must be an infinite merit about His death—a merit unutterable, immeasurable! I think if there had been a million worlds to redeem, their redemption could not have needed more than this "sacrifice of Himself." If the whole universe, teeming with worlds as many as the sands on the seashore, had required to be ransomed, that one giving up of the ghost would have sufficed as a full price for them all! However gross the insults which sin may have rendered to the Law of God, they must be all forgotten since Jesus magnified the Law so abundantly and made it so honorable by His death. I believe in the special design of our Lord's atoning death, but I will yield to no one in my belief in the absolutely infinite value of the offering which our Lord Jesus has presented! The glory of His Person renders the idea of limitation an insult.

Next, consider the perfection of our Lord's Character. In Him was no sin, nor tendency to sin. He was "holy, harmless, undefiled and separate from sinners." In His Character we see every virtue at its best! He is incomparable. If He, therefore, died, "the Just for the unjust," what must be the merit of such a death? His righteousness has such sweetness in it that all the ill-savor of our transgression is put away—it is no wonder that by the obedience of such a One as this "Second Adam" many are made righteous! Think next, dear Friends, of the nature of the death of Christ and you will be helped to see how effectual it must be. It was not a death by disease, or old age—but a death of violence, well symbolized by the killing of the victim at the altar. He did not die in His bed, sleeping Himself out of the world—He was taken by wicked hands, scourged, spit upon and then fastened up to die a felon's death! His was a cruel doom! Human malice could scarcely have invented any method of execution more sure to create pain and anguish than death by hanging on a tree, fastened by nails driven through hands and feet!

In addition to His physical pain, our Lord was sorely vexed in spirit. His soul-sufferings were the soul of His sufferings—"He was exceedingly sorrowful even unto death." Heaven refused its smile. His mind was left in darkness. To be frowned upon of God was a part of the punishment of our sin and Jesus Christ was not spared that direst and bitterest woe. God, Himself, turned away His face from Him and left Him in the dark! He died a dishonorable death, yes, a cursed death—"As it is written, cursed is everyone that hangs on a tree." Now, for the Son of God to die, and die in such a manner, was a marvel! Never martyr died crying that he was forsaken of his God! That desertion was the lowest depth of the Savior's grief. And since He died thus, I can well understand that He has, thereby, made an ample Atonement for the sins of all who believe in Him. Oh, great Atonement of my blessed Lord, my sins are swallowed up in You! Looking to the Cross and to the pierced heart of Jesus, my Lord, I am assured that if I am washed in His blood I shall be whiter than snow!

And then think of the spirit in which our Lord and Savior bore all this. Martyrs who have died for the faith have only paid the debt of Nature a little before its time, for they would have died, sooner or later. But our Lord needed not to have died at all! He said of His life, "No man takes it from Me, but I lay it down of Myself." The pouring out of His soul unto death was not in the power of man until the Lord was pleased to yield Himself a Sacrifice. "He gave Himself for me." He laid down His life for His sheep. Out of love to God and man He willingly drank of the appointed cup—the only compulsion which He knew was His own desire to bless His chosen. "For the joy that was set before Him, He endured the Cross, despising the shame." Oh, it was splendidly lived, that life of our Lord! The Spirit which guided it, lights it up with an unrivalled brightness! Oh, it was splendidly died, that death of our Lord, for He went up to the Cross with such willing submission that it became His Throne!

The crown of thorns was such a diadem as emperor never wore! It was made of the ended sorrows of His people—sorrows ended by their encircling His own majestic head! On the Cross He routed His enemies and made a show of them openly, triumphing over them in it! In the act of death He nailed the handwriting of ordinances that were against us to His Cross and so destroyed the condemning power of the Law of God. O glorious Christ, there must be infinite merit in such a death as Yours, endured in such a style! And then I bid you to remember, once more, the Covenant Character which Christ sustained, for when He was crucified, we thus judge that One died for all, and in Him all died. He was not slain as a private individual, but He was put to death as a Representative Man.

God had entered into Covenant with Christ and He was the Surety of that Covenant, therefore His blood is called "the blood of the Everlasting Covenant." Remember the expression of the Apostle where he speaks of "the blood of the Covenant with which we are sanctified"? Neither the First nor the Second Covenant were dedicated without blood—but the New Covenant was established by no blood of beasts, but by the blood of our Lord Jesus Christ, that great Shepherd of the sheep! When He offered Himself, He was accepted in that Character and capacity in which God had regarded Him from before the foundations of the world, so that what He did, He did as the Covenant-Head of His people. It was meet that He should die for us, seeing He had assumed the position of the Second Adam, being constituted our federal Head and Representative. The chastisement of our peace was upon Him because He condescended to be one flesh with us—and with His stripes we are healed because there is a Covenant union between us.

Thus much upon the effectual prevalence of that great Sacrifice—a theme so vast that one might enlarge upon it throughout all time!

III. Beloved Friends, it seems to me that no one will now forbid my saying, thirdly, that the fact of the necessity for the death of the Lord Jesus is *intensely instructive.* Listen while I repeat the lessons very briefly—you can enlarge upon them when you go from here to meditate in solitude.

Must the victims die? Must Jesus bleed? Then let us see what is claimed by our righteous God. He claims our life—He claimed of the offering its blood, which is the life thereof—He justly requires of each of us our whole life. We must not dream of satisfying God with formal prayers, or occasional alms-deeds, or outward ceremonies, or a half-hearted reverence. He must have our heart, soul, mind and strength—all that makes our true self—the very life of our being. Dead works are worthless before the living God. He claims our life and He will have it one way or another—either by its being perfectly spent in His service, or else by its being smitten down in death as the righteous punishment of rebellion! Nor is the demand unjust. Did He not make us and does He not preserve us? Should He not receive homage from the creatures of His hands?

Next, must the sacrifice die? Then see the evil of sin. It is not such a trifle as certain men imagine. It is a deadly evil, a killing poison. God, Himself, in human form, took human guilt upon Himself—the sin was none of His—it was only imputed to Him, but when He was made sin for us and bore our iniquities, there was no help for it, He must die! Even He must die! It was not possible that the cup should pass from Him. A voice was heard from the Throne of God—"Awake, O Sword, against My Shepherd, and against the Man that is My Fellow, says the Lord of Hosts: smite the Shepherd!" So unflinching is Divine Justice that it will not, cannot spare sin, let it be where it may! No, not even when that guilt is not the Person's own, but is only taken up by Him as a Substitute. Sin, wherever it is, must be smitten with the sword of death—this is a Law of God fixed and unalterable. Who, then, will take pleasure in transgression? Will not every man who loves his own life awaken himself to fight against iniquity? Sinner, shake off your sin, as Paul shook off the viper into the fire! Do not dally with it. Pray God that you may have done with it. It is a horrible and a grievous thing and God says to you "Oh, do not this abominable thing which I hate." God help you to flee from all iniquity.

Next, learn the love of God. Behold how He loved you and me! He must punish sin, but He must save us—and so He gives His Son to die in our place. I shall not go too far if I say that in giving His Son, the Lord God gave Himself, for Jesus is One with the Father. We cannot divide the Substance though we distinguish the Persons—thus God, Himself, made Atonement for sin committed against Himself! The Church is "the flock of God which He has purchased with His own blood." Wonder of wonders! Truly love is strong as death as we see it in the heart of God! "Scarcely for a righteous man will one die: yet perhaps for a good man some would even dare to die. But God commends His love toward us, in that, while we were yet sinners, Christ died for us." This is a heaped-up marvel! Behold what manner of love the Father has bestowed upon us!

Next, learn how Christ has made an end of sin. Sin is laid on Him and He dies—then sin is dead and buried! If it is sought for, it cannot be found. Speak of finality—this is the truest and surest finality that ever was, or ever shall be! "If a man dies shall he live again?" Not as before. If Christ died, what is there after death? Nothing but the Judgment and lo, He comes to that judgment—"Being raised from the dead He dies no more, death has no more dominion over Him." This is our joy because neither sin nor death can have dominion over us for whom Christ died, and who died in Him! Christ has made an end of sin. His one offering has perfected, forever, the set-apart ones. These are but a few of the great lessons which we may learn from the necessity that the Sacrifice should be slain. I pray you learn them well. May they be engraved on your hearts by the Holy Spirit!

IV. And so I shall close by saying that this blessed subject is not only full of instruction, but it is *energetically inspiring*. First, this inspires us with the spirit of consecration. When I think that I could not be saved except by the death of Jesus, then I feel that I am not my own, but bought with a price. I remember reading of Charles Simeon, the famous evangelical clergyman of Cambridge, that he was, one day, thrown from his horse and was fearful that he had sustained serious injury. When he had recovered from the force of the fall, he stretched out his right arm, felt it, and finding that there was not a bone broken, he consecrated that arm, anew, to the living God who had so graciously preserved it.

Then he examined his left arm and found it all right—and so held that up and dedicated it anew unto Divine service. He did the same with his head, his legs and his whole body. As I was thinking over this subject, I felt as if I must go over my body, soul and spirit, and dedicate all to that dear Savior by whose blood I am altogether redeemed from death and Hell. "Bless the Lord, O my Soul: and all that is within me, bless His holy name!" As I am not cast away from God. As I am not destroyed. As I am not in torment, not in Hell—I dedicate to God my blood-bought spirit, soul and body from this day forth to be the Lord's as long as I live! Brothers and Sisters, do you not feel the same? I pray God the Holy Spirit to make you do so in a very practical manner. This doctrine of the death of Christ ought to inspire you till you sing—

"Jesus, spotless Lamb of God,
  You have bought me with Your blood.
I would value nothing beside Jesus—
  Jesus crucified!

I am Yours and Yours alone.
  This I gladly, fully own.
And, in all my works and ways,

43

Only now would seek Your praise."

Next, this Truth of God should create in us a longing after the greatest holiness, for we should say, "Did sin kill my Savior? Then I will kill sin! Could I not be saved from sin except by His precious blood? Then, O sin, I will be revenged upon you! I will drive you out by the help of God's Spirit! I will not endure you, nor harbor you. I will make no provision for the flesh. As sin was the death of Christ for me, so Christ shall be the death of sin in me." Does not this inspire you with great love for the Lord Jesus? Can you look at His dear wounds and not be wounded with love for Him? Are not His wounds as mouths which plead with you to yield Him all your hearts? Can you gaze upon His face, wet with bloody sweat, and then go away and be ensnared with the world's painted beauties? Heard you ever of a ruler dressed in such robes of love as those which Jesus wore? Did ever Love use such sacred means to win the beloved heart as Christ has done? What can any one of us do but answer Him thus—

"Here, Lord, I give myself away,
'Tis all that I can do"?

Do you not think that this solemn Truth of God should inspire us with great zeal for the salvation of others? As Christ laid down His life for us, should we not lay ourselves out for perishing souls and, if necessary, lay down our lives for the Brethren? Should we not practice self-denial in our labors to bring men to Jesus? Should we not joyfully toil and cheerfully bear reproach, if by any means we may save some? I think if this subject should go home to our hearts, it would be beneficial to us in a thousand ways and make us better soldiers of the Cross, closer followers of the Lamb. I pray that God the Holy Spirit may place it in the center of our souls and keep it there! It will bring with it peace and rest. Why should we be troubled, since Jesus died? It will fill our mouths with praises!

Hallelujah to the Lamb that was slain, who has redeemed us by His blood! It will draw us into closer communion with Him. If He loved us and died for us, we must live with Him, and in Him, and to Him. Surely it will also make us long to behold Him! Oh, for the vision of the Crucified! When shall we see the face that was so marred for us? When shall we behold the hands and feet which still bear the nail marks? And when shall we look into the wounded side bejeweled with the spear wound? Oh, when shall we be done with all our sins and griefs, forever to behold Him shine and see Him still before us? Oh, when shall we be—

> "Far from a world of grief and sin,
> With God eternally shut in?"

Till then our hope, our solace, our glory, our victory are all found in the blood of the Lamb, to whom be glory forever and ever. Amen!

3

Salt or Sacrifice

"And every oblation of your meat offering shall you season with salt; neither shall you suffer the salt of the Covenant of your God to be lacking from your meat offering: with all your offerings you shall offer salt." (Leviticus 2:13)

I T IS TAKEN FOR GRANTED that all true Israelites would bring many oblations and offerings of different kinds to God. And so they did who were truly devout and really grateful. I am sure that if the Lord has set our hearts on fire with His own love, we, also, shall be frequently saying, "What shall I render unto the Lord for all His benefits toward me?" It will be the habit of the Christian, as it was the habit of the devout Israelite, to be continually bringing oblations to his God.

How is this to be done? That is the point. We have need, each of us, to say with Paul, "Lord, what will You have me to do?" And we may add another question, "How will You have me do it?" For will-worship is not acceptable with God. If we bring to God what He does not ask, it will not be received. We must only present to Him that which He requires of us and we must present it to Him in His own way, for He is a jealous God.

I call your attention to the fact that, in this verse, the Lord three times expressly commands that with the meat offerings and all other offerings they were to offer salt. Does the great God that made Heaven and earth talk about salt? Does He condescend to such minute details of His service as to enact that the absence of a handful of salt shall render a sacrifice unacceptable—and the presence of it shall be absolutely necessary to its being received by Him? Then, my Brethren, nothing in the service of God is trifling! A pinch of salt may seem to us exceedingly unimportant, but before the Lord it may not be so. In the service of God, the alteration of an ordinance of Christ may seem to be a pure matter of indifference, and yet in that alteration there may be the taking away of the very vitals of the ordinance—and the total destruction of its meaning. It is yours and it is mine to keep to the letter of God's Word, as well as to the spirit of it, remembering that it is written, "Whoever shall break one of these least commandments and shall teach men so, he shall be called the least in the Kingdom of Heaven." It is not for the servant to say, "This order of my master is unimportant and the other is binding." The servant's duty is to act in all things exactly as he is bid. Since our Master is so holy and so wise, it is impossible for us to improve upon His commandments. Yes, God enters into detail with His servants and even makes orders about salt.

If you will read the chapter through, you will note that other things were needed in connection with the sacrifices of the Israelites. Their sacrifices were, of course, imperfect. Even on the low ground which they occupied as symbols and emblems they were not complete, for you read, in the first place, that they needed frankincense when they offered their sacrifice to God. God did not smell sweet savor in the bullock, or the ram, or the lamb, unless sweet spices were added. What does that teach us but that the best performances of our hands must not appear before His Throne without the merit of Christ mingled with it? There must be that mixture of myrrh, aloes and cassia with which the garments of our Prince

47

are perfumed to make our sacrifice to be a sweet savor to the Most High! Take care in your sacrifices that you bring the sacred frankincense.

Another thing that was enjoined constantly was that they should bring oil—and oil is always the type of the blessed Spirit of God. What is the use of a sermon if there is no unction in it? What is unction but the Holy Spirit? What is prayer without the anointing that comes of the Holy Spirit? What is praise unless the Spirit of God is in it to give it life, that it may rise to Heaven? That which goes to God must first come from God. We need the oil—we cannot do without it. Pray for me that I may have this oil in the sacrifice of my ministry, as I pray for you that in all that you do for the Lord Jesus, your sacrifice may continually have the sacred oil with it.

Then came a third requisite, namely, salt. If you read the preceding verses, you will see that the Lord forbids them to present any honey. "No meat offering, which you shall bring unto the Lord, shall be made with leaven: for you shall burn no leaven, nor any honey, in an offering of the Lord made by fire. As for the oblation of the first fruits, you shall offer them unto the Lord: but they shall not be burnt on the altar for a sweet savor." Ripe fruits were full of honey, full of sweetness—and God does not ask for sweetness, He asks for salt. I shall notice that as we go on farther. Not honey, but salt, must be added to all the sacrifices which we present before the living God.

What is the meaning of all this? We may not pronounce any meaning of the types with certainty unless we have Scripture to direct us, but still, using our best judgment, we do, first of all, see that the text explains itself. Observe, "neither shall you suffer the salt of the Covenant of your God to be lacking from your meat offering."

I. It appears, then, that salt was *the symbol of the covenant.* When God made a Covenant with David, it is written, "The Lord gave the kingdom to David forever by a Covenant of salt"—by which was meant that it was an unchangeable, incorruptible Covenant which would endure as salt makes a thing to endure, so that it is not liable to putrefy or corrupt. "The salt of the Covenant" signifies that whenever you and I are bringing any offering to the Lord, we must take care that we remember the Covenant. Standing at the altar with our gift, serving God with our daily service, as I trust we are doing, let us continually offer the salt of the Covenant with all our sacrifices. Here is a man who is doing good works in order to be saved. You are under the wrong Covenant, my Friend, you are under the Covenant of Works and all that you will gain in that way is a curse, for, "Cursed is everyone that continues not in all things which are written in the Book of the Law, to do them." "Therefore," says the Apostle, "as many as are of the works of the Law are under the curse." Get away from that and get to that other Covenant which has salt in it, namely, the Covenant of Grace, the New Covenant of which Christ is the Head! We must not come to God without the salt of faith in Christ, or our offerings will be a sort of antichrist. A man who is trying to save himself is in opposition to the Savior. He that thinks of the merits of his own good works, despises the merit of the finished work of Christ! He is offering to God that which has no salt with it and it cannot be received.

We need this salt of the Covenant in all that we do, in the first place, to preserve us from falling into legality. He that serves God for wages forgets the Word—"The gift of God is eternal life." It is not wage, but gift, by which you are to live. If you forget that you are under a Covenant of pure Grace, in which God gives to the unworthy and saves those who have no claim to any Covenant blessing, you will get on legal ground. And, once on legal ground, God cannot accept your sacrifice. With all your offerings you shall offer the salt of the Covenant of Grace, lest you are guilty of legality in your offering.

The Covenant is to be remembered, also, that it may excite gratitude. Whenever I think of God entering into Covenant that He will not depart from me and that I shall never depart from Him, my love to Him overflows. Nothing constrains me to such activity and such zeal, in the cause of God, as a sense of Covenant love. Oh, the gratitude one feels for everything which comes to us by the Covenant of Grace! Remember the old Scottish wife who thanked God for the porridge and then thanked Him that she had a Covenant right to the porridge, since He had said, "Verily, you shall be fed?" Oh, it makes life very sweet to take everything from the hands of a Covenant God and to see in every mercy a new pledge of Covenant faithfulness! It makes life happy and it also inspires a Believer to do great things for his gracious God. Standing on Covenant ground we feel consecrated to the noblest ends!

This tends to awaken our devotion to God. When we remember that God has entered into Covenant with us, then we do not do our work for Him in a cold, chilly, dead way—neither do we perform it after a nominal, formal sort—for we say, "I am one of God's covenanted ones." He has made an everlasting Covenant with me, ordered in all things and sure; therefore my very soul goes after Him and this which I am about to do, though it is only to sing a hymn, or to bow my knees in prayer, shall be done intensely, as by one who is in covenant with God, who is, therefore, bound to serve with all his heart and with all his soul, and with all his strength. Covenanted service should be the best of service. The covenanting saints of old stopped not at death, itself, for Him to whom they were bound!

My time will not allow me to enlarge, but I pray the people of God will always keep the Covenant in view. That Covenant will claim the last accent of our tongues on earth. It shall employ the first notes of our celestial songs. Where are you if you are out of Covenant with God? You are under the curse of the Old Covenant if you are not under the blessing of the New! But if the Lord Jesus Christ has stood Surety on your behalf and made the Covenant sure to you, you will serve God with alacrity and delight—and He will accept your service as a sweet savor offering in Christ Jesus. That is the first meaning of the text.

II. But, secondly, salt is *the token of communion*. In the East, especially, it is the token of fellowship. When an Oriental has once eaten a man's salt, he will do him no harm.

Whenever you are attempting to serve God, take care that you do it in the spirit of fellowship with God. Take care that you suffer not this salt to be lacking from your meat-offering. Offer it in fellowship with God.

And this is a very important point, though I cannot dwell upon it at any length. Beloved, we never serve God rightly, joyfully, happily, if we get out of fellowship with Him. "His servants shall serve Him and they shall see His face." There is no serving God acceptably unless you see His face. Once you feel your love to God dying out and the Presence of God withdrawn from you, you can live by faith, but you cannot work with comfort. You must feel a sweet friendship with God or else you will not so heartily give yourself to God's service as the saints of God ought to do. I want you to live always in the sense of God's nearness to you. Live always in the delightful conviction that God loves you. Never be satisfied to have a doubt about your being one with Christ, or that you are dear to the heart of God. You cannot sing, you cannot pray, you cannot teach a Sunday school class—you cannot preach in a fit and proper style if you lose this salt of communion! You may limp, but you cannot run in the ways of God if your fellowship is broken. "The joy of the Lord is your strength." Have plenty of this salt of fellowship to heap upon every oblation.

Then, feel fellowship with God as to all His purposes. Does God wish to save souls? So do I. Did Christ die to save souls? So would I live to save them. Can you say that? Does the Holy Spirit strive against sin? So would I strive against sin. Feel all this. Endeavor to run on parallel lines with God as far as the creature can keep pace with the Creator. And when you do—when all your aims and designs are the aims and designs of God—then, Brother, you will plow and you will sow—and you will reap with joy and gladness of heart! There must be this fellowship with God in His designs. This is the essential salt of sacrifice.

I would have you especially have fellowship with God in Christ Jesus. Does God love Jesus? So do we. Does God desire the Glory of His Son? So do we. Does God determine that His Son shall put down all power, authority, rule and be King? We, too, wish Him to reign over us and over all mankind. "Your Kingdom come" is our prayer, even as it is God's will that the kingdoms of this world should become the Kingdoms of our Lord and of His Christ.

Now, if you can always work in fellowship with God, what a grand thing it will be! For lack of this, many workers know not their position and never realize their strength. We are laborers together with God. If we are in our right state, we take a brick to lay it on the wall and a Divine hand has lifted that brick. We use the trowel and it is the great Master Builder that grasps the tool. We wield the sword and the Captain of the Lord's host is strengthening our arm and guiding our hand that we may do valiantly in the day of battle. What an honor to have the Lord working with us and by us!

But oh, Beloved, do not get out of fellowship with God! If you have done so, before you do another stroke of work for Him go and get into fellowship with Him. If I were captain of the host and I saw that you were out of fellowship and yet you were marching to the battle, I would say, "Brother, go back." When we bring our sacrifice, we are to leave it till we are reconciled to our brother—and much more must we leave it till we have a sense of being reconciled to God. I can- not go on serving God if I do not know that I am His child. I cannot go on preaching to you if I have any doubt of my own salvation. At any rate, it would be very wretched work to preach of freedom while myself in chains! He preaches best who is at liberty and can, in his own person, tell the captives how Christ makes men free. When you know that you are in union with God—and when your heart feels a blessed friendship to Him—then it is, dear Friends, that your oblation will come up acceptably before Him and you can do your work as it ought to be done before Him.

III. But I must get your minds to another point. Salt is the *emblem of sincerity*. "With all your offerings you shall offer salt." There must be an intense sincerity about all we do towards God.

I bade you note that you were not allowed to present honey before the Lord. I really wish that some of our Brethren who are over-done with honey, would notice that. There is a kind of molasses godliness which I can never stomach. It is always, "Dear this," and, "Dear that," and, "Dear the other," and, "This dear man," and, "That dear woman." There is also a kind of honey-drop talk in which a person never speaks the plain truth. He speaks as familiarly as if he knew all about you and would lay down his life for you, though he has never set eyes on you before and would not give you a half- penny to save your life! These people avoid rebuking sin, for that is "unkind." They avoid denouncing error. They say, "This dear Brother's views differ slightly from mine." A man says that black is white and I say that it is not so. But it is not kind to say, "It is not so." You should say, "Perhaps you are right, dear Brother, though I hardly think so." In this style some men think that our sacrifice is to be offered! If they hear a sermon that cuts at the roots of sin and deals honestly with error, they say, "That man is very narrow-minded."

Well, I have been so accustomed to be called a *bigot* that I, by no means, deny the charge! I feel no horror because of the accusation. To tell a man that if he goes on in his sin, he will be lost forever and to preach to him the Hell which God denounces against the impenitent is no unkindness! It is the truest kindness to deal honestly with men. If the surgeon knows very well that a person has a disease about him that requires the knife and he only says, "It is a mere trifle: I dare say that with a little medicine and a pill or two we may cure you," a simpleton may say, "What a dear kind man!" But a wise man judges otherwise. He is not kind, for he is a liar! If, instead of that, he says "My dear Friend, I am very sorry, but I must tell you that this mischief must be taken out by the roots and, painful as the operation is, I beg you to summon courage to undergo it, for it must be done if your life is to be saved."

That is a very unpleasant kind of person and a very narrow-minded and bigoted person—but he is the man for us! He uses salt and God accepts him—the other man uses honey and God will have nothing to do with him. When honey comes to the fire, it turns sour. All this pretended sweetness, when it comes to the test, turns sour—there is no real love in it. But the salt, which is sharp and when it gets into the wound makes it tingle, nevertheless does sound service.

Whenever you come before God with your sacrifices, do not come with the pretense of a love you do not feel, nor with the beautiful nonsense of hypocrites, but come before the Lord in real, sober, earnest truth. If you are wrong and feel it, say so, and out with it! And if God has made you right through His Spirit, do not deny it, lest you deny the work of the Holy Spirit and so dishonor Him.

What is meant is that in all our sacrifices we ought to bring our hearts with us. If we sing, let us sing heartily as unto the Lord—not with our voices only, but with our very souls! If we preach, let us preach with all our might—we have such precious Truth to handle that it ought not to be dealt with in a trifling manner. If we try to win a soul, let us throw our whole strength into the work. Though we would not scheme, like the Pharisees, to make a proselyte to our sect, yet let us compass sea and land to bring a man to Christ, for such we should do.

And when we bring our heart and throw it intensely into the service of God, which is one form of the salt, let us take care that all we do is spiritually performed—not done with the external hand, or lips, or eyes, but done with the soul, with the innermost heart of our being! Otherwise it will be mere flesh and, without salt, it will be viewed as corrupt and rejected at God's altar.

When you attempt to pray and rise from your knees feeling that you have not prayed, then do not leave the Mercy Seat, but pray till you pray! When you are singing a hymn and do not feel quite in tune for singing, sing yourself into tune! Do not leave an ordinance till you have tasted the salt of that ordinance. I admire that resolution of John Bradford the martyr. He said that he made a rule that he never ceased from a holy engagement till he had entered into the spirit of it. Too often we treat these things lightly. There is no soul in them and yet we are satisfied with them.

We eat our unsavory devotions without salt—and the Lord rejects them. We have had a few minutes in prayer in the morning and, perhaps, just a few weary minutes at midnight. We have run through a chapter, or perhaps we have taught a class on the Sabbath afternoon and taught it perfunctorily without any life and yet we have been content. Or we have preached, but it has been a mere saying of words—there has been no life or vigor in it.

Oh, do not so! Bring not to God your unsalted sacrifices, but let the salt of sincerity savor all. It is better to say, "I did not pray," than it is to say, "I did pray," and yet only to have gone through a form. It is better to have to confess, "I did not sing," than to follow the tune when your heart is not in it. You had better leave off the external form than keep it up if your soul is not in it—lest you be found to mock the Most High God! Pile on the salt! Let it season the whole of your sacrifice through and through! Be sincere before the heart-searching God.

IV. Lastly, salt is *the type of purifying power* and with all our sacrifices we have need to bring a great deal of this salt. The salt eats into the meat. It drives away corruption. It preserves it. We require a deal of this. Brothers and Sisters, if we come before God with holy things while we are living in sin, we need not deceive ourselves—we shall not be accepted! If there is any man of whom it can be said that he is a saint abroad and a devil at home, God will estimate him at what he is at home—and not at what he is abroad. He may lay the sacrifice upon the altar, but if it is brought there with foul hands and an unholy heart, God will have nothing to do with it! "Without holiness no man shall see the Lord" and, certainly, without holiness can no man serve the Lord. We have our imperfections, but known and willful sin, God's people will not indulge. From this God keeps them. As soon as they know a thing to be sin and their attention is called to it, that which they have committed in inadvertence causes them grief and sorrow of heart and they flee from it with all their souls.

But do not be deceived! You may be a great man in the Church of God and hold office there—and even be a leader—but if you lead an unholy life, neither you nor your sacrifice can ever be accepted by the Most High. God abhors that His priests should serve Him with unwashed hands and feet. "Be you clean that bear the vessels of the Lord." I constantly preach to you free, rich and Sovereign Grace without the slightest condition—and I preach the same at this time. But remember that the Grace of God brings sanctification with it and that the gift of God is deliverance from sin—and if we abide in sin and remain in it, we cannot be the children of God! We must, dear Friends, bring with all our oblations that salt in ourselves which shall purify our hearts from inward corruption and which shall have a power about it to purify others. Know you not that the saints are the salt of the earth? And if we are salt to others, we must have salt in ourselves. How can we conquer sin in others if sin is unconquered in ourselves? How can we give a light we have never seen? How can we have seed as sowers if we have never had bread as eaters?

You know what the woman said concerning the well—"Father Jacob," she said, "gave us the well and drank thereof himself." You cannot give other people wells if you do not drink from this yourself! You cannot benefit a man by Grace if you are not first benefited by Grace yourself. Can anything come out of a man that is not in him? There must be a holy, sanctifying power about the child of God, making him to be as salt, or else he cannot act upon the putrid masses round him as the salt ought to do.

With all your oblations, then, bring this salt. God give it to us! Let us cry to Him for it! I bless God for this Church that God has made you a power in the neighborhood—that God is making you a power all over this country! Those hundreds of ministers who came up this week, whom we have educated here and whom all of you have helped to educate—are not these a purifying salt? Our Brothers and Sisters by thousands are scattered all over the world. Not a week passes without some of our number going far away and I always say, "Yes, go, dear Brethren. Salt should not remain in the box. It ought to be scattered all over the meat. Wherever you go, mind that you are salt, so that people do not say, 'Is this one of the Tabernacle people? He is a poor, lukewarm creature.'" Do not have it so, but do, now that God blesses you so largely, take care that the salt is in you all.

"I have no greater joy than to hear that my children walk in truth," and I have no greater sorrow than this—that there are some among you who are no credit to your profession. There are some among you who do not live, even, as well as the world expects you to live. I mean not only poor ones, but rich ones among us are a dishonor to us. There are a few of all degrees among us who are not spiritually-minded but are worldly and carnal. They come to this place and sit among us with their faces turned towards Heaven while they, themselves, are going the way of the ungodly. They know what I mean while I speak it! God grant that they may bear the rebuke—and repent and turn to the Lord! They are looking one way and rowing another—trying to be the people of God, if they can, and yet, at the same time, acting as common sinners act!

The Lord bless you, Beloved, by making you all holy! And if you will not be holy, may He take that great fan into His hand and blow the chaff away! If it cannot be that this shall be a pure heap lying upon His floor to His honor and Glory, then may He still continue that great purgation which is always going on in every Church where He is really present! Brothers and Sisters, we must be holy! We must be holy, or else cease to be what we are. God bring us to this—that with every oblation we may offer huge handfuls of salt! May we always be accepted in Christ, accepted with our sweet savor—holy, acceptable to God because His Spirit has made us holy and keeps us right before Him. The Lord bless you always! Amen.

4

The Sin Offering

"If the anointed priest sins, bringing guilt on the people; then let him bring for his sin, which he has sinned, a young bullock without blemish unto the Lord for a sin offering." (Leviticus 4:3)

I N THE PREVIOUS CHAPTERS of the Book of Leviticus you read of the burnt offering, the peace offering, and the meat offering—all types our Lord Jesus Christ, as seen from different points of view. Those three sacrifices were sweet savor offerings, and represent the Lord Jesus in His glorious Person and perfect Righteousness as an offering of a sweet smell unto God. The Chapter before us, the whole of which we shall require as a text, describes the sin offering, which, although quite distinct from the sweet savor offerings, is not altogether to be separated from them, for the Lord Jesus Christ viewed in any light is very dear unto His Father; and even when beheld as a Sin Offering is Elect and Precious unto God, as we shall have to show you in the type before us still, the sin offering does not set forth the acceptance of the substitute before the Lord, but rather brings out the abhorrence which God has towards sin, the putting away from His Holy Presence of everything upon which sin is laid. This morning, if God shall enable us, we hope to impress upon your minds, first of all, the great evil of sin; and secondly, the great and wonderful power of the blood of Atonement by which sin is put away.

Without any further preface we shall invite you, in meditating upon the type before us, first, to consider our Lord Jesus as made sin for us; secondly, we shall ask you to observe, carefully and prayerfully, His blood in its efficacy before the Lord; and thirdly, we shall bid you look at His Substitution in the shame which it involved.

I. First, Brothers and Sisters, let us, by the aid of the Holy Spirit, view our *blessed Lord as made sin for us*, as He is here typified in the bullock.

His Personal Character is set forth before us in the victim chosen, namely, a young bullock without blemish. It was a bullock, the most valuable of the sacrifices, an animal laborious in life and costly in death; it was a young bullock in the fullness of its strength and vigor; it was without blemish—and the slightest fault disqualified it from being laid upon the Altar of God. Behold, O Believer, your Lord Jesus, more precious by far than ten thousands of the fat of fed beasts—a Sacrifice not to be purchased with gold, or estimated in silver. Full of vigor, in the very prime of Manhood, He offered up Himself for us! Even when He died, He died not through weakness; for that cry of His at His death, "with a loud voice," proved that His life was still firm within Him, and that when He gave up the ghost, His death was not one of compulsion, but a voluntary expiring of the soul. His Glory is as the firstling of the bullock, full of vigor and of strength. How distinctly was our Lord proved to be without blemish! Naturally born without sin, practically He lived without fault. In Him there was neither deficiency nor excess. In no virtue did He come behind, and no fault could be found in Him. The prying eyes of the prince of this world could find nothing in Him, and the still more accurate search of the All-Seeing God found no fault in Him.

This spotlessness was necessary, for how could He have been made an Offering for our sin, if it had not been true that personally, "He knew no sin?" Shall one bankrupt stand in the debtor's court as a substitute for another? How shall one penniless wretch pay the debt of another who is about to be cast into prison? If the king requires service of any man, how shall another from whom service is equally due, offer himself as a substitute for him? No, the Savior of others must have no obligations of His own; He must owe no personal debts; there must be no claims on the part of justice against Him, on His own account, or He cannot stand "the Just for the unjust," to expiate the sins of men. You holy souls, feast your eyes upon the spotless Son of God. You pure in heart, delight your purified vision with a sight of His perfections. You shall one day be like He—this will be your Heaven; meanwhile, make it your rapture, your paradise on earth, to gaze upon the unrivaled beauties of the Altogether Lovely. "In Him was no sin." In Him was all excellence. His body and soul are alike—white as the lily for holiness, though made by suffering red as the rose. Alabaster, and bright ivory overlaid with sapphires are but dull and soiled types of His Purity. Come, you virgin souls, and let the eyes of your holy love survey Him, that you may see how fit He was to suffer as "the Just for the unjust, to bring us to God." The act of transference of sin to the victim next calls for our attention. You will have noticed, in reading the chapter, that our Lord's being made sin is set forth to us by the very significant transfer of sin to the bullock, which was made by the priest, or by the elders of the people, as the case might be. We are expressly told, "He shall lay his hands upon the bullock's head," which act, our good Dr. Watts has interpreted in his well-known verse—

> "My faith would lay her hands
> On that dear head of Yours,
> While like a penitent I stand;

And there confess my sin."

This laying of the hand does not appear to have been a mere touch of contact, but in some other places of Scripture has the meaning of leaning heavily, as in the expression, "Your wrath lies hard upon me" (Psa. 88:7). Surely this is the very essence and nature of faith, which does not only bring us into contact with the Great Substitute, but teaches us to lean upon Him with all the burden of our guilt; so that if our sins are very weighty, yet we see Him as able to bear them all; and mark, the whole weight of our iniquity taken off from us, who must would been crushed to the lowest hell thereby, and laid on Him who took the weight and bore it all, and then buried it in His sepulcher forever. From of old it was decreed, "The Lord has laid on Him the iniquity of us all." Jehovah made to meet upon the head of the Substitute all the offenses of His Covenant people; but each one of the chosen is brought personally to ratify this solemn covenant act of the great God, when by Grace he is enabled by faith to put his hands upon the head of the "Lamb slain from before the foundation of the world." My fellow Believers, do you remember that rapturous day? My soul recalls her day of deliverance with delight; laden with guilt and full of fears, I saw my Savior willing to be my Substitute, and I laid my hand, oh, how timidly at first, but as my courage grew and confidence was confirmed, I leaned my soul entirely upon Him; and now it is my unceasing joy to know that my sins are no longer imputed to me, but laid on Him, and like the debts of the poor wounded traveler, Jesus, like the Good Samaritan, has said of all my future sinfulness, "Set that to My account." Oh, blessed discovery, sweet solace of a repenting heart!—

"My numerous sins transferred to Him,
Shall never more be found,
Lost in His blood's atoning stream
Where every crime is drowned!"

We must now beg your notice of the sins transferred. In the case of the type, they were sins of ignorance. Alas, the Jew knew nothing about a sin offering for sins of presumption, but there is such a Sin Offering for us. Our presumptuous sins were laid on Christ; our willful sins; our sins of light and knowledge, are pardoned by His blood. The mention of sins of ignorance, suggests a very comfortable reflection, that if there are any sins which I know not, they were, notwithstanding my ignorance, laid on my Substitute and put away by His Atonement. It is not sin as we see it which was laid on Christ, but sin as God sees it; not sin as our conscience feebly reveals it to us, but sin as God beholds it, in all its unmitigated malignity, and unconcealed loathsomeness. Sin in its exceeding sinfulness Jesus has put away. Not sham sin, but real sin; sin as before the Lord; sin as sin, Jesus has made an end of. Child of God, you will not misuse this Truth of God and deny the need of repentance, for you well know that you cannot practically feel the power of this blood, except as your sin is known to you; this, indeed, is intimated in the type, for, according to verse fourteen, the bullock was only offered when the sin was known. It was to be laid by the elders upon the head of the bullock, when the sin was no longer hidden from the eyes of the congregation. Sin unknown, the sacrifice is unheeded. It is only as you know and perceive sin that you can consciously know and prize the Atonement by which it is taken away. Mark, it is when you perceive sin that then you are to trust the blood; not when you perceive holiness in yourself, and goodness and virtue, but when you perceive sin, and iniquity, and defilement—it is then you are to lay your hand upon the head of the Great Atoning Sacrifice. Jesus is a sinner's Savior. "If any man sin, we have an Advocate with the Father, Jesus Christ the Righteous."

It is not written, "If any man is holy, he has an Advocate," but, "if any man sin, we have an Advocate," so that in all our sin and iniquity, blackness, and defilement—when overwhelmed with our own vileness, we may still come to Christ, and believe that our most horrible and detestable sins were laid upon Him, and over and above that, those sins which we do not feel, which may be even more detestable, even these, and what is more, the sinfulness of our nature itself—that black and polluted fount from which the streams of our trespasses take their rise; the guilt of all actual and original sin was laid upon Jesus, and by Him forever put away.

Passing on, still keeping to the same point, we would remark that the sin was laid upon the bullock most conspicuously "before the Lord." Did you notice the frequent expressions: "shall bring him to the door of the congregation before the Lord;" "kill the bullock before the Lord;" "shall sprinkle the blood seven times before the Lord, and shall put some of it upon the horns of the Altar of Sweet Incense before the Lord?" Clearly the most important part of the sacrifice was not before the people, but before the Lord. All that the onlookers outside could have seen was the bullock, when dead, carried by the priests outside the camp. Some of them who came nearer might have seen the pouring of the blood at the bottom of the Bronze Altar, but they certainly never did and never could see the priest sprinkle the blood towards the veil, nor yet see him put it upon the horns of the golden altar, for the Court of the Priests was concealed from their view. We are very much mistaken if we think that the ceremonies of Jews were much seen by the people. They were mainly unseen except by the priests. The ritual of the Old Covenant must have been very little a matter of sight; for the Israelite, pure and simple, never penetrated beyond the first court; he stood before the Bronze Altar, but he never went further; and all that was done in the next Court of the priests, and especially all that was done in the Most Holy Place, must have been entirely a matter of faith to all the people. The fact was, the sacrifices were not so much for men to look at as for God Himself to gaze upon, and though this may seem to you a strange observation, there is no little value in it.

You will hear men nowadays say that the purpose of Atonement has reference to men, and not to God. Depend upon it there is a fatal error in this doctrine, and we must denounce it. Although its advocates take a few expressions from some of our hymns, and pretend to believe that we teach that the blood placated an angry God, we never taught anything of the kind, and they know we never did; yet we are not to be frightened into denying or qualifying our assertion that the action of God towards man has been wondrously affected by the Atonement of Christ. God the Judge would have condemned us to punishment had not Jesus suffered in our place, so that, in justice, we might be permitted to go free. Not only is man made willing to love God by the manifestation of the Love of God in Christ Jesus, but it has become possible for God to extend the hand of amity towards sinful man through the Atonement; and this would not have been possible, consistently with the Divine Attributes, if it had not been for the Atoning Sacrifice. We must still stand to it, that the blood is not merely a comfort to the wounded conscience, but is really a satisfaction to Divine Justice; a covering, a Propitiation, a Mercy Seat for the Most Holy God.

That is a striking passage concerning the Passover and the destroying angel in Egypt. Thus spoke Jehovah, "When I see the blood, I will pass over you;" not, "When you see the blood." The spared ones did not see the blood at that moment; for, you will remember, they were all inside the house feasting upon the lamb. The father of the family had put the blood outside upon the lintel and the side-posts, not for the inhabitants to see, but for God to see; and so, though a sight of the precious blood, thanks be to God, does bring us faith, and joy, and peace, yet the real work of our salvation is not the effect of the blood upon us, but the effect of the blood upon God Himself; not, it is true, a change produced in God, but a change which is thus produced in the action of Divine Justice. Apart from the blood, we are guilty and condemned; washed in the blood, we are accepted and beloved. Without the Atonement, we are aliens and strangers, heirs of God's Wrath even as others; but, as seen in the Eternal Covenant purpose, through the precious blood of Jesus, we are accepted in the Beloved. The great stress of the transaction lies in its being done "before the Lord."

Still, further, carefully observe that as soon as ever the sin was thus "before the Lord," laid upon the bullock, the bullock was slain. "He shall lay his hands upon the bullock's head, and kill the bullock before the Lord." So, in the 15th verse, "The elders of the congregation shall lay their hands upon the head of the bullock before the Lord, and the bullock shall be killed before the Lord." Ah, yes; as soon as the sin is transferred, the penalty is transferred too. Down fell the pole-axe the minute that the priestly hands had been laid on the bullock. Unsheathed was the bloody knife of sacrifice the moment that the elders had begun to lean upon the sacrificial head. So was it with our Savior; He must smart, He must die, for only as dying could He become our Sin Offering. Ah, Beloved, those who would preach Christ, but not Christ Crucified, miss the very soul and essence of our holy faith. "Let Him come down from the Cross, and we will believe in Him," is the Unitarian cry! Anything but a Crucified God! But there, indeed, lies the secret of that mystery, and the very core and kernel of our confidence. A Reigning Savior I do rejoice in—the thought of the splendor yet to come makes glad our eyes; but after all, it is a bleeding Savior that is the sinner's hope. It is to the Cross, the center of misery, that the sinner turns his eyes for comfort, rather than to the stars of Bethlehem, or to the blazing sun of the millennial kingdom. I remember one joining this Church who said, "Sir, I had faith once in Christ Glorified, but it never gave me comfort: I have now come to a faith in Christ Crucified, and I have peace." At Calvary there is the comfort, and there only. That Jesus lives is delightful; but the basis of the delight is, "He lives who once was slain." That He will reign forever is a most precious Doctrine of our faith, but that the hand that wields the silver scepter, once was pierced, is the great secret of the joy. O Beloved, abide not in any place from which your eyes cannot behold the Cross of Christ! When you are thinking of the Doctrines of the Gospel, or the Precepts of the Word, or studying the Prophecies of Scripture, never let your mind relinquish the study of the Cross! The Cross was the place of your spiritual birth; it must always be the spot for renewing your health, for it is the sanatorium of every sin-sick soul.

The blood is the true balm of Gilead; it is the only catholicon which heals every spiritual disease. Come, sin-sick Soul, and breathe the air which was purified when the blood of the heart of Jesus fell from His wounds to the ground, for no spiritual disease can abide the Presence of the healing blood. Hurry, you weak ones, to Calvary, and partake in God-given strength and vigor. It is from Calvary that you shall see the Sun of Righteousness arising with healing beneath His wings. The Beloved Physician meets His patients at the foot of the Cross, and relieves them from all their ills.

I shall not ask you to dwell on any further details of the type, as they refer to the Substitution, but I cannot leave the topic till I have asked each one this all-important question: "Is the Lord Jesus made a Sin Offering for you? It is written, "He has made Him to be sin for us," and from this it appears that sin was laid upon Jesus by God Himself; but still it is true that each Believer by faith lays his own sins there, and the hymn, "I lay my sins on Jesus," is quite Scriptural. Have you, dear Friend, seen your sins laid on Jesus? Has your faith laid its hand upon His head? My dear Hearers, we shall soon, each one of us, have to pass through the Valley of Death; it may be but a very short time before some of us will know what are the solemnities of our last, departing hour. Are you ready? Quite ready? You have been a professor of religion for years—are you now ready to die? Can you hope that if at this moment the summons were given, sitting where you are, can you hope you are so really and truly resting in the precious blood, that sin would not disturb your dying peace because it is forgiven and put away? Search the ground of your hope, I pray you, and be not satisfied unless your faith is surely built upon the Rock of Ages. Get as much Assurance as you can, my Brothers and Sisters, but beware of presumption. I have seen some of those fine Christians who will not say—

"Rock of Ages, cleft for me,
Let me hide myself in Thee!"

And I think very little of them. It is their boast that no hymns will suit them but those which are full of Assurance and conscious enjoyment. I admire their confidence, if it is the Fruit of the Spirit; but I fear, in many cases, it is the offspring of proud, unhumbled self-conceit. I know that in shaking times, when I am sorely vexed with bodily pain and mental dis- tractions, I am glad enough to say—

"Let me hide myself in You!
Let the water and the blood,
From Your riven side which flowed,
Be of sin the double cure,
Cleanse me from its guilt and power!"

Without boasting, I can declare as much about strong faith in God as most men; and I can usually rejoice in the fullest confidence of my acceptance in the Beloved; but there are times with me of deeply awful depression of spirit, and horror of great darkness—and at such periods my joyous confidence takes the form of humbly pleading the blood once shed for sinners, and saying, with a broken heart—

"Nothing in my hands I bring:
Simply to Your Cross I cling."

It seems to me, that humbly resting upon Jesus is the best position for us; and I ask each of you, very affectionately, whether that is your position at this present moment? Does your heart rejoice in the Substitute? Do you rejoice in the language of these two precious verses?—

"When Satan tempts me to despair,
And tells me of the guilt within,
Upward I look, and see Him there
Who made an end of all my sin.

Because the sinless Savior died,
My sinful soul is counted free,
For God, the Just, is satisfied
To look on Him, and pardon me."

II. Let us turn to the second part of the subject. The Chapter sets forth before us *the efficacy of the precious blood of Jesus.* As soon as the bullock was slain, the priest carefully collected the blood. The bullock was slain in the Court of the Israelites; look, there it lies at the foot of the Bronze Altar, with the blood in a basin. The priest passes into the Court of the Priests, passes by the Golden Altar of Incense, which stood in the Holy Place, and proceeds to dip his finger in the basin and to sprinkle the blood seven times towards the veil which concealed the Holy of Holies. Whether the blood fell on the veil or not, we are not certain; but we have good reason to believe that it was cast upon the veil itself. The veil, of costliest tapestry, would thus become by degrees more and more like a vesture dipped in blood. Seven times towards the veil the blood of the sin offering was sprinkled by the priest. Why did he begin there? It was to show that our communion with God is by blood. The veil was not then, of course, torn. It showed that the way of access to God was not then revealed. The sprinkling of the blood showed that the only thing that could open the way of access to God was the blood; that the blood, when it would be perfectly offered, seven times sprinkled, would tear the veil. The blood of Jesus has to the letter fulfilled the type. When our Lord had sprinkled, if I may say so, seven times His own heart's blood upon the veil, He said, "It is finished," and "the veil of the Temple was torn in two from the top to the bottom." Beloved, through the perfect offering of the precious blood, we have access with boldness into this Divine Grace where we stand; and we who have faith in that blood have intimate communion with the Living God, and come near to His Mercy Seat to talk with Him, who dwells between the cherubim, as a man talks with his friend.

The priest began at the innermost point, because the first thing which a Christian loses through sin is communion with God, and free access to Him, and consequently the first thing to be restored to him must be this communion with his God. Suppose, my Brother, my Sister, you backslide, there are some things which you will not lose at once. You will still be able to pray in a feeble style; you will still have some sense of acceptance, but certainly your enjoyment and fellowship with God will be suspended as soon as you have fallen from your first estate. Therefore the blood is sprinkled upon the veil to show you that through the blood, and through the blood only, you can renew your access. You advanced Christians, you who have lived in the very heart of God, and have stood like Milton's angel in the sun; you who have been made to sit at the banqueting table, and to drink of the wines on the lees well refined; you who have been the King's favorites, and, like Mephibosheth, have always been made to sit at the King's own table, and to eat of the choice portions of His dainties—if you have lost your heavenly fellowship, it is through the blood, and only through the blood, that you can again have access unto the heart of God.

The next act of the priest was to retire a little from the veil to the place where stood the Golden Altar of Incense, adorned with four horns of gold, probably of a pyramidal shape, or fashioned like rams' horns, and the priest, dipping his finger in the basin, smeared this horn and the other, until the four horns glowed with crimson in the light of the golden candlestick. The horn is always, in the Oriental usage, indicative of strength. Then why was the blood put upon the altar? That incense altar was typical of prayer, and especially of the intercession of Christ; and the blood on the horn showed that the force and power of all-prevailing intercession lies in the blood. Why was this the second thing done? It seems to me that the second thing which a Christian loses is his prevalence in prayer. Whereas, first he loses communion with God when he backslides; the next thing he loses is his power in supplication. He begins to be feeble upon his knees; he cannot win of the Lord that which he desires. How is he to get back his strength? Here the great Anointed Priest teaches us to look to the blood for renewed power, for look, He applies the blood to the horns of the altar, and the sweet perfume of frankincense ascends to Heaven and God accepts it. O Beloved, think of this, Christ's intercessory power with God lies in His precious blood, and your power and mine with God in prayer must lie in that blood, too. Oh, to see the horns of that altar smeared with blood! How can you ever prevail with God unless you plead the blood of Jesus? Believer, if you would overcome in prayer, tell the Lord of all the groans of His dear Son; never dream of arguing except with arguments fetched from Jesus' wounds—these are potent pleas with God—the bloody sweat, the flagellation, the nails, the spear, the vinegar, the Cross—these must be the mighty reasons with which to overcome the Infinite One. Let the altar of your incense be smeared with our Savior's blood!

This being finished, the priest goes backwards still further and enters the Court of the Israelites. There stood the great Altar of Brass, whereon was consumed the burnt offerings; and now the priest, having his basin full of the blood of which only a small quantity had been used in sprinkling the veil and touching the horns of the Golden Altar, pours the whole of the remaining blood in a great stream at the foot of the Altar of Burnt Offering. What does that typify? Did he not thus teach us that the only ground and basis (for mark, it is put at the foot of the altar), of the acceptance of our persons and of our thank offerings is found in the blood of Jesus? Did it never strike you how the whole Tabernacle must have been smeared with blood everywhere? Blood was on every side. The priest himself, when at his work, with garments on which showed every stain, must have looked as though all smeared with gore. You could not look at his hands or at his vestments without seeing blood everywhere; indeed, when consecrated, he had blood on his ear, blood on his foot, blood on his hand—he could not be made a priest without it. The Apostle says, "Almost everything under the Law was sprinkled with blood." It was blood, blood everywhere. Now, this could have been very far from a pleasant sight, except to the spiritual man who, as he looked at it, said, "What a holy God is the God of Israel! How He hates sin! See, He will only permit sinners to approach Him by the way of blood!" And then the inquiring mind would ask, "What blood is this which is here intended?" We know that the blood of bulls and of goats was but the visible symbol of the sufferings of Jesus, the Great Sacrifice, whom God has set forth to be a Propitiation for our sins. All the blood-marks pointed to the "Lamb of God, which takes away the sin of the world." Let us rejoice in the precious blood of Christ the Lamb without blemish and without spot, who was foreordained from the foundations of the world, but was manifest in these last days for us.

Will you now make a summary of what has been spoken? Come with me outside the Tabernacle. Let us begin at the opening in its curtains leading to the Outer Court. We have sinned, and desire acceptance with God; that must be the first blessing. The Bronze Altar of Burnt Offerings is standing before us, and we wish to offer our thank offering, may we do so? How can we be accepted? Look at the bottom of the Altar! What do you see there? A pool of blood all around it, as though the altar stood in blood! What does this mean? Surely the blood of Jesus is the basis of our acceptance before God, and here we stand as citizens of Heaven, not accursed, but beloved; not rejected and abhorred, but elect and blessed through the blood which is the ground of our acceptance as Believers and citizens of Zion. Now we have come so far, we remember that we are not only citizens of the New Jerusalem, but priests unto God, and as priests we desire to enter the Court of the Priests, and offer the incense of praise and prayer. Here we stand as priests, and there is the Golden Altar, but where is our power to minister before the Lord? How shall we approach with the love of our hearts, our joyful thanks, and our fervent intercessions? Behold the answer to our inquiries! Observe with joy the blood-marks on the four horns! It is not our prayers that will be in themselves prevalent, nor our praises, nor our love; but the *blood* gives prevalence, acceptance, and power to all. Come here, then, and let us lay our heart itself, all bleeding, upon that altar, and let our prayers and praises rise to Heaven, like pillars of smoke, accepted through the blood!

But, Beloved, this is not all, we are something more than priests—we are children of God, dear to His heart; let us, then, seek fellowship with our Father who is in Heaven. How can we enter into the Most Holy Place and commune with the God who hides Himself? What is the mode of entrance into that which is within the veil? We look, and lo, the veil is torn, and on the floor, right across where the veil used to hang, we see a line of blood, where, times without number, the blood had been sprinkled; and on the two pieces of the veil through which we pass, we can see many distinct traces of blood; yes, and when we come right up to the Mercy Seat we can see the blood there, too! What does this mean but that the blood is the means of access to God, and by no other means is He to be approached? When we shall be nearest to God, and see Him face to face, and dwell with Him in Heaven forever, it will be because Jesus Christ loved us and died for us, and sprinkled His blood for us that we are permitted to have this close and wonderful communion with God which even angels never had, for even they can only veil their faces with their wings, and must not dare to look upon God as we shall do, when our eyes shall see Him as our Father and our Friend!

Thus I have tried to set forth the threefold prevalence of the precious blood, but let it not be forgotten that the blood also put away sin; for you find at the end of the Chapter, "His sin shall be forgiven." First forgiven, then accepted, then prevalent in prayer, and then admitted into access with boldness to God; what a chain of blessings! All, all through the blood of Jesus!

III. Thirdly, the most painful part of our sermon remains, while I beg you to view *the shame which our Lord endured.* While it is all so well for us, so sweet for us, I want you now to reflect how bitter, how shameful it was for our Lord! The offerer who brought the sin offering has been forgiven; he has been accepted at the Bronze Altar; his prayers have been heard at the Golden Altar; and the veil has been sprinkled on his behalf: but what of the Victim? Draw near and learn with holy wonder! In the first place, albeit that our Lord Jesus Christ was made sin for us, it is noteworthy that, though nearly all the bullock was burned outside the camp, there was one portion left and reserved to be burnt upon the Altar of Burnt Offering—the fat. Certain descriptions are given as to the fat which was to be consumed upon the altar, by which we believe it was intended to ensure that the richest part of the fat should be there consumed. As much as if God would say, "Though My dear Son must be made sin for this people, and consequently I must forsake Him, and He must die outside the camp, yet still He is most dear and precious in My sight, and even while He is a Sin Offering, yet He is My Beloved Son in whom in Himself I am still well pleased." Brothers and Sisters, whenever we speak about our Lord as bearing our sins, we must carefully speak concerning Him—not as though God ever did despise or abhor the prayer of His afflicted Son, but only seemed to do so while He stood for us, representatively made sin for us, though He knew no sin. Oh, I delight to think that the Lord smelled a sweet savor even in the Cross, and that Jesus Crist is this day a sweet savor unto God, even as a Sin Offering; the fat, the excellence of His heart, the consecration of His soul, were acceptable to God, and sweet in His esteem, even when He laid upon Him the iniquity of His people! Still, here is the shameful part of it; the priest then took the bullock, and gathering up all the innards, every part of it, the skin, the dung—all mentioned to teach us what a horrible thing sin is, and what the Surety was looked upon as being when He took our sin—he took it all up, and either himself personally, or assisted by others, took it away out of the camp. We are told that in the wilderness, so large was the camp, that it may have been the distance of four miles that this bullock had to be carried. I think I see the sad procession—the priest all smeared with blood, carrying the carcass of the bullock, taking it right away down the long line of tents, first through the abodes of one tribe and then of another, through the long streets of tents, while the people stood at their doors and saw the ghastly sight. It was killed at the Altar of Burnt Offering. Why was it not burnt there? That altar was holy, and as soon as ever sin was laid upon the bullock, it ceased to be any longer looked upon as a holy thing; it could not, therefore, be burnt in the holy place, it must be taken away. So the priest carried it away—a terrible load—till he reached the usual place where the ashes were kindled, and he put the bullock there, and heaped the hot ashes upon it till the whole smoked up to Heaven, and was utterly consumed as a sin offering.

My Beloved, try if you can to grasp the idea of Jesus being put away from God. I cannot give you the thoughts, but if you could hear the air pierced with the dreadful cry, "Eloi, Eloi, lama Sabacthani?" (meaning, "My God, My God, why have You forsaken Me?"), you would see Christ put away because He was made sin. It was not possible for God to look upon sin, even when it was in Christ, with anything like complacency. "It pleased the Father to bruise Him; He has put Him to grief." If you have read the order of the burnt offering, you will have noticed that when the bullock of the burnt offering was offered, it was washed, to show the perfection of Christ as He is a sweet savor, all pure and clean; but in this case there is added that humiliating word, "with the dung." What a humiliating type of Christ! Ah, but what are your sins and mine that were laid upon Jesus? How could our iniquities and transgressions be better set forth than by that bleeding, mangled mass which the High Priest had to carry out away from the camp, as though it were a thing abhorred, which could not be endured in the camp any longer? It is your Savior made sin for you and put away on your behalf.

After the removal, they gathered the hot ashes, they kindled the fire, and burnt it all. See here a faint image of the fire which consumed the Savior upon Calvary! His bodily pains ought never to be forgotten, because there is so intimate a relation between physical suffering and mental grief, that it were hard to draw the line; but still the sufferings of His soul must have been the very soul of His sufferings, and can you tell what they were? Have you ever suffered from a raging fever? Have you felt at the same time the pangs of some painful disease? Has your mind refused to rest? Has your brain been tossed like the waves of a sea of fire within your head? Have you questioned whether you should lose your reason or not? Have you ever been near unto distraction? Have you ever been near unto the breaking of the cords of life? If so, you may feebly guess what He suffered when He said, "My soul is exceedingly sorrowful, even unto death," and when He "began to be sorrowful and to be very heavy." Those were the coals of juniper which were being heaped over the sin offering. As you see Jesus scourged by Herod and by Pilate, and afterwards bleeding on the accursed tree, you see the fire of Divine Wrath consuming the Sin Offering because our sin had been laid upon Him. I will not dwell longer on this, only ask the Holy Spirit to make you feel the shame that Christ suffered for you. Sometimes I cannot grasp the thought, when I have tried to think that He who made the heavens, to whom the whole blue arch is but as a span, and the depths of the seas as the hollow of His hand, should be made flesh, and then suffer for such an insignificant worm as I am! That He should suffer, however, never amazes me as much as that He should bear my sin. Oh, amazing Grace! The angels say, "Holy! Holy! Holy! Lord God of Sabaoth!" What could they have said when He, whom they hymned as "glorious in holiness," bowed His head and gave up the ghost, because "made sin for us?" Blessed Son of God! Where we cannot understand we will adore!

The Apostle Paul suggests to us the most practical conclusion of our sermon. He tells us that as our Savior, having given His blood to be sprinkled within the Tabernacle for us, was then taken outside the camp, so it is our duty, yes, and our privilege, to go forth unto Him outside the camp also, bearing His reproach. You have heard how He was reproached for you; are you unwilling to be reproached for Him? You have heard how He went outside the camp in that shameful manner—are you unwilling to go outside the camp for Him? Too many Christians try to be Christians in the camp, but it cannot be done. "Be not conformed to this world, but be you transformed by the renewing of your minds." There is so much of worldly conformity among us; but the promise is not to worldly-minded Christians, but, "Come you out from among them; be you separate; touch not the unclean thing; and I will receive you, and will be a Father unto you." How much we lose by affinities with the world! How much of distance there is between us and God because of the nearness there is between us and the world! Come out, you lovers of the Savior, and tread the separated way which your Savior walked before you!

And now, should there be any here who are unsaved, I should not wonder but what some of them will make the remark, the almost, no, the quite profane remark, "Why, he spoke so much of blood!" Ah, Sinner, and we need to speak much of it to you, for it is your only hope! God will either have your blood or Christ's blood, one of the two. If you reject Christ, you shall perish in your sin. "The blood is the life thereof," says the Word of God; and your life must be taken unless Christ's life shall die for you. The very heart of Christ was broken to find out the way to save a sinner; and, Sinner, there is no other; if you refuse the purple road, you shall never reach the pearly gate. Trust in the blood of Jesus. Do you doubt? How can you? Is there not efficacy enough in the blood of the Son of God to take away sin? Do you contradict God's declared Truth, "The blood of Jesus Christ, His Son, cleanses us from all sin"? Oh, believe it, and cast your soul upon it, and we will meet within the veil, one of these days, to sing, "To Him who loved us, and washed us from our sins in His own blood . . . to Him be glory forever and ever!" Amen.

5

The Sprinkling of the Blood
of the Sacrifice

"And the priest shall dip his finger in the blood, and sprinkle of the blood seven times before the Lord, before the veil of the sanctuary. And the priest shall put some of the blood upon the horns of the altar of sweet incense before the Lord, which is in the tabernacle of the congregation; and shall pour all the blood of the bullock at the bottom of the altar of the burnt offering, which is at the door of the tabernacle of the congregation." (Leviticus 4:6-7)

I HAVE PREACHED, BEFORE, to you upon the types of our Lord's Sacrifice—the subject is as large as it is important. We began with the laying of the hands upon the offering and we went on to the all-important matter of the slaying of the victim.* Now we come to the use which was made of the blood of the sacrifice after it had been slain. In thinking upon this subject, I seem to hear a voice saying to me, "Put off your shoes from off your feet, for the place whereon you stand is holy ground." This is the central mystery of our religion. It becomes us to be reverent in heart as we approach it. The Doctrine of Substitution is the

---

* See chapters 1 and 2.

heart of the whole matter—our whole heart needs to be awakened while we speak upon it. The Son of God, Himself, assuming human nature and, in that Nature bleeding and dying in our place, is the Revelation of Revelation, the wonder of wonders, the Glory of the glorious God! Solemnity and awe may well fill us while we meditate on such a theme.

Oh, that the Spirit of God may rest upon us now! May His melting power be over this vast assembly! May the speaker feel it and may the hearers experience it, so that we may, with one consent, in spirit and in truth, look to Him who, by the Eternal Spirit, offered up Himself without spot unto God! The sacrifices under the Law of God were varied according to the uppermost thoughts in the offerers' minds and their peculiar conditions before God. A burnt offering, a peace offering, or a sin offering might be brought, according as men wished to give unto the Lord, to have fellowship with Him, or to confess their sin to Him. There was a sacrifice specially arranged for the anointed priest, another for all the congregation, another for a ruler and yet another for one of the common people—in truth the typical sacrifices all pointed to the one Great Sacrifice, but they indicated various marks and characteristics of the undivided Lamb of God.

The victims varied from a bullock or a lamb down to a pair of turtle doves or two young pigeons. We take different views of the Sacrifice of Christ according to our capacity to see it, but all these views may be quite in accordance the Truth of God, for the Atonement is many-sided and operates in many directions. The Levitical types represent the different views which believing minds take of our Lord Jesus Christ. They set forth but one Christ, but that one Christ from various standpoints. The mercy is that the Sacrifice of our Lord Jesus is suitable to you and equally suitable to me—and to all that come to Him by faith. The rich, the poor, the brave, the timid, the amiable and the immoral all find, in Jesus, that which fits their individual case. You may be a person of great mind and profound thought, but you shall find, in Jesus, all that your high intelligence can desire! I may be a person of slender education and of narrow powers of thought, but I shall find the Lord Jesus humbling Himself to my limited capacity.

The manna is said, by the rabbis, to have pleased every man's taste and, even so, the Christ of God is every man's Christ, so that no man who comes to Him shall be disappointed, but each shall find His needs supplied. Each man shall find his case perfectly met by the Savior's Atonement, as much so as if Jesus were prepared for that man, only—as if that man were the only sinner under Heaven—or Jesus a Redeemer sent to him, alone, of all the family of man! Oh, the depth of the wisdom and of the Grace of God in the Person and work of our Lord Jesus Christ! Note particularly, with great interest, that there were sacrifices provided for sins of ignorance under the Law—therefore we safely conclude that a sin of ignorance is a sin. There is not that intensity of evil in a sin of ignorance which is to be seen in willful, deliberate transgression, but still, there is sin in it—for no law can allow ignorance to be an excuse for trespass since it is the duty of the subject to know the law. Even if I do that which is wrong with a sincere wish to do right, still, my wrong act has a measure of sin in it. No amount of sincerity can turn injustice into righteousness, or transform falsehood into truth.

You can illustrate this by the stern facts of Nature. Certain inventors have thought that they could fly and they have, in perfectly honest faith, leaped from a lofty crag. But their honest belief has not saved them from the result of violating the law of gravity—they have fallen to the ground—and have been dashed in pieces just as surely and terribly as if they had felt no real belief in their powers of flight. If a man partakes of a deadly poison believing it to be a health-giving medicine, his sincerity will not hinder the natural course of Nature—he will die in his error. It is precisely so in the moral and spiritual world. Sins committed in ignorance must be, still, sins in the sight of the Lord, or else no expiation would have been provided for them. Without shedding of blood, there is no remission even for sins of ignorance!

Paul persecuted the saints ignorantly, but he thereby incurred sins which required to be washed away—so Ananias told him and so he felt—for he called himself the chief of sinners because he persecuted the Church of God. When the people sinned through ignorance and the thing was hid from the eyes of the assembly, they were to bring an offering as soon as the sin was known. If you have transgressed ignorantly, my Brothers and Sisters, the time may come when you will find out that you were sinning—and it will then rejoice your heart to find that the Lord Jesus has made Atonement for your sins before you knew them to be sins! I am greatly rejoiced to think there should be such a Sacrifice provided, since it may yet turn out that the larger number of our sins are sins of which we have not been aware because our heart has prevented our discovering our error. You may have sinned and have no conscience of that sin at this present time—yes, and you may never have a conscience of that particular offense, in this world—yet it will be sin all the same.

Many good men have lived in an evil habit and remained in it unto death—and yet have not known it to be evil. Now, if the precious blood of Jesus only put away the sin which we perceived in detail, its efficacy would be limited by the enlightenment of our conscience and, therefore, some grievous sin might be overlooked and prove our ruin. But inasmuch as this blood puts away all sins, it removes those which we do not discover as well as those over which we mourn. "Cleanse You me from secret faults" is a prayer to which the Expiation of Christ is a full answer. The Atonement acts according to God's sight of sin and not according to our sight of it, for we only see it in part, but God sees it all and blots it all out.

When we discover our iniquity, it is ours to weep over it with true and deep repentance. But if there are some sins which, in detail, we have not discerned and, consequently, have not, by a specific act of repentance, confessed them separately, yet, for all that, the Lord puts away our sin, for it is written, "The blood of Jesus Christ His Son cleanses us from all sin." Those unknown sufferings of Christ which the Greek Liturgy mentions so wisely, have put away from us those unknown sins which we cannot confess in detail because we have not yet perceived them. Blessed be God for a Sacrifice which cleanses away, forever, not only our glaring faults, but those offenses which the most minute self-examination has not yet uncovered!

After the blood had been spilt by the killing of the sacrifice and thus atonement had been made, three several acts were to be performed by the priest—we have them described in our text—and if you will kindly look, you will see that very much the same words follow in the 17th and 18th verses, as, also, in the 25th verse and the 34th verse, where, with somewhat less detail, much the same act is set forth. "And the priest shall dip his finger in the blood and sprinkle it seven times before the Lord, before the veil of the sanctuary. And the priest shall put some of the blood upon the horns of the altar of sweet incense before the Lord, which is in the tabernacle of the congregation; and shall pour all the blood of the bullock at the bottom of the altar of the burnt offering, which is at the door of the tabernacle of the congregation."

All this is symbolic of the work of the Lord Jesus and the manifold effects of His blood. There were three things—first, "the priest shall dip his finger in the blood and sprinkle it seven times before the Lord, before the veil of the sanctuary." This represents the atoning sacrifice in its reference to God. Next, "The priest shall put some of the blood upon the horns of the altar of sweet incense before the Lord." This sets forth the influence upon the offering of intercessory prayer. Thirdly, we read, "He shall pour all (the rest) of the blood of the bullock at the bottom of the altar of the burnt offering." This displays the influence of the blood of Christ on all our service for the Lord. Oh, for the Spirit's power to us to show the things of Christ!

I. We begin with *the sacrifice of Christ in its relation to the Lord God of Israel.* In the type before us the prominent thing before God is the blood of atonement. No mention is made of a meat offering, or a drink offering, or even of sweet spices upon the golden altar—the one conspicuous object is blood. This was sprinkled before the Lord before the veil of the Most Holy place. I am well aware that some persons cry out, "The preacher continually talks about blood and, this morning, from the first hymn to the last, he has brought before us constant allusions to blood. We are horrified by it!" I wish you to be horrified for, indeed, sin is a thing to shudder at—and the death of Jesus is not a matter to be treated lightly! It was God's intent to awaken in man a great disgust of sin by making him see that it could only be put away by suffering and death.

In the Tabernacle in the wilderness, almost everything was sanctified by blood. The purple drops fell, even, on the Book and all the people. The blood was to be seen everywhere. As soon as you entered the outer court you saw the great bronze altar—and at the base of it bowls of blood were constantly being poured out! When you passed the first veil and entered the Holy Place, if you saw a priest, he was spattered from head to foot with blood—his snow-white robes bringing the crimson spots most vividly before your eyes. If you looked around, you saw the horns of the golden altar of incense smeared with blood—and the gorgeous veil which hid the innermost sanctuary was bedewed with a frequent sprinkling of the same! The holy tent was by no means a place for sentimentalists—its emblematic teachings dealt with terrible realities in a boldly impressive manner—its ritual was not constructed to gratify the taste, but to impress the mind!

It was not a place for dainty gentlemen, but for broken-hearted sinners. Everywhere, the ignorant eye would see something to displease—but the troubled conscience would read lessons of peace and pardon! Oh, that my words would cause triflers with sin to be shocked at the abominable thing! I would have them filled with horror of that detestable thing which cannot be put away except by that which is infinitely more calculated to shock the instructed mind than rivers of the blood of bulls and of goats—I mean the sacrifice of God's own Son—whose soul was made an offering for sin!

The blood of the sacrifice was sprinkled before the veil seven times, signifying this—first, that the Atonement made by the blood of Jesus is perfect in its reference to God. All through the Scriptures, as you well know, seven is the number of perfection, and in this place it is doubtless used with that intent. The seven times is the same as once and for all—it conveys the same meaning as when we read, "For Christ also has once suffered for sins." And again, "We are sanctified through the offering of the body of Jesus Christ once." It is a complete act. In this text we understand that the Lord Jesus offered unto the justice of God an absolutely complete and satisfactory Atonement by His vicarious suffering and death for guilty men. There is no need of further offering for sin. "It is finished." He has purged our sins! In old times—before the coming of our Lord—the veil hung darkly between the place of God's glorious Presence and His worshipping people. It was only lifted for a moment, once a year, and then that only one of all living men might enter into the Holy of Holies for a brief time—the way into the Holiest not yet being made manifest. But still, the blood was sprinkled towards the place where the Glory of God was pleased to dwell indicating that access to Him could only be by the way of the blood.

Albeit that modern thought will contradict me, I shall not cease to assert perpetually that the greatest result of the death of the Lord Jesus was Godward. Not only does He reconcile us unto God by His death and turn our enmity into love, but He has borne the chastisement of our peace, and thus magnified the Law and made it honorable. God, the Judge of All, is enabled without the violation of His justice to pass by transgression, iniquity and sin. The blood of the sin offering was sprinkled before the Lord because the sin was before the Lord. David says—"Against You, You only, have I sinned," and the prodigal cries, "I have sinned against Heaven and before you." The Sacrifice of Christ is so mainly a Propitiation before God, so thoroughly a vindication of Divine Righteousness, that this one view of the Atonement is sufficient for any man, even if he obtains no other!

But let him beware of trusting to a faith which does not look to the great Propitiation! This is the soul-saving view—the idea which pacifies conscience and wins the heart! We believe in Jesus as the Propitiation for sin. The lights which stream from the Cross are very varied, but as all the colored rays are found in the white light of day, so all the varied teachings of Calvary meet in the fact that Jesus suffered for sin—the Just for the unjust! Do not your hearts feel glad to think that the Lord Jesus Christ has offered a perfect Atonement, covering all, removing every obstacle to the mercy of God—making a clear way for the Lord most justly to justify the guilty? No man need bring anything more, or anything of his own with which to turn away the anger of God—he may come just as he is— guilty and defiled, and plead this precious blood which has made effectual Atonement for him. O my Soul, endorse the doctrine! Feel the sweet experiences that flow from it and stand, now, in the Presence of God without fear—for seven times has the blood spoken for you unto God!

Note next, that not only is the Atonement, itself, perfect, but that the presentation of that Atonement is perfect, too. The sevenfold sprinkling was typical of Christ, as a Priest, presenting Himself unto the Father as a

Sacrifice for sin. This has been fully done. Jesus has, in due order, carried the Propitiation into the sanctuary and appeared in the Presence of God on our behalf. Here are the Apostle's own words, "by His own blood He entered in once into the Holy Place, having obtained eternal redemption for us." It is not our presenting of the blood, but Christ's presenting of the blood which has made the Atonement—even as it is not our sight of the blood, but Jehovah's sight of it which causes us to escape—as it was written concerning the Passover, "When I see the blood, I will pass over you." Jesus at this moment sets His Atonement within view of a righteous God and, therefore, the Judge of all the earth is able to look on the guilty with eyes of mercy! Let us rest perfectly satisfied that all we require to bring us near to God has been done for us—and we may now come boldly unto the Throne of the heavenly Grace—

> "No longer far from God, but now,
> By precious blood made nigh,
> Accepted in the Well-Beloved
> Near to His heart we lie."

We now pass on to a few thoughts about ourselves in relation to this type. This sevenfold sprinkling of the blood upon the veil meant that the way of our access to God is only by virtue of the precious blood of Christ. Do you ever feel a veil hanging between you and God? In very truth, there is none, for Jesus has taken it away through His flesh. In the day when His blessed body was offered up, the veil of the Temple was torn in two from the top to the bottom, showing that there is now nothing to divide the Believer from his God. But still, if you think there is such a separating veil; if you feel as if the Lord had hidden Himself; if you are so despondent that you are afraid you will never draw near to the Mercy Seat, then sprinkle the blood towards the Throne of Grace—cast it on the very veil which appears to conceal your God from you! Let your heart go towards God, even if you cannot reach Him, and let this blood go before you, for rest assured nothing can dissolve obstacles and furnish you with an open access to God except the blood of Jesus Christ the Son of God!

Rest assured that you are already come unto God if boldly, yes, even if timidly with trembling finger, you do but sprinkle the blood in the direction which your faith longs to take! If you cannot present the Atonement of Christ, yourself, by the firm hand of an undaunted faith—remember, Christ's own hand has presented the Propitiation long before—and, therefore, the work will not fail because of your feebleness! O that by a simple confidence in the Lord, your Redeemer, you may, this day, by His Grace, imitate the example of the priest under the Law, for Jesus makes you a priest by the Gospel! You may now look towards the Lord and plead that all-prevailing blood which makes us near, who were once afar off! I have often admired that blessed Gospel precept, "Look unto Me, and be you saved, all the ends of the earth," for suppose I cannot see, yet if I look, I have the promise of being saved! If there should be a mist and a cloud between me and the bronze serpent, yet if I look that way I shall be healed! If I cannot clearly discern all the glories of my Lord and Savior, yet if I look with the glance of trust, blessed be God, He saves me!

Turn, then, your half-opened eyes which only at one corner admit light! Turn them, I say, Godward and Christ ward—and know that by reason of the atoning blood you are saved! The blood-spattered way is the only one which a sinner's feet can traverse if he would come to God! It is easy, plain and open. See, the priest had the Gospel at his finger-tips—at every motion of his hand, he preached it, and the effect of such preaching remained wherever the drops found a resting place!

I further think that the blood was sprinkled on the veil seven times to show that a deliberate contemplation of the death of Christ is greatly for our benefit. Whatever else you treat lightly, let the Sacrifice of Calvary be seriously considered again and again—even unto seven times let it be meditated on! Read the story of our Lord's death in the four Evangelists and ponder every detail till you are familiar with His grief. I would have you know the story by heart, for nothing will do your heart so much good! Read over the 22nd Psalm and the 53rd of Isaiah every day if you are in any kind of trouble of heart about sin—and pray to God for enlightenment that you may see the exceeding greatness of His Grace to us in Christ Jesus! Oh, that you may with all your heart believe in the Lamb of God! Angels desire to look into these things, therefore, I pray you, do not neglect so great a salvation! Think lovingly of the atoning Sacrifice. Earnestly consider it a second time, do it a third time, do it a fourth time, do it a fifth time, do it a sixth time, do it a seventh time!

Remember, too, that this sets out how great our guilt has been, since the blood must be sprinkled seven times before the work of Atonement is fully seen by you. Our guilt has a sevenfold blackness about it and there must be a sevenfold cleansing. If you plead the blood of Jesus once and you do not obtain peace thereby, plead it again! And if the burden still lies upon your heart, still go on pleading with the Lord the one prevailing argument that Jesus bled! If for the present you do not gain peace through the blood of the Cross, do not conclude that your sin is too great for pardon, for that is not the fact since, "all manner of sin and blasphemy shall be forgiven unto men." A fuller acquaintance with Him who has made peace by His blood will calm the tempest of your mind. Christ is a great Savior for great sinners and His precious blood can remove the blackest spots of iniquity. See it sprinkled seven times for a seven-times polluted sinner and rest your soul on Him though seven devils should have entered into you! God, who bids us forgive unto 70 times seven, sets no limit to His own forgiveness.

Reflect that if your case seems to yourself to be very difficult, it is provided for by this sevenfold sprinkling of the blood. If you say, "My heart is so hard! I cannot make it feel." Or if you say, "I am so frivolous and foolish I seem to forget what I once knew," then continue to look to the blood of Jesus and draw hope from it even to seven times. Do not go away from that, I charge you—where else can you go? The devil's desire will be to keep you from thinking about Christ, but remember, thoughts about anything else will do you very little good. Your hope lies in thinking about Jesus, not about yourself! Masticate and digest such a text as this every morning—"He is able to save them to the uttermost that come unto God by Him." Go to bed at night with this verse upon your tongue, "The blood of Jesus Christ His Son cleanses us from all sin." Or this, "Him that comes unto Me I will by no means cast out."

That dear man of God, Mr. Moody Stuart, somewhere tells us that he once talked with a woman who was in great trouble about her sins. She was a well-instructed person and knew the Bible thoroughly, so that he was in a little difficulty what to say to her, as she was so accustomed to the all-saving Truth of God. At last he urged upon her, very strongly, that passage, "This is a faithful saying, and worthy of all acceptation, that Jesus Christ came into the world to save sinners," and he noticed that she seemed to find a quiet relief in a gentle flow of tears. He prayed with her and when she rose from her knees, she seemed much comforted. Meeting her the next day and seeing her smiling face—and finding her full of rest in the Lord—he asked, "What was it that worked you deliverance?" "Oh," she said, "it was that text, 'Jesus Christ came to save sinners.'" "Did you not know that before?" asked Mr. Stuart. Yes, she knew the words before, but she found that in her heart of hearts she had believed that Jesus came to save saints and not sinners!

Do not many awakened persons abide in the same error? Well, I want you, poor troubled heart, yes, and you, also, who are of a joyful spirit, to keep on with this sevenfold presentation of the Sacrifice of Christ unto God. And even if a veil should hang between you and the Lord, I beg you to continue to sprinkle the veil with blood until, before the eyes of your faith, the veil tears in two and you stand in the Presence of your reconciled God, rejoicing in Christ Jesus!

II. Our second head is this—*the blood in its influence upon prayer.* "The priest shall put some of the blood upon the horns of the altar of sweet incense before the Lord." The priest, in this case, goes from the inside of the Holy Place towards the outer court, having dealt with the veil of the Holy of Holies. He turns round and finds close at his side the altar of incense made of gold and surmounted with a golden crown—to this he goes deliberately and places a portion of the blood upon each of its horns. Horns signify power and the explanation of the symbol is that there is no power in intercessory prayer apart from the blood of expiation.

Remember, first, that the intercession of Christ Himself is based upon His Atonement. He is daily pleading before the Throne of God and His great argument is that He offered Himself without spot unto God. It seems to me most clear and blessed that our Lord Jesus makes this the main plea with the Father on our behalf—"I have finished the work which You gave Me to do." He has suffered in our place and every day He pleads these sufferings for us. His blood speaks better things than that of Abel. He seeks no new plea, but always urges this old one—His blood shed for many for the remission of sins. "It pleased the Father to bruise Him," and now it pleases the Father to hear Him! The bruised spices of His passion are an incense of sweet smell and derive a double acceptance from the blood-smeared altar upon which they are presented.

And now take the type to yourselves. You and I are to offer incense upon this golden altar by our daily intercession for others, but our plea must always be the atoning blood of Jesus. I pray you, dear Friends, to urge this much more than you have been accustomed to do in your prayers. We are to cry to God for sinners and we are to cry to God for saints—but the sacrifice of Jesus must be our strength in petitioning. Intercession is one of the most excellent duties in which a Christian can be engaged—it has about it the honor both of priesthood and kingship. The incense altar ought to be continually smoking before the Lord God of Israel, not only in our public Prayer Meetings, but in our private supplications. We should be continually pleading for our children, for our friends, for our neighbors, for those who are hopeful and those who seem hopeless. But the great plea must always be, "By Your agony and bloody sweat! By Your Cross and passion."

Offer sweet spices of love, faith and hope, and lay on the burning coals of strong desire. But on the horn of your altar smear the blood—

> "Blood has a voice to pierce the skies!
> 'Revenge,' the blood of Abel cries.
> But the rich blood of Jesus slain
> Speaks, 'Peace' as loud from every vein."

Take care you never advance another plea, or if another, let it be very subsidiary to this master reason. We may say, "O Lord, save men because their immortal souls are precious. Save them that they may escape from endless misery and that they may display the power of Your Grace. Save them, also, that Your Word may not return unto You void, and that Your Church may be built up by their means." But we must never be content with these pleas! We must go on to plead the name of Jesus, for whatever we ask in that name we shall receive. He who once poured out His soul unto death and now makes intercession for the transgressors, will see to it that our pleas shall not be rejected! In all our intercessions we must remember Calvary—the incense altar, for us, must, on the horn of its strength, be always sprinkled with the blood!

And, dearly Beloved, as this must be the plea of our intercession, so it must be our impulse in making intercession. When we pray, we come, as it were, to this golden altar and we look thereon—what do we see? Stains of blood! We look again, and again see crimson spots, while all the four horns are red with blood. Did my Lord pour out His soul unto death for men and shall not I pour out my soul in living earnest when I pray? Can you now bow your knee to plead with God and not feel your heart set upon the good of men when you see that your Lord has laid down His life that they may be saved? Cold prayers and dull pleas would vanish if we would but remember how Jesus loved—how being in an agony He sweat, as it were, great drops of blood.

Brothers and Sisters, we are sadly blameworthy for neglect of intercessory prayer! I cannot tell how much of a blessing is being withheld because we do not pray importunately for our fellow men! May the Lord awaken us! May He never permit us to neglect the precious use of the Mercy Seat! When the late Dr. Bacchus was ill and near to death, a surgeon visited him. And as he left the room, he was observed to speak to the servant. The good old Divine begged the attendant to tell him what the surgeon said. After some pause, he said, "Dear Sir, he told me not to leave you, for you could not live more than another half-hour." "Then," said the saint, "help me out of bed, let me get upon my knees and spend my last half hour on earth in praying for the Church of God and for the salvation of men."

What a blessed way of spending one's last half-hour! Let me rather say—what a blessed way of spending half-an- hour at any time! Try it this afternoon! I do not know any method of benefiting our friends which is more constantly open to us all than that of intercessory prayer. And I cannot give you a better argument for why you should use it than this—

your Lord has sprinkled the golden altar of intercession with His own blood! Where He poured out His blood, will you not pour out your tears? He has given His bleeding heart for men—will not you give your pleading lips?

I think, too, I must say that this smearing of the horns of the altar with blood is meant to give us very great encouragement and assurances whenever we come to God in prayer. Never give anybody up, however bad he may be. If you know a man that is as much like the devil as two peas in a pod, still have hope for him, because when you come to the golden altar to offer your prayers on his behalf what do you see? Why, there is the blood of Christ! What sin is there which it cannot remove? "Oh," you ask, "did Jesus die for sinners like this man and shall I despair of him and, therefore, refuse to pray for him?" This is logical argument. We are slow to labor for men because we are slow of heart in expecting their salvation—and this arises out of our narrow views of our Lord Jesus. I pray you enlarge your ideas of God's mercy and of Christ's power to cleanse! Pray not with a phantom hope, but with solid confidence, and say, "Lord, I do but follow with my tears where You have been with Your blood. I am pleading for this man's pardon and You are also making intercession for transgressors. I am pleading for those whom You have bought with Your blood and, therefore, I am confident that my desire is in consonance with Your will and that I shall be heard in Heaven, Your dwelling place."

When we pray, let us with vehement desire plead the blood of Jesus Christ! Perhaps fewer petitions and more urging of the merit of Christ would make better prayers. If we were shorter in what we ask for but longer in pleading the reason why we should obtain it, we might prevail more easily. I suggest that we use fewer nails, but take care that those nails are driven in with Calvary's blood-stained hammer and clenched with this argument—"For Jesus' sake." May this sort of prayer be used by all of us in private and in public—and then we must and shall prevail!

III. Time flies too quickly this morning and, therefore, I must pass over many things I had thought to dwell upon. The last point is, *the blood in its influence upon all our service.* You see we have been coming outwards from the veil to the golden altar and now we pass outside the Holy Place into the outer court. And there in the open air stands the great bronze altar—the first object that the Israelite saw when he entered the sacred precincts. As soon as he entered into the first enclosure, his eye lighted upon the great altar of brass upon which burnt offerings were burned and oblations were presented unto the Lord. It was at the foot of this bronze altar that the bowls of blood were continually poured out—so that the altar was encrimsoned with it—and the soil around was soaked with the sanguine flood.

That altar represents a great many things and among the rest of them, our Lord Jesus presenting Himself to God as an acceptable Sacrifice. Whenever you think of our Lord as being an offering of a sweet smell unto God, never dissociate that fact in your mind from His being slain for sin, for all our Lord's service is tinged by His atoning death. It is a great mistake, when you are trying to explain any one of the Levitical sacrifices to run entirely upon one line, for there is a blessed union of all of them in Christ. The offerings of a sweet savor were, all of them, in a sense, sin offerings—there are clear indications of this. At the same time the sin offering was not altogether an abomination, but, in part, a sweet savor offering, for the fat, as we have seen in our reading, was presented upon the altar. What God has joined together let no man put asunder. You may look at your Lord under various headings and separately think of His life and of His death—but never stereotype even that division, for His death was the climax of His life—and His life was necessary to His death. Always think of Jesus, in all your meditations upon Him, as

95

presenting Himself to God and pouring out His soul unto death by way of atonement. When I see that great bronze altar, I do not forget how our Lord was accepted of God, but when I see the floods of blood at the foot of the altar, I am reminded of the fact that, "He His own self bore our sins in His own body on the tree."

Viewing the type in reference to ourselves, let us learn that whenever we come to offer any sacrifice unto the Lord, we must take care that we present it by virtue of the precious blood of Christ. The worship of this morning—God knows our hearts—He knows how many have really adored Him. And He knows, out of those who worship, how many of us have presented our sacrifice, thinking only of the merit of Jesus as the reason why it should be received.

When you rise from your knees after your morning prayer, have you really pleaded the precious blood? Your petitions will not be acceptable to God if you have not. When you are praying at eventide and speaking with your heavenly Father, have you your eyes upon Christ? If not, your devotion will be rejected. As it is with worship in the form of prayer, so is it with worship in the form of praise. Sweet sounds are very delightful when we sing the praises of God, but unless the altar is blood-stained upon which we lay our Psalms and hymns, they will not be accepted for all their music! We also bring to God our gifts as He prospers us. I trust we are all ready to give Him a portion of our substance—but do we present it upon the altar which sanctifies the giver and the gift? Do we see the blood of Christ upon it and present our gold and silver through that which is more precious by far? If not, we might as well keep our money. When you go, this afternoon, to your Sunday school classes, or go out into the streets to preach, or go round with your tracts, will you present your holy labor to God through the precious blood? There is but one Altar on which He will accept your services—that Altar is the Person of His dear Son—and in this matter Jesus must be viewed as pouring out His blood for us.

We must view the Atonement as connected with every holy thing. I believe that our testimonies for God will be blessed of God in proportion as we keep the Sacrifice of Christ to the forefront. Somebody asked our Brother, Mr. Moody, how it was that he was so successful. And he is said to have replied, "Well, if I must tell you, it is, I believe, because we come out fair and square upon the Doctrine of Substitution." In that remark he hit the nail on the head. That is the saving doctrine! Keep that before your own mind. Keep it before the minds of those whom you would benefit. Let the Lord see that you are always thinking of His dear Son.

And, Beloved, do you not think that this pouring of the blood at the foot of this bronze altar indicates to us how much we ought to bring there? If Jesus has brought His life, there, and laid Himself thereon, ought we not to bring all that we are and all that we have—and consecrate all to God? Let us not offer a lean, scraggy sacrifice, or one that is half dead, or broken, or diseased—but let us bring our best at its best—and cheerfully present it unto the Most High through the precious blood of Christ. One said of a young man who had lately joined the Church, "Is he O and O?" And another answered, "What do you mean by that?" "Why," said the first, "I mean—is he *out* and *out* for Christ? Does he give himself—spirit, soul and body, to Jesus?" Surely, when we see the altar with Christ Himself upon it and His blood poured out there, we must acknowledge that if we could spend our whole life in zealous labor, and then die a martyr's death, we should not have rendered even half what such amazing love deserves! Let us be stimulated and quickened by the sight of the blood upon the bronze altar!

Lastly, you notice the blood was poured out at the bottom of the altar. What could that mean but this—that the altar of thank offering stood upon and grew out of a basis of blood. So all our deeds for God and our sacrifices for His cause must spring out of the love which He has manifested in the death of His dear Son. We love Him because—you know the "because"—because He first loved us. And how do we know that He loves us? Behold the death of Jesus as the surest proof! I long to put my whole being upon that altar and I should feel, as I did so, that I was not giving my God anything, but only rendering to Him what His dear Son has bought a million times over by once shedding His life-blood! When we have done all, we shall be unprofitable servants and we shall say so. All that we have given to God has been presented out of gratitude for the fact that God so loved us that He gave His only-begotten Son to die for us that we might live through Him.

Load the altar! Heap it high! Let sacrifices smoke thereon, for it is built upon God's unspeakable Gift! When sin is removed, service is accepted—"then shall they offer bullocks upon Your altar." Attempt no offering of your own works till then, for unpardoned sinners bring unaccepted offerings! First, let the blood be recognized and let the full Atonement be rejoiced in. Service rendered to God with a desire for personal merit is abominable in His sight. But when our merit is all found in the Divine Person of His Son, then will He accept us and our offering, too, in Christ Jesus! God grant unto you, dear Hearers, to be accepted in the Beloved. Amen.

6

Blood Even on the Golden Altar

"And the priest shall put some of the blood upon the horns of the altar of sweet incense before the LORD, which is in the Tabernacle of the Congregation." (Leviticus 4:7)

ALL THROUGH HOLY SCRIPTURE you constantly meet with the mention of "blood." "Without shedding of blood is no remission." "The blood of Jesus Christ, His Son, cleanses us from all sin." "You were not redeemed with corruptible things, as silver and gold, from your vain conversation received by tradition from your fathers, but with the precious blood of Christ." The word, "blood," is recorded over and over again, and if any complain of the preacher that he frequently uses this expression, he makes no kind of apology for it—he would be ashamed of himself if he did not often speak of the blood! The Word of God is as full of references to blood as the body of a man is full of life and blood.

But what does, "the blood," mean in Scripture? It means not merely suffering, which might very well be typified by blood, but it means suffering unto death. It means the taking of a life. To put it very briefly, a sin against God deserves death as its punishment, and what God said by the mouth of the Prophet Ezekiel still stands true, "The soul that sins, it shall die." The only way by which God could fulfill His threatening sentence and yet forgive guilty men was that Jesus Christ, His Son, came into the world and offered His life instead of ours. His life, because of the dignity of His Person, and the majesty of His Nature, was so vast in its value that He could give it not only for one man, but for the whole multitude of men who should believe in Him! Now, that by which men are saved is the suffering of Jesus Christ even unto death, as Peter writes, "Christ, also, has once suffered for sins, the Just for the unjust, that He might bring us to God." Paul puts it, "Christ has redeemed us from the curse of the Law, being made a curse for us: for it is written, Cursed is everyone that hangs on a tree." And again, "He has made Him to be sin for us, who knew no sin; that we might be made the righteousness of God in Him."

All the sacrifices under the Law of God, when their blood was poured out, were typical of the life of Christ given for men as a Sacrifice in the place of those who had offended unto death against the Law of God and, therefore, were doomed to die. You who hear me constantly know very well what I mean. Have I ever given any uncertain sound about this great central Truth of God? There is no way of salvation under Heaven but by faith in the Substitutionary Sacrifice of Jesus Christ! And the way by which we are redeemed from eternal wrath is by Christ having stood as Substitute for us and having died in our place, as it is written, "The chastisement of our peace was upon Him, and with His stripes we are healed." It is worthy of note that in the death of Christ, the shedding of blood was made very conspicuous, as if to refresh our memories about the teaching of the types of the Mosaic Law. Jesus was scourged unto bleeding. His temples were pierced and lacerated with a crown of thorns. His hands and feet were nailed with iron to the Cross. His side was opened by the soldier's spear and forthwith there flowed blood and water. There are many ways by which men may die without the shedding of blood—the capital punishment of our own country is free from this accompaniment—but our Savior was ordained to die by a death in which the shedding of blood was conspicuous, as if to link Him forever with those sacrifices which were made as types and symbols of His great atoning work! My dear Brother, Mr. Pearce, in his prayer, seemed to set forth Christ evidently crucified among you. I wish that even though you have to use your imaginations a little, you would think that you see Jesus on the Cross. Picture Him here, tonight, and lovingly watch Him. You will need few words from me if you do but catch sight of Him. Behold your Savior pouring out His life's blood that He might bear your guilt away, dying for you that you might live forever!

In the verse before our text we read that the priest was to take of the blood of the bullock of the sin offering and sprinkle it seven times "before the Lord, before the veil of the sanctuary." The veil concealed the inner dwelling place of God and this veil was to be sprinkled seven times, that is, perfectly. There was to be a perfect presentation of the precious blood before the place where God was concealed. After that was done, the priest was to take some of the blood of the bullock and smear with it the four horns of the golden altar which stood just in front of the veil, and near the golden candle- sticks. This altar was intended for the burning of sweet incense upon it and the priest was to smear with blood the four horns of it. What was meant by that act? Let me read the text again and then at once seek to explain it. "The priest shall put some of the blood upon the horns of the altar of sweet incense before the Lord."

I.   My first observation is this—*the atonement was presented with a view to the Lord.*

Have you not often heard it said that all the Atonement accomplished was something in relation to us? We think upon the death of Christ and it stirs our affections, but some teachers say that is the only result—it brings us to God, but it does not bring God to us! That is what they say, but when we turn to Holy Scripture we find that the blood shedding was with reference to God, Himself, as well as with reference to us, because in the text it is distinctly said, "The priest shall put some of the blood upon the horns of the altar of sweet incense before the Lord."

Its place was where the Lord would especially see it. I would like the young people, when they get home, to take a pencil and mark in the first chapters of the Book of Leviticus how often the expression is used, "before the Lord." The bringing of the bullock, the killing of the sacrifice, the sprinkling of the blood—all was to be done, "before the Lord." Whether any man saw it or not, was of small account, for it was, "before the Lord." True, it was done in the presence of the congregation, but it is specified over and over, again, that it was, "before the Lord." I would remind you that in the memorable type of the paschal lamb, the Lord gave special instructions as to where the blood was to be sprinkled. Was it to be within the house? Remember that all the people were inside the house—on the Passover night there was not a man outside! Where, then, was the blood put? Upon the interior walls of the house where they could see it? Might it not tend to comfort them if they could look upon it? That was not the Lord's plan—the blood was not put where the people could see it—it was sprinkled outside the house! And the Inspired account tells us that the Lord, Himself, said to Moses and Aaron, "And they shall take of the blood, and strike it on the two side posts and on the upper door post of the houses . . . and when I see the blood, I will pass over you." It was put where God could see it, and, as if to show that that was the main point, it was put where the people could not see it—that it might be distinctly said to them, "It is, after all, God's sight of the great sacrifice which saves you."

Next, the place of the blood is where the Lord sees it in reference to us. Understand where the Lord sees it with reference to us. They charge us with teaching that the Atonement in some way changes the Nature of

God. We have never said so and we never dreamed anything of the kind! Above all things, we have always taught that God is Immutable and cannot be changed either in His Nature or in His purpose. They tell us that we teach and, they tell others that we teach, that the Sacrifice of Christ was offered to make God love His people. We have, over and over and over again, denied this, and declared that—

> "'Twas not to make Jehovah's love
> Towards the sinner flame,
> That Jesus, from His Throne above,
> A suffering Man became!
>
> "'Twas not the death which He endured,
> Nor all the pangs He bore,
> That God's eternal love procured,
> For God was love before."

Christ in His Sacrifice is the result of God's love, not the cause of it! Yet, dear Friends, we do confess, without any hesitation, to this fact, that the death of Christ has a reference to God's dealing with us in this way— the claims of Divine Justice must be met. The Judge of all the earth must do right and He cannot suffer sin to go unpunished! Our own conscience confirms that Truth of God—there is no sinner, even when he is most hardened, who deep down in his soul does not know that to be true! And when he lies dying, it causes him great trouble to think that he is going where God must visit his sin upon him!

Now, what Christ has done is this—the Father has given us, in Christ, that which satisfies the claims of Infinite Justice. God can be just and yet the Justifier of him that believes. Executing the death penalty upon our Surety, He declares that whoever believes on Him shall not perish, but have everlasting life! Oh, dear Friends, it is God's looking on and seeing in His Son the vindication of His law, the honoring of His holiness—it is this which is the very essence of Christ's Sacrifice as to its result upon us!

I believe that the great Lord, the just Judge of all, looks on Jesus Christ with extreme delight as having suffered for His people. He sees in the sufferings of Christ the honoring of His own holiness. Jesus loved holiness so much that He would sooner die than that holiness should be impugned. He was so true, so upright, so just, that He would rather suffer to the death on the tree than that God should, in the least degree, violate His Word, or infringe His Justice. The Father looks on Christ's great Sacrifice and He takes great delight in it because He sees in it His own holiness honored and glorified!

And what a delight He must take in the love of Christ when He sees that Jesus loved us with a love which many waters could not quench, and which death, itself, could not drown! The great Father looks to the death of Christ and sees Christ's love triumphant on the tree, and He is charmed with it. I do not think that you and I can ever tell what pleasure the Father has in the finished work and Sacrifice of His dear Son. We read that He "smelled a savor of rest" in what was only a typical sacrifice—but what a savor of rest must the great heart of the Infinite Jehovah find in the Infinite Sacrifice of His Well-Beloved! You look upon it with bleared and bedimmed eyes, yet you see enough to make you wonder and adore. But what does God see in the Atonement of Jesus? Ah, Beloved, we cannot fully answer you, but we know that He sees there that which He eternally looks upon with infinite complacency and, for the sake of it, He looks upon us, poor guilty ones as we are, with complacency, too! He loves us because of what Christ has done in reference to us!

That is my first remark and though I have but feebly set it forth, yet, Beloved, it is a great and glorious Truth of God! The Atonement has a bearing towards the Lord, Himself, and, therefore, in this ancient type, the blood was smeared upon the altar of sweet incense before the Lord.

II. But now, secondly, coming to the very heart of the text—*the atonement give power to the intercession of the Lord Jesus Christ.*

That altar of sweet incense was the type of Christ pleading for men, making intercession for the transgressors. The horns of the altar signify the power of His intercession and the power of Christ's intercession lies in His Sacrifice—lies in the blood. If I might be allowed to picture such a scene, I seem to see the Divine Son pleading with His Father and He pleads the merit of His own blood.

The Father sees it, first, as a reason why the Son should plead with Him, for the blood shows His nearness of kin to man. Has Jesus blood? "Forasmuch, then, as the children are partakers of flesh and blood, He, also, Himself, likewise took part of the same." Here is the token to His Father that He is truly Man! Here is the sure testimony of His identification with His people for whom He makes intercession! The mark is made by His own blood upon the horns of the altar and its presence there proves that He is qualified to plead for men, seeing that, while He is God, His blood shows that He is evidently also Man!

I hear Him begin to plead and if Justice would stay Him and say, "How can You plead for the guilty? Before this Great White Throne, unsullied by a stain, how can You ask that God should bless the impure and foul?" Jesus points to His own blood as the token of His removal of impeding sin. "The Lamb of God, that takes away the sin of the world," has taken it away by the shedding of His own blood! "The blood of Jesus Christ, His Son, cleanses us from all sin." "Hear Me, My Father," He cries, "hear My plea on behalf of the penitent sinner! I have put away his sin. Answer My prayer and bless him, for I have taken away the sin that cursed him. I have borne its penalty and made expiation for it by My death."

Do you not think, also, that this blood, which is the very power of Christ's intercession, signifies His fulfillment of Covenant engagements? We read of "the blood of the Everlasting Covenant." Jesus had engaged with His Father "to finish the transgression and to make an end of sins, to make reconciliation for iniquity and to bring in everlasting righteousness," and He has done so! By His death, He could say, of His work as the Messiah, "It is finished!" By that death He had fulfilled His Suretyship engagement to His Father in connection with the Covenant of Grace and this, Beloved, is the very sinew of His strength in interceding for His people—this is the very essence of His pleading! He has done all that He agreed to do, therefore He asks the Father to fulfill His part of the Everlasting Covenant and to save the people redeemed by the blood shed on Calvary.

And, it seems to me, that Christ also uses His blood as the great power of His pleading in His claim of reward. "Have I not died for My people? Then will You not let them live, O My Father? Behold, O Justice, with uplifted sword, if you seek Me, let these go their way." Jesus seems to say, "My Lord, My God, I have become Your Servant. I took upon Myself the form of a Servant and was made in the likeness of sinful flesh. And I have performed all the service You did lay upon Me. Reward Me, then, for all My toil. Let Me see of the travail of My Soul. Let Me be satisfied according to the promise which You did make to Me when I undertook this work."

Do you not see, then, my Brothers and Sisters, that the blood on the horns of the altar means this—that Christ's blood is the very strength of His pleading with God? Because He died for guilty men, therefore, today, when He asks for the sinner's salvation, He will have it granted to Him, for the blood prevails with God, speaking better things than that of Abel!

III. And now, in the last place, I want to say to you that *this blood gives acceptance to our worship.*

We bring to God sweet incense through Jesus Christ our Savior. Our prayers, our praises, our services are like the mixture of sweet perfumes which were burnt of old upon the altar before God. But it is the blood-mark on the altar that makes the incense acceptable. It is the atoning Sacrifice of our Lord Jesus Christ that gives prayer, praise and service acceptance in the sight of God.

In beginning to speak upon this point, I want you to notice that the blood is on the altar before we begin to pray. It was the blood that gave acceptance to the incense burnt upon the altar—it was not the stacte onycha and galbanum—those, "sweet spices with pure frankincense," that, by themselves, ascended with fragrance unto the Lord. There must be the blood of the sacrifice sprinkled on the horns of the altar! What does this mean? Why, Beloved, that God accepts us in Christ because of Christ, Himself, and Christ, alone! It is true that we are to bring forth good works, for faith without works is dead. Still, the reason of our acceptance with God is not our good works, but Christ and His atoning Sacrifice, alone! As we come to Him, we sing—

"Nothing in my hand I bring,
Simply to Your Cross I cling."

Before you have performed a single work of holiness, before you have felt any of those sweet emotions which come out of the possession of Divine Love shed abroad in your heart, if you believe in the Lord Jesus Christ, you are accepted with God—Christ has saved you! Therefore is it that a man is justified by faith without works, for it is the faith that justifies him as it lays hold on Christ. There shall be an abundance of sweet spices on the altar, by-and-by, but apart from them, and before there has been a living coal smoking there, the altar has been consecrated unto God by the sprinkling of the blood of the Sacrifice! I like to think of that glorious fact! Let your good works be multiplied, but keep all of them at a distance from the Sacrifice of Christ! Never dream of adding them to Christ's Sacrifice to make it complete, for it is perfect without anything of yours. When you repent of sin, if you begin to trust in your repentance, away with your repentance! When you serve God, if you begin to trust in your service, away with it! Away with it! It becomes an antichrist if it takes the place that should be occupied by Jesus, only, for His precious blood, alone, can put away sin!

But now I want you to note, dear Friends, that whenever you come to God with your worship, you must take care that you notice the blood on the altar, because it removes the sin of our worship. The best worship that we ever render to God is far from perfect. Our praises, ah, how faint and feeble they are! Our prayers, how wandering, how wavering they are! When we get nearest to God, how far off we are! When we are most like He, how greatly unlike He we are! This I know, that my tears need be wept over, and my faith is so mingled with unbelief that I have to repent of that sad admixture! Brothers and Sisters, keep your eyes fixed on the blood of Jesus! There is no prayer, no praise that can come before God, of itself, for it is so imperfect. Therefore, keep your eyes on the blood of Jesus, that even the sin of your holy things may be put away by the Sacrifice once offered on Calvary.

Do you not think, also, that we would pray a great deal better if we thought more of the blood on the altar as our plea in prayer? I remember a Primitive Methodist Prayer Meeting at which a Brother could not get on with his supplication. He was very earnest and fervent, but he could not make any progress. He did not seem as if he had power to pray.

He shouted, as Methodists do, but there is not much in that—yet he could not get on with real praying till a friend at the back end of the room cried out, "Plead the blood, Brother! Plead the blood!" He did so and then he began to pray with mighty power! Here lies the force of all your pleas in prayer—if you can plead for Jesus' sake and in His name, by His agony and bloody sweat, by His Cross and passion—then you have discovered the great secret of prevailing with God! Your hand is on the lever and you can move the world if you will!

Should we not, also, make the precious blood of Jesus the highest note of our praises? When we are praising God, we think a great deal of the music. I do not blame anybody for doing that, especially if he is the leader of the Psalmody, but, Brothers and Sisters, we may come to think more of the melody and the harmony than we do of the heart and soul of praise! Keep your eyes on the crucified Christ and then sing as loudly as you like. Fix your gaze on those five precious wounds—they shall help you to praise Christ better than all the notes of the scales, for what higher note can we ever reach than this, "Unto Him that loved us, and washed us from our sins in His own blood?" Now you have sounded out the very highest note in the scale! Oh, the precious blood, the atoning Sacrifice, the great Substitution of our Lord Jesus Christ! The Hallelujah Chorus of all the redeemed shall have no nobler note than this, "He loved us and saved us. He loved us and died for us and we are washed in His blood."

Let me here say that every sort of worship, not only prayer and praise, but every kind of worship that we can render to the Lord, will be acceptable with God in proportion as we exhibit, with it, the blood upon the altar. I find it a very sweet way of worshipping God to sit down and meditate. I hope you feel the same. You do not need any words at such seasons. You have been reading a chapter of the Bible and God has spoken to you and you, perhaps, have knelt in prayer and have spoken with Him. Now you sit down and meditate. I like to sit quite still and look up, or sit quite still with closed eyes, and just think. Now, the thinking, the meditating, the contemplation which will be best for you and most acceptable with God is that which keeps close to the Cross and near the precious sacrifice. Do you notice what holy men and women say when they come to die? You stand at their bedside and talk to them. If they are in any trouble and distress of conscience, what do they begin to talk about? Why, about the precious Sacrifice of Christ upon the Cross! It does not matter to what sect they belong, or to what denomination they have been joined in life—they always come back to this point at the last. There is no passing out of this life with comfort—there is no hope of entering into Heaven with delight—except as we are resting upon the precious blood of Christ!

Ah, dear Friends, there may be some here who do not think much of this theme. There always were such. It is nothing to you that Jesus should die. But if there is anything that sanctifies, any Truth of God that digs deep into the heart and puts the Seeds of Life into the very center of our being—if there is anything that makes the Christian devout, humble, holy—it is the Doctrine of the Cross! I can almost gauge your piety to a certainty by what you think of the bleeding Savior. If He is nothing to you, you are not in the blessed secret. But if Jesus Christ is first and last with you. If you preach Christ crucified—if you love Christ crucified—in that proportion God dwells in you and you dwell in Him! This is not theory that I am talking—this is no Truth of God that lies upon the borders of the Christian religion and may, or may not be accepted! This is the very heart of the Gospel and if you take this away, you have killed it!

You are no Christian if you disbelieve this Truth of God! If you are not saved by the precious blood of Christ, you are damned! There is but one gate of life and that is sprinkled with the blood of Christ. If you turn away from that door, you have chosen the broad road that leads to destruction. O you who feel your guilt, come to my Lord for pardon! O you who confess your sin, come to His blood for cleansing! It is still true that, "There is life for a look at the Crucified One! There is life at this moment for you."

How many years have I come to this pulpit, telling this old, old story, telling it very poorly and very imperfectly, and yet you are not tired of hearing it! Look how the crowds still throng this house! I might have given you some pretty novelties every now and then, but had I done so, I believe I would have lost you! But this old Truth of God, even if you do not accept it, commands your attention. You cannot help coming to hear it—oh, that you would also believe it! It has made me supremely happy. I was about to say that it has given me an angel's happiness and, sometimes, I could even say without exaggeration it gives me solid peace with which I can live, and with which, by-and-by, I hope to die!

It enables me to stand alone against unnumbered foes and feel as happy as if everybody were with me, for, in this great Truth that Jesus died for me, that Jesus bore my sins in His own body on the tree, there is a rock beneath my feet!

He who is on that rock may stand there and defy even death and Hell! Oh, that you would come and trust my Lord, you restless ones, you who do not know what peace means! Trust Him! Believe that He died for you! Trust Him and you shall have peace like a river—and righteousness like the waves of the sea!

May we now come to the Communion Table thinking much of the precious blood once shed for many for the remission of sins!

Exposition of Leviticus 16:1-3

Verse 1, 2. *And the LORD spoke unto Moses after the death of the two sons of Aaron, when they offered before the LORD, and died, and the LORD said unto Moses, Speak unto Aaron, your brother, that he come not at all times into the Holy Place within the veil before the Mercy Seat, which is upon the Ark, that he die not: for I will appear in the cloud upon the Mercy Seat.* The way into the heavenly places was not yet made manifest. The inner shrine called the Holy of Holies, was specially guarded from human access. No one could have said, in those days, *"Let us come boldly unto the Throne of Grace,"* for only the High Priest could approach the Mercy Seat at all—and he must go within the veil strictly in accordance with the instructions given to Moses by the Lord. Nadab and Abihu appear to have entered into the Presence of God wrongfully. They had probably been drinking, for there was a command, afterwards, given that no priest should drink wine or strong drink when he went into the House of the Lord. God, in His righteous anger, slew these young men at once and now, lest any others should intrude into the secret place of communion, a Law was given to tell when and how man might approach his God.

3. *Thus shall Aaron come into the Holy Place: with a young bullock for a sin offering, and a ram for a burnt offering.* There is no access to God except by sacrifice—there never was, and there never can be any way to God for sinful man except by sacrifice!

4. *He shall put on the holy linen coat, and he shall have the linen breeches upon his flesh, and shall be girded with a linen belt, and with the linen miter shall he be attired: these are holy garments; therefore shall he wash his flesh in water, and so put them on.* Our great High Priest offered Himself without spot to God and He is, Himself, without sin. But the Jewish High Priest must make himself typically pure by putting on the snow-white garments of holy service and, before doing so, he must wash himself with water, that he might come before God acceptably. None might approach the Holy God with impurities upon them.

5, 6. *And he shall take of the congregation of the children of Israel two kids of the goats for a sin offering, and one ram for a burnt offering. And Aaron shall offer his bullock of the sin offering, which is for himself, and make an Atonement for himself, and for his house.* These priests were

112

sinful and, therefore, they must first, themselves, be purged from guilt be- fore they could come near to God; but the true High Priest of God, our Lord Jesus, needed to offer no sacrifice for Himself, for He was pure and without blemish or stain or sin.

7. *And he shall take the two goats, and present them before the LORD at the door of the Tabernacle of the Congregation.* These two goats were not for himself, but for the people. You must regard them as if they were but one offering, for it needed both of them to set forth the Divine Plan by which sin is put away—one was to die and the other was, typically, to bear away the sin of the people.

8. *And Aaron shall cast lots upon the two goats; one lot for the LORD, and the other lot for the scapegoat.* One goat was to show how sin is put away in reference to God by sacrifice, and the other goat was to show how it is put away in reference to us, God's people, by being carried into oblivion.

9-14. *And Aaron shall bring the goat upon which the LORD's lot fell and offer him for a sin offering. But the goat on which the lot fell to be the scapegoat, shall be presented alive before the LORD, to make an Atonement with Him, and to let him go for a scapegoat into the wilderness. And Aaron shall bring the bullock of the sin offering, which is for himself, and shall make an Atonement for himself, and for his house, and shall kill the bullock of the sin offering which is for himself: and he shall take a censer full of burning coals of fire from off the altar before the LORD, and his hands full of sweet incense beaten small, and bring it within the veil: and he shall put the incense upon the fire before the LORD, that the cloud of the incense may cover the Mercy Seat that is upon the testimony, that he die not: and he shall take of the blood of the bullock, and sprinkle it with his finger upon the Mercy Seat eastward; and before the Mercy Seat shall he sprinkle of the blood with his finger seven times.* This was his first entrance within the veil, with holy incense to denote the acceptance which Christ has with God, though He is always well-beloved, dear and precious to His Father. This incense sent up a cloud that veiled the Glory of the Shekinah which shone between the two wings of the cherubim and so the High Priest was better able to bear the wondrous brilliance by which God revealed His Presence. When Aaron had thus filled the place with the sweetly- perfumed smoke, he took the blood of the bullock of the sin offering and carefully sprinkled it seven times on the Mercy Seat, and on the ground around the Mercy Seat. What a mercy it is for you and me that the spot where we meet with God is a place where the blood of the Great Sacrifice has been sprinkled, yes, and that the ground of our meeting with God, the place on which the Mercy Seat rests, also has the blood mark upon it!

15. *Then shall he kill the goat of the sin offering, that is for the people, and bring his blood within the veil, and do with that blood as he did with the blood of the bullock, and sprinkle it upon the Mercy Seat, and before the Mercy Seat.* Twice, you see, is the Holy Place thus sprinkled, first with the blood of the bullock and then with that of the goat.

16. *And he shall make an Atonement for the Holy Place because of the uncleanness of the children of Israel, and because of their transgressions in all their sins: and so shall he do for the Tabernacle of the Congregation that remains among them in the midst of their uncleanness.* If God is to dwell in the midst of sinful men, it can only be through the blood of the Atonement. Twice, seven times, were the Holy Place and the tabernacle to be sprinkled with blood, as though to indicate a double perfectness of efficacy of the preparation for God's dwelling among sinful men.

17-19 *And there shall be no man in the Tabernacle of the Congregation when he goes in to make an Atonement in the Holy Place, until he come out, and has made an Atonement for himself, and for his household, and for all the congregation of Israel. And he shall go out unto the altar that is before the LORD, and make an Atonement for it; and shall take of the blood of the bullock, and of the blood of the goat, and put it upon the horns of the altar round about. And he shall sprinkle of the blood upon it with his finger seven times, and cleanse it, and hallow it from the uncleanness of the children of Israel.* Even this altar to which we bring our prayers and our thank offerings has sin upon it. There is some defilement, even, in the saltwater of our penitent tears! There is some unbelief, even, in our most acceptable faith! There is some lack of holiness about our holiest things! We are unclean by nature and by practice, too—what could we do without the sprinkling of the blood? See how the Lord insisted upon it in the case of His ancient people, yet there are some in these modern times who deride it. God forgive their blasphemy!

20, 21. *And when he has made an end of reconciling the Holy Place, and the Tabernacle of the Congregation, and the altar, he shall bring the live goat: and Aaron shall lay both his hands upon the head of the live goat and confess over him all the iniquities of the children of Israel, and all their transgressions in all their sins, putting them upon the head of the goat, and shall send him away by the hand of a fit man into the wilderness.* Notice the, "all," in this 21st verse—"Aaron shall lay both his hands upon the head of the live goat and confess over him all the iniquities of the children of Israel, and all their transgressions in all their sins, putting them upon the head of the goat, and shall send him away by the hand of a fit man into the wilderness." This was the second part of the Atonement showing not sacrifice, but the effect of sacrifice, and explaining what becomes of sin after the sacrifice has been accepted and the blood has been presented within the veil.

22-25. *And the goat shall bear upon him all their iniquities unto a land not inhabited: and he shall let go the goat in the wilderness. And Aaron shall come into the Tabernacle of the Congregation and shall put off the linen garments which he put on when he went into the Holy Place, and shall leave them there: and he shall wash his flesh with water in the Holy Place, and put on his garments, and come forth, and offer his burnt offering, and the burnt offering of the people, and make an Atonement for himself, and for the people. And the fat of the sin offering shall he burn upon the altar.* Only the fat of it, the best of it, was burnt upon the altar, for sin offerings were not acceptable to God. They were regarded as being filled with impurity by reason of the sin which they brought to mind. For this reason the bullock and the goat of the sin offering had to be burnt outside the camp—"Therefore Jesus, also, that He might sanctify the people with His own blood, suffered outside the gate," as our Sin Offering. Yet, inasmuch as the fat was accepted upon the altar, so is Christ, even as our Sin Offering, acceptable before God.

26, 27. *And he that let go the goat for the scapegoat shall wash his clothes, and bathe his flesh in water, and afterward come into the camp. And the bullock for the sin offering and the goat for the sin offering, whose blood was brought in to make Atonement in the Holy Place, shall one carry forth outside the camp; and they shall burn in the fire their skins, and their flesh, and their dung.* All must be burnt—and the last is mentioned because it more strikingly sets forth the impurity of the sin connected with the sin offering! All must be burnt right up. There must not be a particle of the sin offering left unconsumed.

28. *And he that burns them shall wash his clothes, and bathe his flesh in water, and afterward he shall come into the camp.* Everything that has to do with God's service must be clean and purified by fire, and purified by water. An Atonement cannot be made by that which is, itself, defiled—it must be without spot, or wrinkle, or any such thing before it can put sin away. This is the virtue of Christ's Atonement, for He was altogether without sin of any kind.

29-31. *And this shall be a statute forever unto you: that in the seventh month, on the tenth day of the month, you shall afflict your souls, and do no work at all, whether it is one of your own country, or a stranger that sojourns among you: for on that day shall the priest make an Atonement for you, to cleanse you, that you may be clean from all your sins before the* LORD. *It shall be a Sabbath of rest unto you, and you shall afflict your souls, by a statute forever.* This shows what sacredness the Lord attached to the great Day of Atonement and gives us more than a hint of the preciousness of our Lord's atoning work for us. Now let us turn to the Epistle to the Hebrews and see how the Apostle spiritualizes the services of the Mosaic dispensation.

Exposition of Hebrews 9:1-21

Hebrews 9:1 *Then verily the first Covenant had also ordinances of Divine service and a worldly sanctuary.* An external sanctuary, a material structure and, therefore, belonging to this world.

2. *For there was a tabernacle made; the first, wherein was the candlestick, and the table, and the showbread: which is called the sanctuary.* Or, "the Holy Place."

3-8. *And after the second veil, the tabernacle which is called the Holiest of All; which had the golden censer, and the Ark of the Covenant overlaid round about with gold, wherein was the golden pot that had manna, and Aaron's rod that budded, and the Tables of the Covenant; and over it the Cherubims of glory shadowing the Mercy Seat; of which we cannot now speak particularly. Now when these things were thus ordained, the priests went always into the first tabernacle, accomplishing the service of God. But into the Second went the High Priest, alone, once every year, not without blood, which he offered for himself, and for the errors of the people: the Holy Spirit thus signifying that the way into the Holiest of All was not yet made manifest, while as the first tabernacle was yet standing.* Notice especially those words, *"Not without blood."* There could be no approach to God under the old dispensation without the shedding of blood and there is no access to the Lord, now, without the precious blood of Christ.

9-22. *Which was a figure for the time then present, in which were offered both gifts and sacrifices, that could not make him that did the service perfect, as pertaining to the conscience; which stood only in meats and drinks, and divers washings, and carnal ordinances, imposed on them until the time of reformation. But Christ being come an High Priest of good things to come, by a greater and more perfect tabernacle, not made with hands, that is to say, not of this building, neither by the blood of goats and calves, but by His own blood, He entered in once into the Holy Place, having obtained eternal redemption for us. For if the blood of bulls and of goats, and the ashes of an heifer sprinkling the unclean, sanctifies to the purifying of the flesh: how much more shall the blood of Christ, who through the Eternal Spirit offered Himself without spot to God, purge your conscience from dead works to serve the living God? And for this cause He is the Mediator of the new testament, that by means of death, for the redemption of the transgressions that were under the first testament, they which are called might receive the promise of eternal inheritance. For where a testament is, there must also of necessity be the death of the testators. For a testament is of force after men are dead: otherwise it is of no strength at all while the testator lives. Whereupon neither the first testament was dedicated without blood. For when Moses had spoken every precept to all the people according to the Law, he took the blood of calves and of goats, with water, and scarlet wool, and hyssop, and sprinkled both the Book, and all the people, saying, This is the blood of the testament which God has enjoined unto you. Moreover he sprinkled with blood both the tabernacle, and all the vessels of the ministry. And almost all things are by the Law purged with blood; and without shedding of blood is no remission.* That is the great Gospel Truth that was set forth by all the sacrifices under the Law of God—"without shedding of blood is no remission."

7

The Sin Offering for the Common People

"And if any one of the common people sins through ignorance, while he does something against any of the commandments of the Lord concerning things which ought not to be done, and is guilty. Or if his sin, which he has sinned, comes to his knowledge: then he shall bring his offering, a kid of the goats, a female without blemish, for his sin which he has sinned. And he shall lay his hand upon the head of the sin-offering, and slay the sin-offering in the place of the burnt-offering. And the priest shall take of the blood thereof with his finger, and put it upon the horns of the altar of burnt-offering, and shall pour out all the blood thereof at the bottom of the altar. And the priest shall burn it upon the altar for a sweet savor unto the Lord; and the priest shall make an atonement for him, and it shall be forgiven him." (Leviticus 4:27-31)

V ERY MUCH OF INTERESTING truth clusters around the sin-offering. The type is well worthy of the most careful consideration, and I regret that we shall not have time this morning to enter into all its details. The reader of the Chapter will perceive that it gives us four forms of the same sacrifice. These may be regarded as four views of the same thing, probably views taken by four classes of Believers, according to their standing in the Divine Life; for, although all men who are saved have the same Savior, they have not the same apprehensions of Him. We are all cleansed, if cleansed at all, by the same blood, but we have not all the same knowledge of the manner in which it is effectual for cleansing. The devout Hebrew had but one sin-offering, but that was set forth to him under varying symbols.

The following remarks may aid you in understanding the type before us. The Chapter begins with the sin-offering for the anointed priest, and describes it with the fullest detail. It then proceeds, in the 13th verse and onwards, to give the sin-offering for the whole congregation and it is most notable that the sin-offering for the anointed priest is almost in every circumstance identical with the sin-offering for the whole congregation. Is not this designed to show to us that when Christ, our anointed Priest, took upon Himself the sin of all the congregation of God's Chosen as His own, there was demanded of Him the same expiation and atonement as would have been demanded of His people had they been reckoned with in their own persons? His Atonement for sins which were not His own, but which were laid upon Him by the Lord on our behalf, is equivalent to the penalty which would have been required of all the congregation of Believers for whom His blood was especially shed. This is a memorable lesson which ought not to be forgotten; we ought to see herein the inestimable value of the Sacrifice of Christ by which the many offenses of a number that no man can number are forever put away; there was given, in the death of our Lord, as full a recompense to justice as if all the Redeemed had been sent into Hell. No, the truth goes far further than that—they could not have made a complete expiation, for even had they suffered for sin for thousands of years, the debt would "Still be paying, never paid." Glory be to the name of our great Substitute! He by His sin-offering has perfected forever them who are set apart.

In the case of the sin-offering for the priest, we have a fuller picture of the atonement than is offered by the two latter instances, and you will please note that the sin-offering was a victim without blemish. In the first two cases a bullock was to be slain; thus the most precious animal the Hebrew owned, the noblest, the strongest—the image of docility and labor—was to be presented to make atonement. Our Lord Jesus Christ is like the firstling of the bullock, the most precious thing in Heaven, strong for service, docile in obedience, One who was willing and able to labor for our sakes, and He was brought as a perfect Victim, without spot or blemish, to suffer in our place. The priest slew the bullock and its blood was poured forth, for without shedding of blood there is no remission. The vital point of the Atonement of Christ lies in His death; however much His life may have contributed to it, and we are not among those who, in the matter of Salvation, separate His life from His death by a hard and fast line—yet the great point of the putting away of human guilt was the Lord's obedience unto death, even the death of the Cross; the Victim was slain, and so the Atonement was made. Returning to the passage before us, we find that the blood of this victim was taken into the Holy Place which was immediately outside the sacred veil of the sanctuary; and there the priest dipped his finger in the blood, and sprinkled the blood seven times before the Lord, before the veil of the sanctuary. So in making Atonement for sin there is a perfect exhibition of the blood of Jesus before the Lord; that life has been given for life is openly proven where alone the proof is available. Before the offended Lord, the vicarious death is thoroughly exhibited—for was it not written of old in the Book of Exodus, "When I see the blood I will pass over you?" Our sight of the blood Christ gives us peace, but it does not make the satisfaction—it is God's seeing of the blood which makes the Atonement, and, therefore, seven times before the veil was this blood exhibited before the Lord, that a perfect atonement might be made.

The next thing the priest did was to go up to the golden altar of incense which stood hard by the veil, and put some of the blood upon each one of the horns, indicating that it is the blood of the atonement which gives power (for that is the meaning of the horns) to intercession. The sweet perfume of the altar of incense stands for the prayers and praises of the saints, and especially for the intercession of Christ Jesus, and, because the blood is there, Christ's intercession is heard, and, therefore, our prayers and praises come up with acceptance before the Lord.

Then the priest removed to the bronze altar of burnt sacrifice, and all the blood which remained he poured out at the bottom of the altar of the burnt-offering which stood at the door of the tabernacle of the congregation. Full bowls of blood colored the base of the altar. Blood was seen on every side—on the veil, on the golden altar, and now upon the altar of brass. Within and without the Holy Place but one voice was heard, the voice of the blood of atonement crying to God for peace! The whole tabernacle must have been almost at all times so smeared with blood as to have been far from pleasant to the eye! This was intended to teach Israel that God's anger against sin is terrible, and that the dishonored Law will be satisfied with nothing less than the giving of life for life, if sinners are to be saved. The altar of burnt-offerings was the altar of acceptance—it was the place where those sacrifices were presented in which there was no mention of sin, but which were brought as thanksgivings to God. Therefore, as much as to teach us that the very ground and foundation of the acceptance of the Christian and his offering lies in the precious blood of Jesus, full bowls of blood were poured upon the base of the altar. See what wonders the precious blood of Jesus Christ can do; it is the strength of intercession, and the foundation of acceptance!

From the bullock which had been slain certain choice pieces were taken—especially the inward fat, and these were laid upon the altar and consumed, to show us that even while the Lord Jesus was a Sin-Offering He was still accepted of God, and though His Father forsook Him so that He cried out, "Why have You forsaken Me?" He was still a sweet savor unto the Lord in the obedience which He rendered.

But, the most significant part of the whole sacrifice remains to be described, and you will notice that it is only described in the first two forms of the sin-offering. The priest was not allowed to burn the bullock, itself, upon the altar, but he was commanded to take up the whole carcass—its skin, flesh, head, and everything, and carry the whole outside the camp. It was a sin-offering, and therefore it was loathsome in God's sight! And the priest went right away from the door of the tabernacle, past all the tents of the children of Israel, bearing this ghastly burden upon him; went, I say, right away, till he came to the place where the ashes of the camp were poured out, and there, not upon an altar, but on wood which had been prepared upon the bare ground, every single particle of the bullock was burned with fire! The distance the bullock was carried from camp is said to have been four miles; the tracking of which is just this: that when the Lord Jesus Christ took the sins of His people upon Himself, He could not, as a Substitute, dwell any longer in the place of the Divine favor, but had to be put into the place of separation, and made to cry, "Eloi, Eloi, lama Sabacthani?" Paul in his Epistle to the Hebrews puts the matter clearly, "For the bodies of those beasts, whose blood is brought into the sanctuary by the high priest for sin, are burned outside the camp; therefore Jesus, also, that He might sanctify the people with His own blood, suffered outside the gate." Outside Jerusalem our Lord was led to the common place of doom for malefactors, for it is written, (and oh, the power of those Words; I dare not have uttered them if they had not been inspired), "He was made a curse for us, for it is

124

written, cursed is everyone that hangs on a tree." The blessed Son of God was made a curse for us, and put to an accursed death by being hung upon the Cross; and all because sin anywhere is hateful to God, and He must treat it with indignation! The fire of Divine Justice fell upon our blessed Sin-Offering until He was utterly consumed with anguish, and He said, "It is finished," and gave up the ghost. Now this is the only way of putting away sin—it is laid upon Another, and that Other is made to suffer as if the sin belonged to Him; and then, since sin cannot be in two places at once, and cannot be laid upon Another and rest upon the offerer, too, the offerer becomes clear from all sin! He is pardoned, and he is accepted because his Substitute has been slain outside the camp instead of him! I have thus introduced to you the first two forms of the sin-offering; it seemed necessary to begin there.

The third form of the sin-offering was for a ruler, a person of considerable standing in the camp.

There is nothing very remarkable about that third form which needs now detain us; we, therefore, come to the subject in hand: the sin-offering for a common person.

I. And, here, we will begin our discourse upon the text itself by speaking of *the person*, a common person. It gives me unspeakable joy to read these words, "If any one of the common people sin," for which one of the common people does not sin? The Text reminds me that if a common person sins, his sins will ruin him; he may not be able to do as much mischief by his sin as the ruler or a public officer, but his sin has all the essence of evil in it, and God will reckon with him for it. No matter how obscurely you may live, however poor and unlettered you may be, your sin will ruin you if not pardoned and put away! If one of the common people sins through ignorance, his sin is a damning sin; he must have it put away, or it will put him away forever from the face of God. A common person's sin can only be removed by an Atonement of blood. In this case you see the victim was not a bullock; it was a female of the goats or of the sheep, but still it had to be an offering of blood, for without shedding of blood there is no remission. However commonplace your offenses may have been; however insignificant you may be yourself, nothing will cleanse you but the blood of Jesus Christ! That verse is quite correct—

"Could my zeal no respite know,
Could my tears forever flow,
All for sin could not atone.
Christ must save, and Christ alone."

It is true the sins of great men cover a larger space, but yet there must be a bloody Sacrifice for the smallest offenses, for the sins of a housewife or of a servant; of a peasant, or of a crossing-sweeper; there must be the same Sacrifice as for the sins of the greatest and most influential; no other Atonement will suffice; the sins of the common people will destroy them unless the blood of Jesus Christ cleanses them. But here is the point of joy that for the common people there was an Atonement ordained of God! Glory be to God! I may be unknown to men, but I am not unthought of by Him! I may be merely one of the many, but still He has thought of me! As each blade of grass has its own drop of dew, so each guilty soul coming to Christ shall find Atonement for itself in Christ! Blessed be the name of the Lord; it is not written that there is a Sacrifice for the great ones of the earth, alone, but for the common people there is a Sin-Offering so that each man coming to the Savior finds cleansing through His precious blood!

Observe with thankfulness that the sacrifice appointed for the common people was as much accepted as that appointed for the ruler. Of the ruler, it is said, "The priest shall make atonement for him as concerning his sin, and it shall be forgiven him." The same thing is said of the common person; Christ is as much accepted for the poorest of His people as for the richest of them! He as much saves the unknown as He does the apostolic names of high renown! They need the sacrifice of blood, but they need nothing more, and the blood which pleads before the Throne of God speaks as well for the least as it does for the chief of the flock!

Come here, then, you who belong to the common people! If any of you have sinned, come at once to Jesus, the great Sin-Offering! Though you are common in rank, know you not that the common people heard Him gladly? Publicans and sinners pressed around Him to hear Him! Though you are but commoners in your wealth, possessing little of this world's goods, yet come; buy wine and milk without money, and without price! Common in your talents and in your gifts, yet He bids you come, for these things are hid from the wise and prudent; it is not for those who think themselves distinguished that He has especially laid down His life, but, "The poor have the Gospel preached to them," and in their Salvation He will be glorified! Mark, it says, "If any one of the common people sin, through ignorance, or if his sin, which he has sinned, comes to his knowledge, then he shall bring his offering." Has it suddenly come to the knowledge of any person here that he has sinned, though he thought he had not sinned? Has some fresh light broken in upon you, and revealed to you your darkness? Did you come to this House depressed in spirit because you have discovered that you are guilty, and must perish unless the mercy of God prevents it? Then come, you common people who have discovered your sin, and bring your sacrifice; no, it is here already for you! Come and accept the Sacrifice which God provides, and let your sins be put away forever! I wish the words of the Text could provoke the same feelings in every heart that they do in mine, for I could gladly stand here and weep my soul away in joy that for the common people's sin there should be a Sacrifice, for I can put my name down among them! I have sinned! I have come to the knowledge of my sin! And I thank God I need not ask myself any other question—be I who I may, or what I am, though but one of the common people, there is a Sin-Offering for me!

II. Now, pass on from the person to *the sacrifice.* "He shall bring his offering, a kid of the goats, a female without blemish, for his sin which he has sinned."

Observe first, my Brothers and Sisters, that there is a discrepancy between the type and the reality, for first, the sin-offering under the Law was only for sins of ignorance. But we have a far better Sacrifice for sin than that, for have we not read in your hearing this morning those precious words, "The blood of Jesus Christ, His Son, cleanses us from all sin?" Not from sins of ignorance only, but from all sin! Oh, that blessed word "all!" It includes sins of knowledge, sins against the Light and Love of God, sins wantonly perpetrated; sins against man, and against God; sins of body, and of soul; sins of thought, and word, and deed; sins of every rank and character. "Sins immense as is the sea"—all, *all* are removed—no matter what they are! "The blood of Jesus Christ His Son cleanses us from all sin." Yet I do bless God that the type deals with sins of ignorance because we may get a Gospel out of it! We have committed many sins which we know not; they have never burdened our conscience because we have not yet discovered them, and, besides, we do not know them to be sins. But Christ takes those sins, too, and prays, "Father, forgive them, for they know not what they do." "Cleanse me," said David, "from secret faults," and that is just what Jesus does! It used to be a doctrine of the church of Rome that no man could have a sin forgiven which he did not confess; truly, if it were so, there would be no Salvation for any of us, since it is not possible for the memory to charge itself with the recollection of every sin, nor for the conscience to become so perfect as to take cognizance of every form of transgression! But, while we ought to confess to God all sins which we know, and while we should confess them as much as can be in detail, yet, if through ignorance they remain unacknowledged, except in the gross and the bulk, Jesus Christ, the Sin-Offering bears our sins of ignorance—sins which we knew not to be sins when we committed them, or which we still know not to be sins! He takes them away! It must be so, for, "He cleanses us from all sin"—sins of ignorance, as well as sins against light and knowledge. Now, what comfort there is here for all you of the common people! Be your sins what they may, there is a Sin-Offering which takes away all sin from you however you may have defiled yourselves; though you are black as night, and hideous as Hell; yet is there power in the atoning blood of the Incarnate God to make you white as newly-fallen snow! Washed once in the fountain opened for sin and for uncleanness, there shall remain upon you no trace of guilt!

Note another discrepancy, the sinner of the common people in this case had to bring his sacrifice—"He shall bring his offering." But our Sin-Offering has been provided for us! You remember the question of Isaac to his father Abraham, as they went up Moriah? He asked him, "My Father, behold the fire and the wood, but where is the lamb for the burnt-offering?" And Abraham said, "My Son, God will provide Himself a lamb." Isaac's inquiry might have been the eternal question of every troubled heart, "O God, where is the lamb for the burnt-offering?" Who will bear human sin? But Jehovah Jireh God has provided Himself a Lamb for a Burnt-Offering and a Sin-Offering, too; and now we have not to bring a sacrifice for sin, but have simply to take what God provided from before the foundations of the world!

Now, let us notice that in the type the victim chosen for a sin-offering was unblemished; whether a goat or a sheep, it must be unblemished. How could Christ make Atonement for sins if He had had sins of His own? Had He been guilty, it would have required that He should suffer for His own guilt; but, being under no obligation whatever to the Law of God except such as He voluntarily undertook, when He had rendered obedience, He had an obedience to give away, and He has graciously bestowed it upon us! When He suffered, His suffering not being due to God on account of anything that He had personally done, He had much suffering to spare, and He has transferred it to us. The Immaculate Christ has died, the Just for the unjust, that He might bring us to God! His is full of comforts, for if you will study, O seeking Soul, the perfect Character of your blessed Lord as God, and as Man, and see how fairer than the lilies He is in matchless purity, you will feel that if He suffered, there must be in such suffering an unspeakable merit which, being transferred to you, can save you from the wrath to come! In the dear Redeemer we have an unblemished Sacrifice! But I do not understand, and therefore cannot explain why the victim was a female in this case, for most of the sacrifices were males of the first year—but this is peculiar in being a female. Is it because there is neither male nor female, bond nor free, but all are one in Christ Jesus? Or, am I wrong if I conjecture that this was intended to typify a view of Christ taken by one of the common people, and therefore it is purposely made incomplete? It is an incomplete view of Christ to have before you the female as the type, and the type is purposely made incomplete in order that this Truth of God may lie before us—that while a complete view of Christ is very comforting, instructive and strengthening, yet even an imperfect view of Him will save us if accompanied by real faith.

If we should make a mistake upon some point, yet, if we are clear upon the main Truth of His Substitution, it is well with us. On purpose, then, it seems to me that a victim was introduced which did not, with exactness, set forth Christ so that the Lord might say to His people, and to us, "You have not reached the perfect conception of My dear Son, but even an imperfect apprehension of Him will save you if you believe in

Him." Who among us knows much of Christ? Oh, Brothers and Sisters, we know enough to make our hearts love Him; we know enough of Him to make us feel that we owe all to Him, and we desire to live for His Glory; but He is far greater than our greatest thoughts! We have only skirted the shores, and navigated the little bays and creeks of Christ; we have not sailed out into the main ocean, nor fathomed the great deeps as yet—yet what little we do know of Him has saved us, and for His dear sake we are forgiven and accepted in the Beloved! Does not the Lord seem to say to us, "Poor Souls, you have misconceived My Son, and made many mistakes about Him; but you do trust Him, and so I save you." A certain woman thought that there was power in the hem of Jesus' garment to make her whole; she was mistaken in imagining that there was a healing efficacy in His garment; but since it was a mistake of faith, and reflected honor upon Christ, the Lord made it true to her—He made virtue go out of Himself even into the hem of His garment for her sake! And so, though we may err here, and err there in reference to our Lord, yet if our soul does but cling to Him like a child to its mother, knowing little of its mother except that its mother loves it, and that it is dependent upon her—that clinging will, by His Grace, be saving!

But the main point about the sacrifice was it was slain as a substitute; there is nothing said about its being taken outside the camp; I do not think it was in this case. All that the offerer knew was it was slain as a substitute, and, dear Hearers, all and everything that is essential to know in order to be saved is to know that you are a sinner, and that Christ is your Substitute! I beseech the Lord to teach every one of us this, for though we should go to the University and learn all knowledge; though we should ransack all the stores of learning; unless we know this—"He loved me and gave Himself for me," we have not learned the very first principles of a true education for Eternity. God gives us to know this, this very day!

III. But, now thirdly, we pass on from the sacrifice to *the after ceremonies* upon which only a word. In the case of one of the common people, after the victim was slain, the blood was taken to the bronze altar and the four horns of it were smeared to show that the power of fellowship with God lies in the blood of substitution. There is no fellowship with God except through the blood; there is no acceptance with God for anyone of us except through Him who suffered in our place.

But, then secondly, the blood was thrown at the feet of this same bronze altar as if to show that the atonement is the foundation as well as the power of fellowship. We get nearest to God when we feel most the power of the blood. Yes, and we could not come to God at all except it were through that bloody way. After this, a part of the offering was put upon the altar, and it is said concerning it what is not said in any other of the cases, "The priest shall burn it upon the altar for a sweet savor to the Lord." This common person had, in most respects, a dim view of Christ, compared with the others, but yet there were some points in which he had more light than others, for it does not say of the priest that what he offered was a sweet savor. But, for the comfort of this common person, that he might go his way having sweet consolation in his soul, he is told that the sin-offering he had brought is a sweet savor unto God. And oh, what a joy it is to think not only has Christ put away my sin if I believe in Him, but now, for me, He is a sweet savor to God, and I am for His sake accepted, for His sake beloved, for His sake delighted in, for His sake precious unto God! When God had destroyed the earth by the Flood, and Noah came out of the Ark, you will remember that he offered a sacrifice unto God, and it is said, "The Lord smelled a sweet savor," or a savor of rest; and then He said I will no more destroy the earth with a flood, and He entered into a Covenant with Noah. Oh, happy is that soul that can see Christ, his Sin-Offering, as being a savor of rest unto the Lord Most

High, so that a Covenant of Grace is made with him—a Covenant of sure mercies that shall never be removed!

IV. The fourth point is one to which I ask all your heart's attention. I have purposely omitted mentioning why the sacrifice, in order to enlarge upon it now.

Please observe that in all four cases there was one thing which was never left out, "He shall lay his hand upon the head of the sin-offering." It was no use killing the bullock; it was no use slaying the heifer; no use pouring out the blood, or smearing the horns of the altar unless this was done. The guilty person must come, and must himself lay his hands upon the victim! Oh, that while I speak of this, some of you may lay your hands upon Christ Jesus according to the verse of the poet—

"My faith does lay her hand
On that dear head of Yours,
While like a penitent I stand,
And there confess my sin."

Now, that act of laying on the hand signified confession. It meant just this—"Here I stand as a sinner, and confess that I deserve to die. This goat which is now to be slain represents in its sufferings what I deserve of God." O Sinner, confess your sin now unto your great God; acknowledge that He would be just if He condemned you! Confession of sin is a part of the meaning of laying on of the hand.

The next thing that was meant by it was acceptance. The person laying his hand said, "I accept this goat as standing for me; I agree that this victim shall stand instead of me." That is what faith does with Christ—it puts its hand upon the ever-blessed Son of God, and says, "He stands for me; I take Him as my Substitute." The next meaning of it was transference. The sinner standing there confessing, putting his hand on

133

the victim, and accepting it, did by that act, say, "I transfer, according to God's Ordinance, all my sin which I here confess, from myself to this victim." By that act the transference was made. You know there is a blessed passage which says, "The Lord has laid on Christ the iniquity of us all." From this expression an objection has been revised to that blessed hymn—

"I lay my sins on Jesus."

Yet I think the expression is quite correct. Cannot both utterances be true? God did lay sin in bulk upon Christ when He laid upon Him the iniquity of us all, but, by an act of faith every individual, in another sense, lays his sins on Jesus, and it is absolutely necessary that each man should so do if he would participate in the Substitution.

Now, do observe I pray you, that this was a personal act. Nobody could lay his hand upon the bullock, or upon the goat, for another—each one had to put his own hand there. A godly mother could not say, "My graceless boy will not lay his hand upon the victim, but I will put my hand there for him." It could not be! He who laid his hand there had the blessing, but no one else! Had the godliest saint with holy but mistaken zeal said, "Rebellious man, will you not put your hand there? I will act as sponsor for you!" It had been of no avail; the offender must personally come! And so, dear Hearer, you must have a personal faith in Christ for yourself. The word is sometimes interpreted to mean, and some give it the meaning, of leaning hard. What a blessed view of faith that gives us. Sometimes, according to the Rabbis, those who brought the victim leaned with all their might, and pressed upon it as if they seemed to say by the act, "I put the whole burden, weight and force of my sin upon this unblemished victim." O my Soul, lean hard on Christ! Throw all the weight of your sin upon Him, for He is able to bear it, and came on purpose to bear it—and He will be honored if you will lean heavily on Him! And, Beloved, what a simple act it was! The man who would not be absolved from sin in this way deserved to perish—there was nothing but to lay his hand, nothing but to lean—how could he refuse? Faith in Christ is no mystery; no problem needing to be explained in long treatises; it is simply trust Him! Trust Him! Trust Him and you are saved! "There is life in a look at the Crucified One." "Look unto Him, and be you saved, all the ends of the earth." Nothing can be plainer—nothing can be simpler—why is it so many puzzle themselves where God has given us simplicities? It must be that God made man upright, but man has found out many inventions with which to bewilder himself.

The laying on of the hand was the act of a sinner. He came there because he had sinned, and because his sin had come to his knowledge; had he been sinless there would have been no meaning in his bringing a sin-offering. Innocence needs not a substitute or sacrifice for sin; the sin-offering is evidently for the man who has sin, and what if I say there is no soul here to whom Christ is as suitable as the soul that is most full of sin? You that are a great, big, evil sinner; a thoroughpaced sinner, a damnable sinner; you are the very sinner to come to Christ and glorify His Grace! He is a Physician who did not come into this world to cure finger aches, and pinpricks, but to heal great diseases, loathsome leprosies, and burning fevers! Come, you Sinner of the common people, come and rest alone on Jesus! I wish I knew how to speak of this theme so as to move your souls; within a few months or years at the longest, we shall all be before the bar of God, and what if some of us should be there with our sins upon us? I am afraid some of you will be there unforgiven; O you to whom I have so often spoken, will you be there unpardoned? I shall not be able to make excuses for you there, and say you did not know the way of Salvation, for I have preached it with great plainness of speech! I have often cast aside language which contended itself to my taste, to use, instead, more homely words, lest one of you should miss my meaning! God knows I have often forsaken tracks of thought which opened before me, and which might have interested many of my hearers because I have felt while so many of you are unsaved, I must keep on plowing with simplicity and sowing elementary Truths of God! I am evermore telling over and over again the story of the Substitutionary work of the Lord Jesus. What? Do you hate your souls so much that you will damn them to spite Christ? Is there such a hatred between you and yourself that you will reject God's own Sacrifice for sin? You cannot say it is difficult for you to avail yourself of the death of Jesus; it is but to lay your hand of faith on that dear head! What enmity must there be in your hearts that you will not be reconciled to God even when He makes the Reconciliation by the death of His own dear Son! To what a pitch has man's rebellion against his Maker gone, when, sooner than be at peace with Him, he will reject Eternal Love, and will forever ruin his own soul! Oh, may God grant that some this morning may say, "I will stretch out my hand; I will trust in Jesus!" You see that the hand to be stretched out is an empty one, and the heart which leans may be a fainting one; weakness and sinfulness find strength and pardon by taking Jesus to be their All-in-All!

V. The last word I have to speak to you makes the fifth head, namely, *the assured blessing.* Turn to your Bibles, at the 31st verse; let every soul here that is conscious of sin read those last lines—"And it shall be forgiven him." There is the sacrifice; the man must put his hand upon it. The sacrifice is slain and, "His sin shall be forgiven him." Was not that plain speaking? There were no *ifs,* no *buts,* no *perhaps*; but—"It shall be forgiven him." Now, in those days it was only one sin, the sin confessed, that was forgiven; but now, "All manner of sin and blasphemy shall be forgiven unto men." In those days the forgiveness did not give the conscience abiding peace, for the offerer had to come with another sacrifice by-and-by. But now the blood of Christ blots out all the sins of Believers at once and forever; so that there is no need to bring a new sacrifice, or to come a second time with the blood of atonement in our hands. The sacrifice of the Jew had no intrinsic value! How could the blood of bulls and goats take away sin? It could only be useful as a type of the true Sacrifice, the Sin-Offering of Christ; but in our Lord Jesus there is real Efficacy; there is true Atonement; there is real cleansing, and whoever believes in Him shall find actual pardon and complete forgiveness at this very moment! What a joy it is to know that—

"The moment a sinner believes
   And trusts in his Crucified God,
His pardon at once he receives,
   Salvation in full through His blood."

I delight to believe that of Christ Jesus, Kent's verse is true—

"Here's pardon for transgressions past,
   It matters not how black their cast,
And oh, my Soul, with wonder view,
   For sins to come, here's pardon too."

Our sins were all laid on Christ in one bulk, and were all put away at one time! Woe unto any man who should have to take his sins upon himself as they come! The blessing is that as our sins are committed, they are still laid on Jesus, according to the words of the Psalmist, "Blessed is the man whose transgression is forgiven, whose sin is covered; blessed is the man unto whom the Lord imputes not iniquity, and in whom there is no guile." The Believer sins, but the Lord imputes not his sin to him—he lays it still upon the Scapegoat's head who bore our sins of old, even Christ Jesus our Savior!

The meat of all my discourse is this—if there is a child of God here who is in the dark, and burdened with sin; dear Brother, dear Sister, do not stand controverting with the devil as to whether you are a child of God or not! Do not be going over your experience, and saying, "I am afraid I am a hypocrite, and I have been deceived." But, for the moment, suppose the worst; let the devil take for granted his accusations, and then reply to him in words like those of Martin

Luther—"You say I am a great sinner, and a law-breaker, and all this; to which I reply I will cut your head off with your own sword, for what if I am a sinner? It is written Jesus Christ came to save sinners, and I rest my soul as a sinner simply upon Him." I like beginning again; the best way to get back lost evidences is to leave the evidences alone, and go again to Jesus! Evidences are very much like a sundial: you can tell what time it is if the sun is shining, but not if it isn't! And truly, a man of experience can tell the time of day without the sundial if he can but see the sun itself; evidences are clearest when Jesus is near, and that is just the time when we do not need them! Here is God's direction for acting when under a cloud: "If any walk in darkness and see no light, let him"—what? Fret about his evidences? No, "Let him trust." There is the end of it—"Let him trust in the Lord, and obey the voice of His Servant," and the light will soon come to him. Come away, O burdened Believer, to the Sin-Offering! "If any man sin, we have an Advocate with the Father." The fountain that was opened for sin and for uncleanness was not opened for the unregenerate only, but for the people of God, for it was opened "In the house of David," for the "Inhabitants of Jerusalem," that is, for those who are God's people.

If there is a poor soul here who has never believed in Jesus, but is burdened with sin, I invite him, and I pray God the Holy Spirit to make the invitation effectual, to come now to Jesus Christ. I think that when I was seeking the Savior, if I had been in this congregation and had heard

Christ set forth as bearing sin as a Substitute, and heard the plain talk you have listened to this morning, I would have found peace immediately! Instead of which I was months and months hunting after peace because I did not know this—that I had nothing to do, for Christ had done it all— and all I had to do was to take what Christ had done and simply trust in Him! Now that you know it, oh, may God add something to your knowledge! May He give you power to lay your hand on Jesus! Lean on Him, Soul! Lean on Him! If you cannot lean, fall into His arms! Faint away upon the bosom of the Savior! Trust Him! Rest in Him! It is all He asks of you! And then faith shall justify you and cleanse you, and shall give you sanctification, and by-and-by perfection, and shall bring you into His Eternal Kingdom and Glory. The Lord bless you, for Jesus' sake. Amen.

8

Laying the Hand on the Sacrifice

"And he shall lay his hand upon the head of the sin offering." (Leviticus 4:29)

I MIGHT HAVE TAKEN AS my text several other verses in the same chapter, for they all express the same idea as the words I have just read to you. For the sake of emphasis, let me ask you to look at the 4th verse. When a priest had committed sin and brought a sin offering unto the Lord, it is written, "He shall bring the bullock unto the door of the tabernacle of the congregation before the Lord; and shall lay his hand upon the bullock's head." The 15th verse tells us that when the whole congregation of Israel had sinned through ignorance, the Lord said to Moses, "The elders of the congregation shall lay their hands upon the head of the bullock before the Lord." Then, in the 24th verse, we read that when a ruler had sinned through ignorance and brought his sin offering, "He shall lay his hand upon the head of the goat, and kill it in the place where they kill the burnt offering before the Lord." And, in the 33rd verse, you find that if a common person had committed a sin through ignorance, or if his sin should come to his knowledge, he was to bring a sin offering and then it was added, "He shall lay his hand upon the head of the sin offering."

Any one of those verses would, therefore, have sufficed for a text. It seems to have been a necessary part of the proceedings that when a sin offering was presented to the Lord, to be offered up before Him, the offerer should first of all lay his hand upon the head of the animal devoted to this sacred purpose.

I hope I am addressing many persons who wish to know more about the way and plan of salvation and who are anxious to partake in the benefits of Christ's atoning Sacrifice. Possibly they are saying, "We know that there is a Savior for sinners, but how can He be ours? We know that an Atonement has been made for sin, but how can that Atonement really put away our sin so that we may be pardoned and accepted by God?" This is a very natural question and a very proper one. It would be well if it were most solemnly and seriously asked by all who, as yet, remain without being partakers of the blessings which are stored up for us in Christ Jesus.

Beloved Friends, it will be all in vain, so far as we are personally concerned, "that Christ Jesus came into the world to save sinners," unless He shall save us. It will be of no avail to us that Jesus shed His precious blood unless that blood washes away our guilt. It will increase, rather than diminish our misery if we hear that others are saved as long as we ourselves remain unsaved. If we are finally lost, it will not make our lot in hell any more tolerable if we discover that there was a Propitiation for sin, although we never had a share in its expiatory effects. Of all questions in the world, it seems to me that this is the most urgent and pressing one—and that we ought not to rest until we get it satisfactorily answered and put into practice—"How can I be a partaker in the eternal life which Jesus Christ came into the world to procure for sinners by His death?"

Some of you have up to now totally neglected this question. If you had noticed, in *The Times*, an advertisement stating that somebody's next of kin was wanted, and you had suspicion that you were the person to whom the notice referred, I guarantee you that you would not have let the grass grow under your feet—you would have been quick enough to secure the fortune which had been left by your relative! But now that Jesus Christ has died and left a wondrous legacy of Grace among the sons of men, you have allowed a good many years to roll over your head without making an eager and earnest search into the question whether there is anything for you! You have seen a great many persons saved all around you, yet you remain unsaved. You have some of your dear ones who are in Heaven, but you are not pursuing the path which will lead you there and, all this while you have not had the excuse, which many have had, of never having heard that there was a great Savior and great salvation to be had without money and without price!

If you could plead such an excuse as that, it would be better for you than it is now, when you are sinning against light and knowledge in neglecting that which would is most of all for your spiritual and eternal good. Be wise, therefore! You have been trifling far too long! Be serious and bend your whole mind to the earnest consideration at this all-important question, "How can I obtain salvation? How can I get it here and now? How can sin be pardoned? How can my sins be pardoned right now? I have long heard of Christ—how can I come into vital communion with Him? I know that—

> " 'There is a fountain filled with blood,
> Drawn from Immanuel's veins'—

"but how can I be washed therein so that I, personally, may become whiter than snow?" My text says that the guilty person who brought the sin offering laid his hand upon its head. And this act gives a pictorial and symbolical answer to your questions and tells you how you can come into communion with Christ—and how His great Sacrifice can become available for you. You have to do to Christ, spiritually, what these Hebrews did literally! You have to imitate their action and so carry out those words of Dr. Watts which we often sing—

"My faith would lay her hand
On that dear head of Yours
While like a penitent I stand
And there confess my sin."

I shall speak of only two things which we may learn from my text. The first is the intent of this symbol. And the second is, the simplicity of the symbol—this laying of the hand of the offerer upon the head of the victim presented by him to God as a sin offering.

I. First, then, let me try to explain *the intent of the symbol.* What did it mean? These things, of which I shall speak in explaining this symbol, are necessary in order that Christ should become yours. Follow me very carefully and prayerfully, dear Friend, if you do, indeed, desire to be saved, for it may be that the Lord will lead you into Everlasting Life even while I am speaking. I pray that He may do so!

The first meaning of this laying of the hand upon the head of the sacrifice is this—it was a confession of sin. The offering was a sin offering—but for sin it would not have been needed! The man who came and laid his hand on the head of the sin offering, acknowledged, by that act and deed, that he was a sinner. If there had been anyone who was not a sinner, he would have had no right to be there. A sin offering, for a person who had no sin, would have been a superfluity—why should he bring a sin offering to the Lord? So, dear Friends, if you have no sin, you are not fit subjects for Christ's saving power and Grace. If you are not guilty, you do not need forgiveness. If you have never transgressed the

Law of God, you need not come before Him with a sin offering! Only remember that if you do think so, you are under one of the most sorrowful delusions that ever entered the brain of a madman! You are deceiving yourself, depend upon it! If you say that you have no sin, the Truth of God is not in you. But he who brought a sin offering before the Lord said, in effect, "This is what I need, for I am a sinner. I need to have my sins taken away for I am guilty in the sight of God. So I put my hand upon this lamb, or goat, or bull which is about to die, thereby confessing that I need a sacrifice in order that the sin which I confess that I have committed, may be put away."

Are you reluctant to confess that you are a sinner? If so, I pray very earnestly that you may speedily get rid of that reluctance. God does not ask you to confess your sins to any man. It would be a shame for you to do so, for you would pollute that man, whoever he might be, if you poured into his ear the sad tale of your filthiness and sin! God does not ask you to do any man the serious wrong of whispering into his ear the foul story of your transgressions. It is not to your fellow creature, but to your God, that you are to confess your sin! Go straight to Him and say, as the prodigal said to his father, "I have sinned against Heaven, and in Your sight." What makes you so slow to do that? Do you imagine that He does not know about your sin? Do you think that you can hide anything from Him? That is impossible, for "all things are naked and opened unto the eyes of Him with whom we have to do." Is it your pride that keeps you from confessing your sin? How can you hope that God will forgive you if you will not acknowledge that you have sinned against Him?

Think how you act towards your own children. How ready you are to again clasp them to your bosom when they have offended against you! Yet you watch to see in them signs of relenting and repenting. So does the Lord your God watch for tokens of contrition and godly sorrow in you! Why, "take with you words, and turn to the Lord: say unto Him,

Take away all iniquity, and receive us graciously." Are you not willing to do this? Then, alas, you lack the first requisite for obtaining acceptance through Christ! How can you, who will not admit that you have sinned, lay your hand upon the head of the sin offering?

He who thus confessed his sin confessed also that he deserved to die, just as that victim was about to be slain. There stood the priest, with his sacrificial knife, ready to slay the innocent beast and the basin in which to catch the blood of the bull, or goat, or lamb—whichever it might be that was being offered—and he who laid his hand upon its head, thereby said, "This poor animal is about to die and to pour out its blood. And this reminds me that I deserve punishment from God. If He were to destroy me, He would be perfectly justified in doing so." Soul, will you say that? Are you willing to humble yourself in the dust and to say that? Will you put the rope about your neck and confess that you deserve the extreme penalty that the great Judge can inflict? If so, you have begun well, for he who will confess his guilt and will acknowledge that he deserves the punishment of death for it has begun to put his hand upon the head of the great Sacrifice for sin!

Follow me a step further and I trust that we may rejoice together that you, poor, guilty, self-condemned soul, have found deliverance through the one Sacrifice which God has provided for the putting away of sin. In the second place, the laying of the hand upon the head of the sin offering was a consent to the plan of substitution. He who had brought the victim laid his hand upon its head and, though he did not say so, yet his actions, being interpreted, meant, "God has ordained that this animal should take my place and I accept the Divine appointment right heartily. I agree with Him that I should be pardoned through the offering of a sacrifice and that I should be accepted by God by reason of the shedding of the blood of a sacrificial victim." Now, what say you to this plan, O Man? If the Jew was willing to let the death of the bull, or the goat, or the lamb typically stand for his own death, are you willing, with all your heart, to accept God's plan of salvation by the substitution of His only-begotten Son suffering and dying in your place?

Surely you will not quarrel with this method of saving you if God sees it to be the right one! Whenever my conscience has raised any question about the justice of this arrangement, it has always been quite a sufficient answer for me to say that if the thrice-holy Jehovah feels that the Sacrifice of Christ, in the place of sinners, is enough to vindicate His Justice, I may well be satisfied with what satisfies Him. Indeed, to question the righteousness of that method of saving the lost is to assail God upon a matter which lies very near His heart and to attack that wondrous plan of Redemption which is the last and highest display of all His Divine attributes—for the system of Substitution is the apex of the pyramid of God's Revelation, the very highest point of the great mountain chain in which He has manifested His Wisdom, Power, Love, Mercy and even His Justice to the sons of men—"that He might be just, and the Justifier of him who believes in Jesus." O Soul, if the Lord, who is offended, is satisfied with the Expiation offered, you, certainly, need not be so foolish as to raise questions concerning it or to quibble at it!

Besides, if you will but think seriously about this matter, you will see that the Justice of God is abundantly honored by Christ's standing in your place. There is a well-known story of a school master who had one boy in his school whom he could not keep in order by any ordinary discipline. He had threatened to punish him and, indeed, he had done so again and again, but still he remained incorrigible. At last he threatened that if a certain form of disobedience should be repeated, he would be publicly beaten. The time soon came for the fulfillment of the threat, but the master could not bear that the boy should be punished, yet, at the same time, he felt that the honor of the school and the maintenance of his own authority in it required that it should be so. He told the lads that he was willing to spare the erring one, "yet," he said, "discipline will be at an end, my word will be broken, you will never believe in me again and, moreover, the school will be dishonored by this boy being allowed to act as he does without punishment."

Musing for a minute, he took down the ruler, put it into the hand of the disobedient boy and then held out his own hand, bade the boy strike and he received the punishment that was due to the culprit. The effect produced upon the boy was not a matter of surprise to those who know what fervent love will do. He offended no more and the school was maintained in the highest possible condition of discipline. This is a faint picture of what God has done. In the Person of His well-beloved Son, He says, "I will suffer because you are guilty. Somebody must be punished for your sin and if you suffer the just penalty for your evil deeds, it will crush you to the lowest Hell. You cannot endure it, but I, Myself, will bare My shoulders to receive the stripes which are your due. I will take upon Myself your sins. My Law shall have a terrible yet complete vindication—I shall be just and yet I shall be able to fully and freely forgive you and to accept you." Nothing ever displayed all the attributes of God so gloriously and especially His Immutable Justice, as the atoning death of His well-beloved and only-begotten Son! So, Beloved let there be no question about your assenting to the plan of Substitution. God is content with it. You yourself can see how it honors Him, so be satisfied with it! Do not be a skeptic, doubting and questioning.

There is an old proverb which says, "Don't quarrel with your bread and butter," but I may with even greater emphasis say, "Do not quarrel with your own salvation." If I must quibble at anything, surely I will not quibble against my own soul and try to prove that I cannot be saved, putting my wits to work to show the absurdity of God's way of saving me! Oh, never, never let this be the case with you! But rather cheerfully accept what Infinite Wisdom has arranged!

Thus, you see, that the laying of the hand of the offerer on the head of the sacrifice meant the confession of sin and consent to the way of salvation by substitution. It also meant a great deal more than that.

In the third place, it meant the acceptance of that particular victim in the sinner's place. By laying his hand upon it, he practically said, "This animal is to stand instead of me." Here is the main point, the essential point of the whole matter. Will you accept Christ as standing in your place—the Divine yet Human Savior, perfect in His Humanity, yet also perfect in His Deity? He has lived. He has suffered. He has died. He has risen again. He has gone back into Glory at His Father's right hand. God has honored Him with full acceptance—will you also accept Him? The root of the matter lies there! Oh, may His blessed Spirit sweetly guide your will so that you shall say, as I do, "Accept Him? Ah, blessed be His holy name that He permits me to accept Him! Surely I will do so. I will trust Him—He shall be mine." If you have done so, then He is yours, for that is all He asks of you—to receive Him, to lay your hand upon Him and say, "There! Jesus Christ shall be the Sacrifice for me! I will rest in Him and in Him alone."

I hope that I do not need to multiply words in urging this decision upon you. I trust that the softening influence of the Holy Spirit is already at work among you, leading some of you who have delayed until now, to say, "We will accept Jesus as our Substitute and accept Him now." Why should you delay any longer to stretch forth your hand and lay it upon Jesus, by faith, even as the offerer laid his hand upon the head of the sacrifice?

But this laying on of the hand meant even more than that, though that was the very essence of it all. It also meant a belief in the transference of the sin. He who laid is hand upon the sin offering did, as it were, as far as he could, put his sin from himself on that bull, or goat, or lamb which was about to die, because it had become the sinner's substitute. That laying on of his hand was a token of the transference of his guilt to the appointed victim and if you will have Christ to be your Savior, you must believe that He, "His own Self, bore our sins in His own body on the tree." Do you believe this? Then, see what follows from it. Sin cannot be in two places at one time—if it is laid upon Jesus, it is taken off of you! If you do, in your very soul, accept Christ as your Substitute, then it is clear that the Lord has laid upon Him your iniquity and, therefore, your iniquity has passed away from you and your sin is gone forever! Christ has taken all your iniquities and carried them away where they shall never be mentioned against you anymore!

Oh, what a blessed Truth this is! If a man, who has been blind for 50 years could have his eyes opened, and could be taken out to see the stars, or to look up to the sun, how he would clap his hands and cry, "What a wondrous sight it is!" And I know that when I first perceived that Christ stood in my place and that I stood in His place—that I was accepted because He was rejected, that I was Beloved because He endured His Father's wrath on my account—my soul felt as if it had never lived before and had never known anything that was worth knowing till it perceived that wondrous Truth! The Lord give you, dear Heart, to perceive that it is even so in your case, for then you, also, will be truly glad.

That laying of the hand on the head of the sin offering also meant one thing more—it was dependence, a leaning on the victim. According to the Rabbis, the offerer was to lean with great pressure upon the bullock or the goat. If it was so, there is great significance about that act, for it teaches that you should depend like that upon Jesus—lean hard upon Him, lean with all your weight of sin, and all your load of iniquity, upon Him whom God has appointed to stand in the sinner's place. Accept Him as your Substitute, lean upon Him, rest upon Him. Say in your soul, "If I perish," though that can never be, "I will perish leaning upon Christ. He shall be my soul's only Dependence."

The Puritans speak of faith as a recumbency, a leaning. It needs no power to lean—it is a cessation from our own strength and allowing our weakness to depend upon another's power. Let no man say, "I cannot lean." It is not a question of what you can do, but a confession of what you cannot do and a leaving of the whole matter with Jesus! No woman could say, "I cannot swoon"—it is not a matter of power. Die into the life of Christ! Let Him be All-in-All while you are nothing at all!

"Well," says one, "but I can hardly think that I shall be saved simply by depending upon Christ." Then, let me tell you that this was all that any of the saints of old ever had to depend upon—and this is all that any of the children of God who are now alive, have to depend upon! I bear my own personal testimony that my only hope for everlasting life lies in the death of Him who suffered in my place! I have trusted in Him, I have accepted Him as standing in my place. Gladly have I seen my sin transferred to Him and His righteousness transferred to me! I have no other hope, nor even the shadow of another hope! Prayers, tears, repentance, preaching, almsgiving, yes, and faith itself—all these put together are nothing at all as a ground of dependence for the soul! It is the blood and righteousness of Jesus Christ, the one great Substitute for sinners, upon which we all must rely. There, Soul, if you have nothing else to depend upon, you have as much as I have! And if you accept Jesus Christ to be your Savior, you have the same hope that I have. I will even dare to be bonds- man for you and to perish with you if you can perish trusting in Christ! But that can never be. As this blessed Book is true, and as Christ ever lives, there is not a soul, that shall rely upon Him, whom He will not assuredly bless and pardon here below and take to Himself to dwell in His bosom forever and ever in Heaven!

There you see what is the intent of the laying of the hand upon the head of the sin offering. If you have been helped to follow me thus far—if you have really laid your hand upon Christ—I bless and praise the name of the Lord!

II. Now I have only a few minutes left for speaking, in the second place, upon *the simplicity of this symbol*. What was required was just the laying of the hand of the offerer upon the victim's head—that and nothing more.

Notice that there was no preparatory ceremony. There was the animal provided for a sacrifice, just as God has provided our Lord and Savior Jesus Christ to be the Lamb of God. And the one thing to be done was for the sinner to lay his hand upon the head of the sacrifice. In like manner, there is no preliminary ceremony needed before coming to Christ. This is the first thing, Sinner, that you have to do, simply lay your hand upon Him and say, "He is mine." "But must I not be prepared in a certain way, so that I may come to Him aright? Must I not do, or feel, or be something?" No, the Cross is at the head of the Way of Life—it is the true wicket gate which leads unto Everlasting Life. Believing in Jesus is the first thing you have to do—you live not until you believe in Him. Come, then, to Jesus! Come now! The first thing for you to do is to accept Him as your Substitute and to rely wholly upon Him.

You also perceive, dear Friends, that the hand that was to be laid upon the head of the sacrifice had nothing in it. The man who came thus to confess his guilt, did not bring a silver shekel or talent of gold in his hand. That was not at all necessary. All he had to do was to lay his hand upon the sin offering and, in like manner, you must say, with Toplady—

> "Nothing in my hand I bring—
> Simply to Your Cross I cling."

And, as there was to be nothing in the hand of the sinner, so there was to be nothing on his hand. If he had a dozen diamond rings on his fingers, he could not lay his hand on the bull's head any the better. He who had no ornament at all could do it just as well! And if you have no virtues, no excellences—if you are poor, if you are illiterate, if you have even lost your character—if your hand is a foul hand, a black hand, yet if you lay it, by faith, upon the head of Jesus Christ, if you take Him to be your Savior, you have made the all-important decision—

"'Tis done, the great transaction's done!"

You are your Lord's, and He is yours, for, "he that believes on the Son has everlasting life." He has it already in present possession, so let him go in peace, rejoicing in the blessing that he has received from the Substitute and Savior!

Observe, too, that there was nothing to be done with that hand except to lay it on the head of the sacrifice. There were to be no mystic crossings or moving to and fro, no cunning show of skill—the sinner was just to lay his hand upon the head of the animal that was to die as his substitute. You know that in the Revelation, the woman arrayed in purple and scarlet, that is, the Church of Rome, has upon her forehead the name, "Mystery," and you probably recollect what follows, "Babylon the great, the mother of harlots." But the chaste bride of Christ, the Church which He has redeemed by His blood, is not a partaker of that mystery! And Christ, in the Gospel, gives us nothing but simplicities. As the laying of the hand on the head of the sacrifice was all that was needed for the forgiveness of the sinner under the Law, so all that you need now is to take Christ to be your Substitute and Savior! Therefore, by the eternity of bliss or woe which depends upon your decision, in the name of God, who has sent me to proclaim His Gospel, I demand of you, man or woman, that you should come to the right decision upon this all-important matter! Let there be no putting off and no offering to do something else—what is required is that you should lay your hand, by faith, on the head of the sin-atoning Lamb of God. Have you done so? If not, you have neither part nor lot in Him—and if you remain in your present condition, you will perish in your sin! But if you will accept Christ as your Substitute, you need no earthly priest or mediator. So, take Him as yours—"Take Him now, and happy be." The symbol was one of extreme simplicity, for, finally, there was nothing to be done to the man's hand. The priest was not to wash it, or to read the lines upon it by the aid of palmistry, or to tattoo it with some sacred sign. No, the man came, remember, because he was a sinner. And he laid his hand on the sacrifice because he was a sinner. The hand that he laid there was a sinner's hand, and I believe in Jesus Christ with a sinner's faith. I say to Him, at this moment, as I said when first I trusted Him—

> "Just as I am—without one plea
> But that Your blood was shed for me,
> And that you bade me come to You,
> O Lamb of God, I come."

Do not come to Christ as saints—come as sinners! Come just as you are, sinful, vile, and polluted—and lay the hand of simple yet trembling confidence upon the head of Jesus and say, "He shall be mine." If you come to Him thus, He will not refuse or reject you, for He has said, "Him that comes to Me I will in no wise cast out."

There are some of you who have been here a long time and you are not yet converted. If you go to Hell, I am clear of your blood. Often have I wept over you when preaching here and I have set Christ before you as the one only and open door of salvation. And I have entreated and besought you to enter, but if you will not enter, I can do no more—the rest must lie with yourselves. You will melt the wax that seals your own death warrant. The responsibility rests wholly upon you—lay it not upon God. If any man is saved, it is of God's Grace and God's Grace, alone. But if any man is lost, it is by his own free will and his free will alone. The will of man is the source of damnation—the will of God is the source of salvation. Both those statements are true! Therefore, if you reject the Gospel of the Grace of God, you bring upon yourselves the just punishment of your sin.

I do not know that I can say anymore upon this theme except just this. There may be someone who is saying, "This plan of salvation is too simple." Surely you will not quarrel with it on that account! I guarantee you that if a man were going to be hanged and he could be delivered simply by accepting a free pardon, he would not say that such a plan was too simple! After all, the best things in the world are very simple. If I want to go from here to Glasgow, it is a simple method that I have to follow. I have to get to the proper railway station, take my ticket and enter the right carriage. Then, if all goes well, I shall get there all right. If I want to go to Heaven, it is just as simple. I go by faith to Christ and trust myself wholly to Him and so I get there. It is really a matter of trust when you enter a railway carriage and you reach your destination by a power above your own. If I want to communicate with a friend at the very ends of the earth, I have nothing to do but to step into a telegraph office, write down what I want to say, pay the proper charge and the message will go all right. Though I cannot trace the wire which connects the office with my distant friend, I know that he will get my cablegram in due course. There may be some mystery about the matter, yet, practically, it is a very simple thing.

And believing in the Lord Jesus Christ is just as simple as that. If a farmer wants a harvest, all the philosophers in the world cannot tell him how wheat grows, nor can they make it grow—he has only to drop his seed into the earth at the right time and it will grow by night and by day, though he knows not how! Therefore, act in the same simple, common-sense fashion. Leave off enquiring into mysteries which you cannot understand and puzzling over difficulties which your poor brain cannot comprehend—"Let artful doubts and reasoning be Nailed with Jesus to the tree"—and do you, as a little child, fully trust Jesus as your Savior and so you shall be saved! God help you to do this now, for Christ's sake! Amen.

9

Sins of Ignorance

"And if a soul sins and commits any of these things which are forbidden to be done by the commandments of the Lord; though he knew it not, yet is he guilty, and shall bear his iniquity. And he shall bring a ram without blemish out of the flock, with your estimation, for a trespass offering, unto the priest: and the priest shall make an atonement for him concerning his ignorance wherein he erred and knew it not, and it shall be forgiven him." (Leviticus 5:17-18)

I T IS SUPPOSED IN OUR text that men might commit forbidden things without knowing it. No, it is not merely supposed, but it is taken for granted and provided for. The Levitical law had special statutes for sins of ignorance and one of its sections begins with these words, "If a soul shall sin through ignorance against any of the commandments of the Lord." If you will, at your leisure, read the 4th and 5th chapters of Leviticus, you will find, first of all, it is supposed that a priest may sin. They knew nothing of infallible priests and infallible popes under the Mosaic Law! It was known and recognized that priests might sin and sin through ignorance, too.

"The priest's lips should keep knowledge," but as they were compassed with infirmities, they learned to have compassion on the ignorant by being made, themselves, conscious that they were not perfect in understanding. In the 4th chapter a sacrifice is prescribed for "the priest that is anointed, if he sins according to the sin of the people." The highest in office, who ought to be best read in the things of God, might, nevertheless, err through misunderstanding, forgetfulness, or ignorance. The priests were teachers, but they needed, also, to be taught. As Trapp says, "The sins of teachers are teachers of sins" and, therefore, they were not overlooked but had to be expiated by trespass offerings.

Further on in the chapter it is supposed that a ruler may sin (see verse 22). A ruler should be thoroughly acquainted with the Law which he has to dispense, but yet he might not know every point and, therefore, might err. Therefore it is written, "When a ruler has sinned, and done somewhat through ignorance against any of the commandments of the Lord his God concerning things which should not be done, and is guilty. Or if his sin, wherein he has sinned, comes to his knowledge; he shall bring his offering." There existed no fiction among the Jews that the king can do no wrong—however excellent his intentions, he might be misinformed upon the Divine Law and so fall into error. Errors in leaders are apt to breed mischief and, therefore, they were to be repented of and put away by an expiatory sacrifice.

It was, also, according to the Law, regarded as very likely that any man might fall into sins of ignorance, for in chapter four, verse 27, we read, "And if any one of the common people sins through ignorance, while he does somewhat against any of the commandments of the Lord." The sin even of the most common person was not to be winked at and passed over as a mere trifle, even though he could plead ignorance of the Law! It was not to be said, "Oh, he is quite an insignificant person and he did it in ignorance and, therefore, there is no need to take any note of it." No, on the contrary, he was, also, to bring his trespass offering that the priest might make an atonement for him. Ignorance was common enough among the common people, but it did not constitute a license for them, nor screen them from guilt.

But we need not, dear Friends, go to these Scripture references, for we are well assured by our own observation and the verdict of our own experience that sins of ignorance are possible, for we have often, ourselves, sinned in this fashion, and we have had to mourn deeply over the fact when we have been convinced of it. Very much in which we once allowed ourselves we would not do again, for we see the evil of it, though once we judged it to be right enough. An enlightened conscience mourns over sins of ignorance which it would never do if they were innocent mistakes.

The word rendered, "ignorance," may, also, bear the translation of inadvertence. Inadvertence is a kind of acted ignorance—a man frequently does wrong for lack of thought, through not considering the outcome of his actions—or even thinking at all. He carelessly and hastily blunders into the course which first suggests itself and errs because he did not think about whether or not it was right. There is very much sin of this kind committed every day. There is no intent to do wrong and yet wrong is done. Culpable neglect creates a thousand faults. "Evil is worked by lack of thought as well as lack of heart." Sins of inadvertence, therefore, are undoubtedly abundant among us and in these busy, thoughtless, railway days they are apt to increase.

We do not take time enough to examine our actions! We do not take good heed to our steps. Life should be a careful work of art in which every single line and tint should be the fruit of study and thought, like the paintings of the great master who was apt to say, "I paint for eternity." But, alas, life is often slurred over like those hasty productions of the scene painter in which present effect, alone, is studied, and the canvas becomes a mere daub of colors hastily laid on. We seem intent to do much rather than to do well—we want to cover space rather than to reach perfection. This is not wise. O that every single thought were conformed to the will of God!

Now, seeing that there are sins of ignorance and sins of inadvertence, what about them? Is there any actual guilt in them? In our text we have the Lord's mind and judgment—not that of the Church or of some eminent Divine—but of the Lord God Himself and, therefore, let me read it to you once again. "If a soul sins and commits any of these things which are forbidden to be done by the commandments of the Lord; though he knew it not, yet is he guilty, and shall bear his iniquity." Sins of ignorance, then, are really sins needing atonement because they involve us in guilt! Yet let us clearly understand that they greatly differ in degree of guilt from known and willful sins.

Our Lord teaches us this in the Gospels and our own conscience tells us that it must be so. The Savior puts it, "That servant, which knew his lord's will, and prepared not himself, neither did according to his will, shall be beaten with many stripes. But he that knew not, and did commit things worthy of stripes, shall be beaten with few stripes." He who knew not his lord's will was less punished than the intentional offender, but he was still beaten—and beaten with stripes, of which a few will be far more than you and I may wish to bear! The fewest stripes that will come from the hand of justice will be enough to grievously afflict us!

One stroke has made good men lie in the dust and moan in sorrow. Sins caused by ignorance are punished, for the Prophet says (Isa. 5:13), "My people are gone into captivity because they have no knowledge." And again in Hosea, "My people are destroyed for lack of knowledge." Paul, also, tells us, "the Lord Jesus shall be revealed from Heaven with His mighty angels, in flaming fire taking vengeance on them that know not God." These are to be punished, it seems, though their sinful ignorance is mentioned in the threat. Yes, and according to my text there is sin in ignorance, itself, for the 18th verse declares, "the priest shall make an atonement for him concerning his ignorance wherein he erred."

Ignorance of the Law among those who dwelt in the camp of Israel was essentially sinful. The Israelite had no business to be ignorant. The Law was plain and within his reach. If he neglected to study the statute, his breach of the statute could not be excused by his neglect, seeing the neglect was, in itself, an act of omission of a censurable kind. Willful ignorance of the Lord's will is, in itself, sin, and the sin which comes of it is grievous in the sight of the Lord our God. Blessed be God, the solemn declaration of the text concerning the guilt of sins of ignorance needs not drive us to despair, for a sacrifice is permitted for it!

The offender, on discovering his error, might bring his offering and pay the trespass money for any damage which he had caused by his action. And there was a promise given in connection with the atoning sacrifice which was, no doubt, often realized by the contrite in heart—"It shall be forgiven him." Be it ours, this morning not to attempt excuses but to seek forgiveness! May the Spirit of God work in us a tender-hearted confession of that sin which we did not, before, know to be sin. And while we are confessing it, may the Divine Spirit apply the precious blood that we may have a sweet sense of pardon. May the Lord make us rejoice in the Truth of God that, "the blood of Jesus Christ His Son cleanses us from all sin."

The teaching of my text does three things, of which I shall speak. First, by it the commandment is honored. Secondly, by it the conscience is enlightened. And thirdly, by it the Sacrifice is endeared.

I. By the Divine declaration that sins of ignorance are really sins, *the commandment of God is honored*. I need not multiply words to prove it so. The Law of God is, by this solemn sentence, lifted into a place of dignity. If it is really so, that to break one of its precepts involves us in guilt, even if we did not know that we were offending, then is the Law, indeed, enthroned upon a terrible eminence and girt around with fire. Enlarging upon this thought I would observe, first, dear Friends, that hereby the Law is declared to be the supreme authority over men. The Law is supreme, not conscience.

Conscience is differently enlightened in different men and the ultimate appeal as to right and wrong cannot be to your half-blinded conscience or to mine. I might condemn what you allow and you would scarcely tolerate what I approve—we are, neither of us, judges, but both culprits upon trial when we come under the Law. The ultimate appeal will be to, "Thus says the Lord"—to the Law itself, which is the only perfect standard by which the deeds and actions of men can be measured. The Law of God, from the supremacy into which this text lifts it, says to us, "You will not be excused because your conscience was unenlightened, nor because it was so perverse as to put bitter for sweet and sweet for bitter. My demands are the same in every jot and tittle, whatever your conscience may condemn or allow."

Conscience has lost much of its sensitiveness through the Fall and through our actual sins, but the Law is not lowered to suit our perverted understanding. If we break the Law, although our conscience may not blame us, or even inform us of the wrong, the deed is still recorded against us—we must bear our iniquity. The Law is, also, set above human opinion, for this man says, "You may do that," and a second claims that he may do the other, but the Law changes not according to man's judgment and does not bend itself to the spirit of the age or the tastes of the period. It is the supreme judge, from whose infallible decision there is no appeal. Right is right though all condemn, and wrong is wrong though all approve. The Law is the balance of the sanctuary, accurate to a hair, sensitive, even to the small dust of the balance.

Opinions continually differ, but the Law of God is one and invariable. According to the moral sensitiveness of a man will be his estimate of the act which he performs, but would you have the Law of God vary according to man's fickle judgment? If you would desire such a thing, God's infinite wisdom forbids it. The Law is a fixed quantity, a settled standard and if we fall short of it, though we know it not, yet are we guilty and must bear our iniquity unless an atonement is made. This exalts the Law above the custom of nations and periods, for men are very apt to say, "It is true I did so-and-so, which I could not have defended in itself—but then, it is the way of the trade—other houses do so, general opinion and public consent have endorsed the custom. I do not, therefore, see how I can act differently from others, for if I did so, I should be very singular and should probably be a loser through my scruples."

Yes, but the customs of men are not the standard of right! Where they have been, at first, correct through strong Christian influence, the tendency is for them to deteriorate and sink below the proper standard. Habit, perpetuity and universality of wrong at last enable men to call the false by the same name as the true—but there is no real change worked thereby—the customary wrong is still a wrong, the universal lie is still a falsehood. God's Law is not changed! Our Lord Jesus said, "It is easier for Heaven and earth to pass away than one tittle of the Law to fail." The Divine Law overrides custom, tradition and opinion—these have no more effect upon the eternal standard than the fall of a leaf upon the stars of Heaven.

"If a man does any of these things which are forbidden to be done by the commandments of the Lord; though he knew it not, yet is he guilty." All the customs in the world cannot make wrong right! If everybody that ever lived from Adam down to this hour had done a wrong thing and declared it to be righteous, yet would it make no moral difference in the evil deed. A thousand ages of whitewashing cannot make a vice a virtue. God's commands stand fast forever and he who breaks it must bear his punishment. Thus you see that by the declaration of my text, the Law of God is enshrined in the place of reverence.

Note again, if a sin of ignorance renders us guilty, what must a willful sin do? Do you not perceive at once how the Law is, again, set on high by this? For if an inadvertent transgression covers the soul with guilt which cannot be put away without a sacrifice, then what shall we say of those who knowingly and advisedly, with malice aforethought, break the commands of God? What shall we say of those who, again and again and again, being often reproved, harden their necks and go on in their iniquities? Surely their sin is exceedingly sinful! If I may become a transgressor by breaking a Law of God which I did not know, by what name shall I be called if, when I do know, I presumptuously lift up my hand to defy the Lawgiver and violate His statutes?

Thus again, dear Friends, by the teaching of our text, men were driven to study the Law, for if they were at all right-hearted they said, "Let us know what God would have us do. We do not wish to be leaving His commands undone, or committing transgressions against His precepts through not knowing better." They would, therefore, run to the Prophets and other teachers and ask them, "Tell us, what are the statutes of the Law of God? What has Jehovah ordained?" And right-minded men would be led by a desire to obey, to become earnest students of the will of God, as I trust, beloved Friends, we, also, shall be moved to be. Lest we should break the Law through not knowing its commands, let us make it our continual study. Let us search it day and night! Let it be the man of our counsels and the guide of our lives.

Let this be the prayer of each one of us—"What I know not, O my God, teach me. Make me to understand the way of Your precepts. Let me not be as the horse and the mule which have no understanding, but enlighten me in my inmost heart lest I ignorantly transgress Your commandments." Thus, you see, the Law was glorified in the midst of

163

Israel and men were led to search it to know what the Lord required of them. A holy fear, lest they should inadvertently fall into sin, moved them to diligent reading of the commands. Thus they were often checked when about to perform a hasty deed, and were made to ask themselves, "What would the Lord have us do?"

Without such an ordinance as our text, they might have acted hurriedly and so have sinned, and sinned again in the blundering haste of a thoughtless spirit. But by this they were checked in their heedlessness, called to consideration and made to have the fear of God always before them. They were thereby warned to look at their actions and examine their ways lest, through thoughtlessness, they should sin against the Law of God. And you will see at once, Beloved, that this would lead every earnest Israelite to teach his children God's Law, lest his sons should err through ignorance or inadvertence. The pious Jew carefully taught his children all things concerning the Passover and the yearly feasts, the daily sacrifice, the worship in the Temple and what was due to the service of God.

He made him learn the moral Law and endeavored, as far as he could, to enlighten his conscience, knowing that "for the soul to be without knowledge is not good." He said to his son, "Take fast hold of instruction. Let her not go. Keep her, for she is your life." Without knowledge a man will fall into many pitfalls and snares which the true light would have enabled him to avoid. Good men, therefore, spent much of their time in training their families. "Come, children," they said, "hearken unto me. I will teach you the fear of the Lord." They were, also, zealous to make known the Law of God as far as they could, saying each one to his fellow, "Know the Lord." Fear of committing sins of ignorance was a spur to national education and tended greatly to make all Israel honor the Law of the Lord.

I close these thoughts by noting that to me the sin-revealing power of the Law of God is wonderfully displayed as I read my text. I know the Law to be exceedingly broad. I know its eye to be like that of an eagle and I know its hand to be heavy as iron. But when I find that it accuses me of sins which I knew not, that it searches the secret parts of my soul and brings to light what my own eyes of self-examination have never seen, then I am filled with trembling! When I discover that I may stand before the bar of God charged with iniquities which I shall be quite unable to deny, but of which, at this moment, I am not at all conscious, then am I bowed in the dust! What a Law this must be! What a light is this in which our conduct is placed!

If you set your character side by side with that of your fellow man, you may begin to compliment yourself. If you look at it by the dim candlelight of public opinion, you may begin to flatter yourself. If you go no further than a diligent search by the aid of your own judgment, you may still be somewhat at ease. But if the light in which we shall stand at last will be the light of Jehovah's own ineffable purity! If His Omniscience detects iniquity where we have not perceived it and if His justice will visit sin even where we were not cognizant of it, our position is solemn, indeed! What a Law this is by which men are bound! How severe and searching! How holy and how pure must God, Himself, be?

O thrice holy Jehovah, we are filled with awe of You! The heavens are not clear in Your sight and You charged Your angels with folly! How, then, can we be just with You? After reading this, Your own Word, we see how justly You will charge us with folly and how impossible it is for us to hope to be justified in Your sight by any righteousness of our own! Thus, my Brothers and Sisters, we see that the Law of God is honored.

II. Secondly, by the teaching of the text, *the conscience is awakened*. I feel, when I read these words, as if a great gulf opens at my feet! "If a soul sins and commits any of these things which are forbidden to be done by

165

the commandments of the Lord; though he knew it not, yet is he guilty, and shall bear his iniquity." You know, dear Friend, that you are a willful sinner and have broken God's Law consciously. But if you may be a sinner though you knew it not, how the solid earth rolls away from under you as in a dreadful earthquake and, almost like Korah, Dathan and Abiram, you stand in dread as the devouring fire pours forth from the mysterious abyss!

Nothing which is human can be thought certain after this. Think of the sins you may have committed—sins of thoughts which have too rapidly flitted through your mind for you remember them—thoughts which pass over your mind as mere imaginations, like clouds floating aloft in the sky which cast a flying shadow over the landscape and are gone. Think of your evil thoughts, your pleasure in hearing of uncleanness, your desires, wishes and excuses of evil—these are all iniquities. Then, too, our words, our hurried words of anger, of falsehood, of petulance and pride. Our idle words, our murmuring words, our unbelieving words, our irreverent words—words scarcely meant which fell from us without thought! What a multitude of these may be laid at our door and all of them are full of sin!

And actions in which we have excused ourselves very thoroughly because we have never looked at them in God's light, but have been content to regard them in the dim ray of custom—are there not many of these which contain sin? When I think of all the forms of evil, I am compelled to fear that much of our life may have been a continuous sin and yet we may have never condemned ourselves, or even thought about it! Remember that great command, "You shall love the Lord your God with all your heart, and with all your soul, and with all your mind, and with all your strength." How far short of that you and I have come!

Mentally we have not served God to perfection, neither have the affections loved Him with all possible intensity, nor has the soul, with its desires, gone after Him so eagerly as it should. Truly we are guilty, guilty much more than we have ever imagined! And as to that second Commandment, "You shall love your neighbor as yourself"—who among us has done so? Have we loved our fellow man with a love that even approximated to our love to ourselves? O God, amid the varied lights of Your Ten Commandments, all comprehended in the white light of that one word, "love," we stand convicted and we perceive that our ignorance affords no covering for us! We hear Your voice and tremble before it while You say, "Though he knew it not, yet is he guilty, and shall bear his iniquity."

Our ignorance, dear Friends, is evidently very great. I do not suppose that the best instructed Christian here will claim to possess much wisdom. The usual rule is that the more we really know, the more conscious we are of the littleness of our knowledge. Our ignorance, therefore, I may take for granted all round, has been very great. What scope, then, has there been beneath the mantle of that mist of ignorance for sin to hide and multiply! As the conies swarm in the holes of the rocks, the bats in the sunless caves of the earth and the fish in the deep abysses of the sea, so do our sins swarm in the hidden parts of our nature. "Who can understand his errors? Cleanse me from secret faults!"

The ignorance of very many persons is, to a large degree, willful. Many do not read the Bible at all, or very seldom, and then without desiring to know its meaning. Even some professing Christians take their religion from a monthly magazine, or from some standard book written by a human author and adopted by their sect—few go to the Word of God itself—they are content to drink of the muddied streams of human teaching instead of filling their cups at the crystal fountain of Revelation itself.

Now, Brothers and Sisters, if you are ignorant of anything concerning God's mind and will, it is not, in the case of any of you, for lack of the Bible, nor for lack of a willing guide to instruct you in it for, behold, the Holy Spirit waits to be gracious to you in this respect. "If any man lacks wisdom, let him ask of God, that gives liberally, and upbraids not." If we do not know, we may know it. Our ignorance has been willful if, in this privileged country, we remain ignorant of the Gospel. Where there is confessedly such a mass of willful ignorance, who among us can imagine what myriads of evil shapes of sin swarm in the grim darkness? The Prince of Darkness holds his court in the blackness of that ignorance which we, ourselves, have willfully created by refusing to come to the Light of God.

The enemy sows the seed of evil by night and amid Egyptian darkness the accursed grain grows to an awful ripeness and brings forth a hundred-fold! Break in, O eternal Light! Break in upon the dimness of our ignorance, lest it thickens into the eternal midnight of Hell! Now, it will be vain for any man to say in his mind, as I fear some will do, "God is harsh in thus dealing with us." If you say thus, O Man, I ask you to remember God's answer. Christ puts your rebellious speech into the mouth of the unfaithful one who hid his talent. He said, "I knew that you were an austere man, gathering where you had not sown."

What did his master say? Instead of excusing him, which is far beneath the dignity of our great God to do, he took the man at his own confession and said, "You knew that I was an austere man, taking up that I laid not down, and reaping that I did not sow. Why, then, did you not put my money into the bank, that at my coming I might have required my own with interest?" If you know God to be harsh, or say you think so, then remember how earnest you ought to be to come up to His standard, for, call that standard what you like, it is the standard! Count it to be severe if you will, it is binding upon you for all that—and by it you will have to be tried, at the last, so that there is no escape for any of us by impeaching our Maker!

Wiser, far, is it to submit and beg for mercy. Let us remember, in order that our doctrine may appear less strange, that it is according to the analogy of Nature that when God's Laws are broken, ignorance of those Laws should not prevent the penalty from falling upon the offenders. The natural law is an instructive type of the moral and spiritual Laws of God and from it we may gather much teaching. Here is the law of gravitation, by which objects are attracted to each other. It is inevitable that heavy matters will fall to the earth. A man thinks that he can fly—he puts on his wings and climbs to the top of a tower. He is fully persuaded that he is about to fly like a bird. Spectators are invited to behold the wonder and expectations are excited. The law of gravitation is against the inventor, but he does not think so. Poor man, he firmly believes in his ability to fly. But the moment he leaps from the tower he falls to the earth and is gathered up a mangled corpse.

Why did not God suspend His natural law because the man did not intentionally violate it? No, the law is stern and changes not, and he who offends in ignorance pays the penalty. I have read that the Chinese at Peking often endure severe winters. They have coal just under them, but they refuse to dig the coal for fear they should disturb the equilibrium of the earth and cause the celestial empire, which is now at the top of the universe, to turn over to the bottom. The celestials are thoroughly conscientious in this belief, but does the weather alter to suit their philosophy? Does God make them warm in winter without coal? By no means! If they refuse the means of warmth, they will be cold—their ignorance does not raise the temperature so much as half a degree!

A physician, with the best possible motive, endeavors to discover a new drug so that he may alleviate pain. In conducting his experiments, he inhales a deadly gas which he did not know to be fatal. He dies as surely as if he had willfully taken poison. The law is not suspended to reward his benevolence and avert the fatal result of his mistake. Whatever his motives may have been, he has broken a natural law and the appointed penalty is exacted of him. Truly, as it is in the natural so will you find it to be in the spiritual world!

But let us go into the question a little, by way of argument. It is necessary that it should be according to this declaration. It is not possible that ignorance should be a justification of sin, for, first, if it did so, it would follow that the more ignorant a man was the more innocent he would be! It would then assuredly be true that ignorance is bliss, for perfect ignorance would be under no responsibilities and free from all sin! All that you and I would have to do, in order to be perfectly clear from all charges, would be to know nothing. To burn the Bible, refuse to hear the Gospel and rush away from civilization would be the nearest way to freedom from all guilt!

Do you not see that if things were so, knowledge might be regarded as a curse and that the light which Christ comes to bring into the world would be a man's most solemn affliction if it shone upon him? I proclaim that, in my unregenerate state, if I had been sure that ignorance would have rid me of responsibility, I would have closed every avenue of knowledge and would have labored to abide in darkness! But such a supposition is not to be borne—it is inconsistent with the first principles of common sense! If, again, the guilt of an action depended entirely upon a man's knowledge, we should have no fixed standard at all by which to judge right and wrong! It would be variable according to the enlightenment of each man and there would be no ultimate and infallible court of appeal.

Suppose the statute book of our own country should be constructed on the principle that in proportion only to a man's knowing the law should be his guilt in breaking it? We should have numbers of persons truthfully pleading ignorance and a great many more endeavoring to do so—and such a simple and easy method of obtaining acquittal would become popular at once! The art of forgetting would be diligently studied and ignorance would become an enviable inheritance. We would have gentlemen brought up for being drunk and disorderly who had paid 40 shillings and costs a score of times, who would still say that they did not know that they could be punished again since they had paid the fine so often! Ignorance would be so continually pleaded that there would be practically an end of all law and the very foundations of the State would be undermined! The thing cannot be endured—it is absurd upon its very face.

Moreover, ignorance of the Law of God is, itself a breach of the Law, since we are bid to know and remember it. Thus spoke the Lord by His servant Moses—"You shall lay up these, My Words, in your heart and in your soul, and bind them for a sign upon your hand that they may be as frontlets between your eyes. And you shall teach them to your children, speaking of them when you sit in your house and when you walk by the way, when you lie down, and when you rise up. And you shall write them upon the doorposts of your house, and upon your gates." Knowledge of the Law was a duty and ignorance a crime.

Can it be possible, then, that one sin is to be an excuse for another? It is a sin, on a man's part, to refuse to search into the Word of God. Can it be that because he commits this sin, he is to be excused for the faults into which his willful ignorance leads him? It is out of the question! If sins of ignorance are not sins, then Christ's intercession was altogether a superfluity. You remember that our text, last Sunday morning was, "He made intercession for the transgressors," and we illustrated it by the text, "Father, forgive them; for they know not what they do." But if there is no sin when a man does not know what he does, why did our Lord pray for pardon for ignorant transgressors? Why ask forgiveness, if there is no wrong? The correct way of putting it would have been, "Father, I do not ask You to forgive, for there is no offense, seeing that they know not what they do." But by the fact of His having pleaded for forgiveness, it is clearly proved that there is guilt in the sin of ignorance.

The work of the Holy Spirit, too, would be an evil instead of a good work in the hearts of men if ignorance were an excuse for sin, for He has come to convict the world of sin. But if unconvicted of sin they are innocent of sin, why convict them of it? Of what use is it to quicken a conscience and to enlighten it and make it bleed over a transgression if it would be no transgression, provided that conscience had never been made cognizant of it? Who is he that shall so blaspheme the Holy Spirit as to say that His work is needless and even idle? Sins of ignorance, therefore, must be sinful! Look at one other consequence which would follow from the contrary doctrine.

The more wicked a man is, the more hardened he becomes and the more ignorant he grows as to the beauty of holiness. Everybody knows that. A sin which troubles a child when at home with his godly father will not trouble him at all when he gets to be 50 years of age, provided he has indulged in a course of vice. From one sin to another the man descends, and, as he descends, his mental and moral eyes grow dim and he perceives less and less the sinfulness of sin. If a man who has arrived at the utmost pitch of infamy can commit any atrocity without the smallest idea of its being wrong—if he can cheat, lie, swear and I know not what and yet call it all nothing and wipe his mouth—if that man is guilty of less sin because of the growing deadness of his conscience and the limited degree of his spiritual knowledge, then, truly, things are turned upside down!

But it is not so. The test of the guilt of an action is not a man's conscience, nor his perception of evil, nor his knowledge, but the Law itself! Sin is a transgression of the Law of God, whether that Law is known or unknown. The statute stands immovable and immutable—and the sinner, blind though he may be—if he falls upon it shall be broken.

Once again, I am sure that many of us now present must have felt the truth of this in our own hearts. You who love the Lord and hate unrighteousness, must, in your lives have come to a point of greater illumination where you have said, "I see a certain action to be wrong. I have been doing it for years, but God knows I would not have done it if I had thought it wrong. Even now I see that other people are doing it and thinking it right, but I cannot do so any more. My conscience has, at last, received new light and I must make a change at once."

In such circumstances, did it ever come to your mind to say, "What I have done was not wrong because I did not know it to be wrong?" Far from it! You have justly said to yourself, "My sin in this matter is not so great as if I had transgressed willfully with my eyes open, knowing it to be sin." But yet you have accused yourself of the fault and mourned over it. At least I know I have. A man like John Newton, who in his early years had been connected with the slave trade and thought it right, as most Christian men did in those times, did not excuse himself in his later years when his conscience was awakened to the iniquity of slavery.

Do you think that the good man would say, "I was quite right in doing as I did because everybody else did it and I knew no better?" Ah, no! It was right or wrong whether he knew it or not and his conscience, when it became enlightened, told him so. My conscience and your conscience may need to be enlightened about several matters which now we are doing complacently enough, without any notion that we are sinning—but the action bears its own character of right or wrong—whatever our judgment may be. Does not this show us the utter impossibility of salvation by works? If you expect to be saved by keeping the Law of God, you must be a bolder man than I dare to be! I know that I cannot keep the Law of God and the doctrine of my text makes it impossible beyond all other impossibility, because the Law accuses me of doing wrong even when I do not intend it and am not conscious of it!

O you who hope to be saved by works, how can you ever enjoy a moment's peace? If you think your righteousness will save you if it is perfect, how can you ever be sure that it is perfect? You may have sinned ignorantly and that will spoil it all! Think of this and be dismayed! I beseech you, believe our testimony when we assure you that the road to Heaven by your own righteousness is blocked! Ten great Krupp guns which fling, each one of them, a bolt huge enough to dash your soul to Hell, stand pointed against you if you attempt to make your way to Heaven by that steep ascent!

There is another path! Yonder Cross directs you to it, for it is the signpost of the King's highway! That royal road to Heaven is paved with Divine Grace—God freely forgives the guilty because they trust in Christ! That path is so safe that no lion shall be there, neither shall any ravenous beast go up on it—but as for the road of Legal Righteousness, attempt it not, but listen to what we have further to say to you!

III. By the grand and awful truth of the text, *the sacrifice is endeared.* Just according to our sense of sin must be our value of the Sacrifice! God's way of delivering those who sinned ignorantly was not by denying their sin and passing over it, but by accepting an atonement for it. "The priest shall make an atonement concerning his sin wherein he has erred, and knew it not, and it shall be forgiven him." The forgiveness was to come through atonement! How greatly you and I need an atonement for our sins of ignorance, seeing our ignorance is great!

O blood of Christ, how much we need You! O Divine Substitute, how greatly do we require Your cleansing blood! How gracious it is on God's part to be willing to accept an Atonement, for if His Law had said there shall be no atonement possible, it would have been just—but infinite Grace devised the plan by which, through the Sacrifice of Another, pardon is possible for the ignorant sinner! Behold how generous God is, for He has Himself provided this Sacrifice! The man who had erred under the Law had to bring an offering, himself, but ours is brought for us! Jesus, the Son of God, was not spared by the great Father, but He gave Him out of His bosom that He might bleed and die!

The Incarnate God is the great Bearer of the sin of ignorance! And today He can have compassion on the ignorant and on them that are out of the way, for He has made an Atonement for them. Under the Law this atonement was to be a ram without blemish. Our Lord had no sin, nor shade of sin. He is the spotless Victim which the Law of God requires. All that Justice, in his most severe mood, could require from man by way of penalty, our Lord Jesus Christ has rendered, for in addition to His Sacrifice for the sin, He has presented a recompense for the damage, as the person who sinned ignorantly was bound to do.

He has recompensed the honor of God and He has recompensed every man whom we have injured. My Brothers and Sisters, has another injured you? Well, since Christ has given Himself to you, there is a full recompense made to you, even as there has been made to God! Blessed be His name, we may rest in this Sacrifice! How supremely efficacious it is! It takes away iniquity, transgression and sin. My dear Hearers, you are bound to confess your sins to God—but if pardon were offered you upon the condition that you should mention every sin you have committed—not one of you would ever be saved! We do not know, and if we ever did know, we cannot remember all our shortcomings and all our transgressions!

But the mercy is, though we do not know them, He does and He can blot them out! Though we cannot weep over them with a distinct knowledge of them because they are not known to us, yet Jesus bled for them with a distinct knowledge of them all—and they are all put away by His unknown sufferings—all cast into the deeps where an angel's eye can never trace them! By the immense and unsearchable agonies He endured for us and by His merits, infinite as His Divine Nature, our Redeemer has taken away that thick darkness of iniquity which we were not capable of comprehending!

O believing Sinner, the debt you know not, your glorious Surety has nevertheless borne and discharged for you! Blessings on His name. Rest in Him and then go your way and rejoice! Amen.

10

The Clean and the Unclean

"Speak unto the children of Israel, saying, These are the beasts which you shall eat among all the beasts that are on the earth. Whatever parts the hoof and is cloven footed and chews the cud, among the beasts, that shall you eat." (Leviticus 11:2-3)

T HE MOSAIC LAW ATTACHED great importance to meats and drinks—the Christian religion attaches none. The Apostle Peter was shown by the vision of a sheet let down from Heaven, not only that all nations were now to receive the Gospel message, but that all kinds of food were now clean, and that all the prohibitions which had formerly been laid upon them for legal purposes were now, once and for all, withdrawn. A Christian may, if he pleases, put himself under restrictions as to these matters. You will remember that the Apostle Paul says, "I know and am persuaded of the Lord Jesus that there is nothing unclean of itself, but to him who esteems anything to be unclean, to him it is unclean." I know our Apostle was tender of weak consciences, but he could expostulate with the Brothers and Sisters somewhat thus, "If you are dead with Christ from the rudiments of the world, why, as though living in the world, do you dogmatize—touch not this, taste not that, handle not the other—and all about things which perish with the using?"

The Doctrine of the New Testament is expressly laid down, "Every creature of God is good, and nothing to be refused, if it is received with thanksgiving." And as for the practice enjoined upon Believers, "All things are lawful, but all things are not expedient." In the example of Paul we have full liberty; he would put no embargo upon the conscience. But in his example we have also fervent charity—he would put no stumbling block in his Brother's way. "If meat makes my brother to offend, I will eat no flesh while the world stands." The Levitical law enjoined many precepts as to meats and drinks; but those carnal ordinances were imposed until the time of reformation. Since then, this Mosaic institution was not designed to be perpetual; we feel certain that it must have had some use at the time when it was first established, and during the time in which it was sustained. As that was peculiarly a typical dispensation, we feel persuaded that we shall not exaggerate the uses of the Text if we show that there was something instructive to us, and something typical of the better Covenant in the command that the people were to eat no creatures but those which divided the hoof, and those which chewed the cud.

I. It is our firm belief that these distinctions of meats were laid down on purpose *to keep the Jews as a distinct people*, and that herein they might be a type of the people of God, who are also, throughout all ages, to be a distinct and separate people—not of the world, even as Christ was not of the world.

You who are conversant with the old Levitical rule, well know that it was quite impossible for the Hebrews to mix with any other nation without violating the statutes they were commanded to keep. Their food was so restricted that they could not possibly enter into social dealings with any of the neighboring peoples. The Canaanites, for instance, ate everything—even the flesh that had been torn by dogs—and the dogs themselves. Now, a Jew could never sit at a Canaanite's table, because he could never be sure that there would not be the flesh of some unclean and accursed thing upon it. The Jews could not even eat with the Arabs, who were near akin to them, for they frequently partook of the flesh of the camels, the hare and the coney, all which, as we shall see presently, were forbidden to the Jew. The Arabs on the south, and the Canaanite nations all round Palestine, were the most likely people with whom the Jews would associate; but this command about what they should and should not eat prevented them, forever, from mingling with these people, and made them a distinct and isolated republic as long as they were obedient to the Law. We are told by Eastern travelers that the Mohammedan regulations, which are far less strict than those of the Jew, prevent their becoming socially intermingled either with the idolaters or with Christians. It is a well-known fact that no people who have laws about meats and drinks have ever changed their religion to that of another people, because the familiarity which seems necessary, in order to proselyte, is quite prevented by the barrier that precludes from dining at the table! It is at the social table men enjoy the most genial dealings—it is there they pour out their souls with the least reserve, and mix their thoughts, one with another, in the greatest freedom of conversation. Stop them there—prevent their sitting at the same table, and there is no likelihood that they will ever blend or intermingle in any kind of affinity—the races must be distinct!

I believe, dear Friends, though I have been somewhat prosy in explaining myself, that it was God's real intention to keep the children of Israel, until the coming of Christ, separate from all the nations that were upon the face of the earth. They could not join in the worship of other nations, for other nations sacrificed to their gods the very animals which to the Jew were unclean; they could not join in social contact, as we have already seen, and therefore marriage with any other nation would be, not only, as it were, prohibited by the Law, but would be actually prevented by the possibilities of the case. It must, in each instance, put the transgressor beyond the pale of his tribe. They would remain as much a distinct people as if a great wall of brass had been built all around them, or as if they had been transported to some island, and an impassable gulf had been put between them and any other kindred upon earth. They were separated forever! Now Friends, you will say, "What is the use of this to us?" I answer, it is the earthly type of a heavenly mystery!

When the Jews were put away as the people of God for a time, then the Gentiles were grafted into their olive branch, and though we did not inherit the ceremonies, we did inherit all the privileges to which those ceremonies point. Thus, all of you who name the name of Christ, and are truly what you profess to be, are solemnly bound to be forever separated from the world. Not that you are to leave off your daily dealings with men. Our Savior did not do so. He was holy, harmless, undefiled, and separate from sinners, yet, you know, He was always in the company of sinners, sitting at their table, seeking their good, and hunting after their souls. He was with them, but He was never of them. He was among them, but always distinct and separate from them—not conforming Himself to them, but transforming them to Himself! He has set us an example. It is not the seclusion of a hermit, nor the exclusion of yourselves in a monastery, where you would be of no service to your fellow men, but it is a higher and more spiritual separation which I claim of Christians tonight. You are to be in the world, and among the world; you are to mingle with all sorts and conditions of men—but still to maintain the dignity of your new-born character, and to let men see that you are among them as a speckled bird, as a light in the midst of darkness, as salt scattered over putridity, as heavenly angels in the midst of fallen men! So are you to be a distinct people, a chosen generation!

But, you will ask of me, in what respects are you to be distinguished? In a pure consistency always—in a vain eccentricity never—this shall be my first reply. Not in your garments, my Brothers and Sisters. All those inventions of broad-brimmed hats, and coats without collars, perish in the using! Let your dress be, nevertheless, so distinguished from that of some other men, that there shall be none of the pride and foolish quality in which they delight. The Apostle Peter has well laid down the regulations by which our Sisters in Christ are to adorn themselves. But I need not mention what you know so well, and practice so little—that chaste and becoming neatness which is always right in the sight of God— and beautiful in the assembly of Christians. Not by any peculiar dialect in your speech are you to be known. For my part, I abhor in any man that sanctimonious tone and sacred whine which many affect—even in the pulpit I despise it! I believe that the reason why the pulpit has lost so much of its former power is because men think they need to mouth our blessed Saxon tongue, and talk as if everything natural were to be eschewed there, and men, metamorphosed into ministers, were to be as unnatural and grotesque in their modes of speech as possible! No, not these, not these; all such artificial separations we leave to the people whose vanity feeds on its own conceit! Nor need you make any straining effort to be distinguished by any stiff rigid formality of your own. Do not try to make yourself look like a Christian! True Christians can do a great many things that sham Christians must not do. As for me, I am never afraid to laugh, for I shall never crack the paint on my face, laugh as I may! A sincere man may do a great many things that a hypocrite dare not do, for he will split the garments of his hypocrisy if he ventures to run as a Christian may. Heavenly realities within do not always need to be plastered up and labeled outside, so that everybody may see and recognize you and say, "There goes a saint." There are other modes of being distinguished from the world than any of these.

What are they, then? Well, Brothers and Sisters, we ought always to be distinguished from the world in the great Object of our life. As for worldly men, some of them are seeking wealth, others of them fame; some seek after comfort, others after pleasure. Subordinately you may seek after any of these, but your main and principal motive as a Christian should always be to live for Christ. To live for glory? Yes, but for His Glory. To live for comfort? Yes, but be all your consolation in Him. To live for pleasure? Yes, but when you are merry, sing Psalms, and make melody in your hearts to the Lord. To live for wealth? Yes, but to be rich in faith; you may lay up treasure, but lay it up in Heaven, where neither moth nor rust corrupt, where thieves break not through, nor steal. It is thought, you know, that ministers live for God—merchants should do the same! I wish, my Brothers and Sisters, that you would trade and do your merchandise for His service. Do your plowing, and sowing, and reaping, and mowing—do it for Christ! Would God you could do this quite as much in His service, as we do ours, when we preach for Christ! You can make the most common calling become really sacred; you may take the highest orders by dedicating your daily life wholly to the service of Jesus. There is such a thing—and let those who deny the possibility stand self-convicted that they obey not the precept—"Whether you eat or drink, or whatever you do, do all to the glory of God."

By your spirit, as well as your aim, you should likewise be distinguished. The spirit of this world is often selfish—it is always a spirit that forgets God that ignores the existence of a Creator in His own world, the land which He makes fat by His own bounty. Men with God's breath in their nostrils forget Him who makes them live! Now, your spirit should be one of unselfish devotion, a spirit always conscious of His Presence, bowed down with the weight, or raised up with the cheer of Hagar's exclamation—"You God see me"—a spirit which watches humbly before God, and seeks to know His will, and to do it through the Grace of God given to you! Such a spirit as this—without the drab of one sect or the phylacteries of another—will soon make you quite as distinct

182

from your fellow men as ever meats and drinks could make the Jews a separate people.

Your maxims, too, and the rules which regulate you, should be very different from those of others. The world says, "Well, it is usual in the trade; there is no use in being over scrupulous; we must not be too Puritanical, or too severe—we shall never get on if we are picking at this, and frowning at that." A Christian never considers what is usual, but what pleases God! He does not estimate a wrong by its commonness—he counts that a fraud, and a falsehood will be a fraud and lie—though all the world shall agree to practice it! The Believer reads things, not in man's light, in the obscurity of which so many blind bats are willing to fly, but he reads things in the sunlight of Heaven. If a thing is right, though he loses by it, it is done! If it is wrong, though he should become as rich as Croesus by allowing it, he scorns the sin for his Master's sake! We want our merchants on the Exchange, our traders in their shops, and our artisans in their factories. Yes, and we want all masters, employers, and overseers, too, to be distinguished as the clean from the unclean, in the maxims that govern their daily life, and thus manifestly separate them from the world!

This will naturally lead to the next point—the Christian should be separate in his actions. I would not give much for your religion unless it can be seen. I know some people's religion is heard of—but give me the man whose religion is seen! Lamps do not talk, but shine. A lighthouse sounds no drum, it beats no gong, and yet, far over the waters its friendly spark is seen by the mariner. So let your actions shine out your religion; let your conduct talk out your soul; let the main sermon of your life be illustrated by all your conduct, and it shall not fail to be illustrious. Have I not told you before that the only bit of ecclesiastical history we have in the whole New Testament is—what? The sermons of the Apostles? No, no, the "Acts of the Apostles." So let your history be written, so that it may have this title—"The acts of such-and-such a man." This will furnish the best proof that you have been with Jesus!

A Christian is distinguished by his conversation. He will often trim a sentence where others would have made it far more luxuriant by a jest which was not altogether clean. Following Herbert's advice—"He pares his apple—he would cleanly feed." If he would have a jest, he picks the mirth, but leaves the sin. His conversation is not use to levity—it is not mere froth—it ministers Divine Grace unto its hearers. He has learned where the saltbox is kept in God's great house, and so his speech is always seasoned with it, so that it may do no hurt but much good. Oh, commend me to the man who talks like Jesus, who will not for the world suffer corrupt communications to come out of his mouth! I know what people will say of you if you are like this—they will say you are straight-laced, and that you will not throw much life into company; others will call you mean-spirited. Oh, my Brothers and Sisters! Bold-hearted men are always called mean-spirited by cowards! They will admonish you not to be singular, but you can tell them that it is no folly to be singular, when to be singular is to be right. I know they will say you deny yourselves a great deal, but you will remind them that it is no denial to you. Sheep do not eat carrion, but I do not know that sheep think it a hardship to turn away from the foul feast! Eagles do not prefer to float on the sea, but I do not read that eagles think it a denial when they can soar in higher atmospheres! Do not talk of self-denial; you have other ends and other aims—you have wells of comfort that such men know not of. It would be a shame for you to be eating husks with swine, when your Father's table is loaded with dainties. I trust, my dear Brothers and Sisters, that you know the value of the gold of Heaven too well to pawn it away for the counterfeits of earth! "Come you out from among them; be you separate, and touch not the unclean thing." By a holiness which merely moral men cannot equal, stand as on a pedestal aloft above the world. Thus, men may know you to be of the seed of Jesus, even as they knew the Jew to be the seed of Israel.

How shall I urge you to give more earnest heed to this holy separation? Let me add the voice of warning to that of entreaty. If we do not see to this matter, we shall bring sorrow on our own souls, we shall lose all hope of honoring Christ, and we shall sooner, or later, bring a great disaster on the world. You know the world is always trying to nationalize the Church. What a mercy it is that there are some who will not have it! If you could once make the Church and the nation one, what would follow? It must be destroyed—it must fall! It was when the Church and the world became one in Noah's day that the Lord sent the flood to destroy all people. No, the proper position of a Christian is not with the world, even in its best state, and its most exalted condition! We are to be separate from this present evil world according to the will of God! Our position today is as much as in Christ's day—outside the camp—not in it. We are still to be protesters, still to be testifiers against the world. "You are of God, little children, and the whole world lies in the Wicked One." Scripture never supposes that the world will get better till the coming of Christ; it does not propose to lift the world up, and marry it with the Church; it always supposes the Church to be as an alien and a stranger here until Christ, her Husband, shall come! On which side will you join? Truce there cannot be! Links between the two there must not be; God and mammon cannot go together. For which will you be—for God—for Truth—for right? Or for Satan—for Hell—for the wrong? Which shall it be? May the Spirit of God whisper in your heart tonight and say, "Believe in Christ Jesus! Take up your cross and follow Him, and be enlisted on His side from now on and forever."

II. We have now a second and an important matter to bring forward. The distinction drawn between clean and unclean animals was, we think, intended by God *to keep His people always conscious that they were in the neighborhood of sin.*

Just let me picture it. I have caught the idea from Mr. Bonar, though I fear I cannot paint it in words as well as he has done. An Oriental Jew, sensible and intelligent, walks out in the fields. He walks along close by the side of the high road, and what should he see but a string of camels going along? "Ah," he says to himself, "those are unclean animals." Sin, you see, is brought at once before his mind's eye. He turns away from the road, and walks down one of his own fields, and as he goes along a hare starts across his path. "Ah," says he, "an unclean animal again. There is sin in my path." He gets into a more retired place; he walks on the mountains; surely he shall be alone there. But he sees a coney burrowing among the rocks—"Ah," he says, "unclean. There is sin there!" He lifts his eye up to Heaven—he sees the osprey, the bald eagle, flying along through the air, and he says, "Ah, there is an emblem of sin there!" A dragonfly has just flitted by him—there is sin there. There are insects among the flowers; now every creeping thing and every insect, except the locust, was unclean to the Jew. Everywhere he would come in contact with some creature that would render him ceremonially unclean, and it were impossible for him, unless he were brutish, to remain even for ten minutes abroad without being reminded that this world, however beautiful it is, still has sin in it! Even the fish, in sea, or river, or inland lake, had their divisions—those that had no scales or fins were unclean to the Jew, so the little Hebrew boys could not even fish for minnows in the brook, but they would know that the minnow was unclean, and so their young hearts were made to dread little wrongs and little sins—for there were little sins in the little pools—even as there were leviathan sins floating in the deep and nude sea! Ah, Friends, we need to have this more before our minds! Look at the fairest landscape that your eyes have ever beheld—see the towering Alps, the green valley and the silver stream—

"These are Your glorious works,
Parent of good, Almighty,"
    but the slime of the serpent is on them all—

"Keep me, O, keep me King of kings,
    Beneath the shadow of Your wings."

When I walk abroad in this temple of Nature and seek to behold Nature's God, I may not light upon a spot in the universe where the curse of sin has never inflicted a blight, or where the hope of redemption should not inspire a prayer! Sometimes, Brothers and Sisters, you get all alone and quiet, but do not imagine that you are even there free from sin! As the most beautiful landscape, so the sweetest retirement cannot shut out uncleanness. As the fly or the insect would intrude into the arbor where the Jew would worship, so sin will haunt and molest us even in the closet of devotion! Get up, Christians, and be upon your watchtowers! You may sleep, but your enemies never will; you may suppose yourselves safe, but then you are most in danger. See that you put on the whole armor of God, and are armed from head to foot, and having done all, watch and pray lest you enter into temptation. Every morning we ought to ask the Lord to keep us from unknown sins, to preserve us from temptations that we cannot foresee, to check us in every part of life if we are about to go wrong, and to hold us up every hour that we sin not. You will say it must have been an unpleasant thing for the Jew always to have sin before his eyes, nor would you wish every aspect of life to be thus fouled before your eyes. But it will not be so unpleasant for you, my Brothers and Sisters, because you know there is a Redemption, and your faith can realize the end of the curse by sin being put away. Shut not your eyes to sin, but keep Christ always before you, and you will walk aright!

I wish that some of my Hearers had sin before their eyes now. Oh, you that trifle with it, you do not know what it is! Fools make a mockery of sin. You laugh at it now—you do not understand what a fire it is that you have kindled to consume your soul! Oh, you that think it is such a little thing, but its deadly poison will soon envenom all your blood—and then you will discover that he that plays with sin, plays with damnation! May the Lord set sin straight before your eyes, and then set the Cross of Christ there, too, and so you will be saved! Two prayers I ask all my hearers to pray—they are very brief—"Lord, show me myself." If there is any man here who says he would pray, but he does not know what to pray for—pray that every night and morning—"Lord, show me myself." And if God hears you, you will soon be in such a wretched state that you will need another prayer. And then, I give you this—"Lord, show me Yourself." And then, if He shall show you Himself hanging on the Cross, the Expiation for guilt, the Great God become Man that He might put away sin—your Salvation will be accomplished! It is all the prayer that is needed—"Lord, show me myself; Lord, show me Yourself; reveal sin and reveal a Savior." Lord, do this for all of us for Your name's sake!

III. And now, I come to show you a third teaching of my Text. As this injunction was meant to separate the Jews from other nations, and to keep the pious Israelite in constant remembrance of his danger of falling into sin, so it was also intended to be *a rule of discrimination by which we may judge who are clean and who are unclean, that is, who are saints and who are not.*

There are two tests, but they must both be united. The beast that was clean was to chew the cud—here is the inner life—every true-hearted man must know how to read, mark, learn, and inwardly digest the sacred Word of God. The man who does not feed upon Gospel Truth, and so feed upon it, too, that he knows the sweetness and relish of it, and seeks out its marrow and fatness—that man is no heir of Heaven! You must know a Christian by his heart, by that which supports his life, and sustains his frame. But then, the clean creatures were also known by their walk. The Jew at once discovered the unclean animal by its having an undivided hoof. But if the hoof was thoroughly divided, then it was clean, pro- vided that it also chewed the cud. So there must be in the true Christian a peculiar walk such as God requires. You cannot tell a man by either of these tests alone—you must have them both. But while you use them upon others, apply them to yourselves! What do you feed on?

What is your habit of life? Do you chew the cud by meditation? When your soul feeds on the flesh and blood of Christ, have you learned that His flesh is meat, indeed, and that His blood is drink, indeed? If so, it is well. And what about your life? Are your conversation and your daily walk according to the description which is given in the Word of believers in Christ? If not, the first test will not stand alone! You may profess the faith within, but if you do not walk aright without, you belong to the unclean. On the other hand, you may walk aright without, but unless there is the chewing of the cud within, unless there is a real feeding upon the precious Truths of God in the heart, all the right walking in the world will not prove you to be a Christian! That holiness which is only outward in moral, and not spiritual, does not save the soul! That religion, on the other hand, which is only inward is but fancy—it cannot save the soul, either. But the two together—the inward parts made capable of knowing the lusciousness, the sweetness, the fatness of Christ's Truth, and the outward parts conformed to Christ's image and Character—these conjoined point out the true and clean Christian with whom it is blessed to associate here, and for whom a better portion is prepared hereafter!

If you read the Chapter through, you will find there were some two or three animals about which the Jew would have some little difficulty. There was the camel that did chew the cud, but did not exactly divide the hoof. Now this animal seems to me fitly to represent—though it may not have been so intended—those men who seem really to feed on the Truth of God, and yet their walk and conversation are not aright. Their feet have been formed rather for the sandy desert of sin than for the sacred soil of godliness. Oh, I know some of you! Come, let us be personal— there are some of you, if I would always preach the Doctrine of Predestination, or some other Doctrine of that kind, how sweet it would be to you! But your lives are not what they should be. Thank God there are not many of that sort who come here. They get angry with me very quickly, and go off to other places where they can get sweet and savory morsels, which exactly suit their taste. They hear no admonitions about their lives whatever! May the Lord, for my Master's sake, deliver my ministry from ever being comfortable and flattering to souls that live in sin! I hope you will sometimes have to say, "I must either give up that sin, or else give up my seat here." I know one who said, "Well! It has come to this—I cannot go there on Sunday evening, and keep my shop open in the morning. It will not do for me to go and sit there, and hear the Word and sing with those people on Sunday evening, and then hear songs, and join in revelries on weeknights."

I hope the Word of God here will be such a searching Word to some of you that you will even gnash your teeth at the preacher! He would sooner for you to do that than for you to say, "Peace, peace, where there is no peace," sucking in sweet Doctrine and yet living in sin. God deliver us from Antinomianism! We do preach against Arminianism, but that is a white devil compared with the black devil of Antinomianism! God save us from that! If there is any religion that will drug consciences, stimulate crime, crowd jails, and turn this world into an Aceldama, it is the religion of the man who preaches Divine Sovereignty, but neglects human responsibility! I believe it is a vicious, immoral and corrupt manner of setting forth Doctrine, and cannot be of God. It would undermine morality and put the very life of society in peril if it were largely believed, or if it were preached by men of any great weight who should have any great numbers to follow them. Oh, dear Friends, be not as the animal which chews the cud, but yet divides not the hoof. Seek not merely to get precious Doctrine, comforting to yourselves—but see that your walk is such as it should be.

Then, there was another animal. It did not chew the cud; still the Jews thought it did. This was the coney—the nearest approach to it is the rabbit of our land—"The coney, because he chews the cud, but divides not the hoof, he is unclean." The coney was a very timid creature, which burrowed in the rocks. "The conies are a feeble folk, but they make their dwellings in the rocks," says Solomon. Now, there are some people who seem as if they like the Gospel Truth, and they may be put down in the class in which Moses puts the coney—which appeared to chew the cud—though it did not really do so. We know there are hundreds of this sort; they like the Gospel, but it must be very cheap. They like to hear it preached, but as to doing anything to extend it, unless it were to lend their tongues an hour, they would not dream of it! The coney, you know, lived in the earth. These people are always scraping; John Bunyan's muck rake is always in their hands. Neither to dig nor to beg are they ashamed. They are as true misers, and as covetous as if they had no religion at all! And many of these people get into our churches and are received, when they ought not to be. Covetousness ought to exclude a man from church fellowship as well as fornication, for Paul says, "Covetousness, which is idolatry." He puts the brand right on its forehead, and marks what it is! We would not admit an idolater to the Lord's Table—nor ought we to admit a covetous man—only we cannot always know him! St. Francis Sales, who had a great many people come to him to confession, makes this note, that he had many men and women come to him who confessed all sorts of most outrageous crimes, but he never had one who confessed covetousness. It is a kind of sin that always comes in at the backdoor, and it is always entertained at the back part of the house. People do not suspect it as an inmate of their own hearts. Mr. Covetousness has changed his name to Mr. Prudent-Thrifty—and it is quite an insult to call him other than by his adopted name. Old vices, like streets notorious for vice, get new names given them. Avaricious grasping, they call that, "the laws of social economy." Screwing down the poor is, "the natural result of competition." Withholding corn until the people curse, oh, that is, "just the usual regulation of the market." People name the thing prettily, and then they think they have rescued it from the taint. These people, who are all for earth, are like the conies, who, though they chew the cud, burrow in the ground. They love the precious Truths of God, and yet they are all for this earth. If there are any such here, in spite of their fine experience, we pronounce them unclean—they are not heirs of Heaven!

The next creature mentioned in the chapter is the hare—"The hare, because he chews the cud, but divides not the hoof, he is unclean." See how he flies with bounding step over the ground! A clapping of the hands, and how he starts and is away! The hare is such a timid creature; she leaves her food and flees before the passerby. I would not say a harsh thing, but there are some people who appear to chew the cud; they love to hear the Gospel preached; their eyes will sparkle sometimes when we are talking of Christ, but they do not divide the hoof. Like the hare, they are too timid to be domesticated among the creatures whom the Lord has pronounced clean. They do not come out from the world, enter into the church, and manifest themselves wholly on the Lord's side.

Their conscience tells them they should be baptized as Believers— but they dare not. They know they should be united with the people of God, and confess Christ before men—but they are ashamed, ashamed, ashamed! One fears lest his wife should know it, and she might ridicule him; some start abashed lest their friends should know it, for the finger of scorn, or the breath of raillery could frighten them out of their senses; others of them are alarmed because the world might, perhaps, give them an ill name! Do you know where the fearful go? Not the fearing, not the doubting—for there are many poor, humble, doubters and fearers who are saved—but do you know where the fearful go? The fearful who are afraid of being persecuted, mocked, or even laughed at for Christ—do you know where they go? You will find it in the Book of the Revelation—"But the fearful and unbelieving shall have their part in the lake which burns with fire and brimstone, which is the second death." Have you ever read that sentence which says, "Whoever shall be ashamed of Me, and of My words, of him shall the Son of Man be ashamed when He shall come in His own Glory, and in His Father's, and of the holy angels"? There you are, young men! You are ashamed of Christ! You have just come up from the country, and you did not pray to God the other night because there was another young man in the room, and you were ashamed of Him! In the name of God I entreat you—no, I *command* you—be not ashamed of your Master, Christ, and of the religion which you learned at your father's knee!

There are others of you who work in large shops, and you do not want to be jeered at, as the other young fellow is who works with you, because he is a Christian. You keep your love as a secret, do you, and will not let it out? What? If Christ had only loved you in secret, and had never dared to come here on earth to be despised and rejected of men, where would you have been? "No man lights a candle and puts it under a bushel." Do you think that Christ has lit a candle in your hearts that you may hide it? Oh, I pray you, be not like the hare; let your hoof be so divided from the rest of mankind that they may say, "There is a man—he is not as bold as a lion, perhaps—but he is not ashamed to be a follower of Jesus Christ. He does bear the sneer and gibe for Him, and counts it his honor to be thought evil of for Jesus' sake." Oh, be not, I pray you, like the timid hare, lest you be found among the unclean!

There is one other creature mentioned—"The swine, though he divides the hoof and is cloven-footed, yet he chews not the cud, he is unclean to you." Now, the swine is the emblem of those who do act rightly. They make a profession—before men they are the most upright and the most devout; but then the inner part is not right. They do not chew the cud. The foot is right, but not the inward part. There is no chewing, no masticating, no digesting the Word of Life. "But," says one, "why pick out a swine, because that does not seem to be a fair comparison." Yes, it is, for there are no people in the world more like swine than those Pharisees who make clean the outside of the cup and the platter—whose hoof is divided enough—but whose inward part is very wickedness! I do not know an animal that might more fitly picture out those vile, unclean Pharisees. You may say you think it is too harsh a picture for you. You are put down, thus, in the catalog, and I have no other place in which to put you. You are like swine, unless the Grace of God is in you. What good does the swine do? Of what concern is life to him but to feed grossly, and slumber heavily? And so your life, since the inward part is wrong, brings no Glory to God—you bring no good to your fellow men. Oh, that the Lord would show you that dead morality, unattended by the Love of God in the soul, will most certainly be of no avail! "You must be born again." "Except you are converted and become as little children, you shall in no wise enter into the Kingdom of Heaven."

My Text seems to be a dividing one—it divides the house in two. Remember, dear Friends, the day is coming when a greater division than any which can be described will occur to all of us! But the same rule will be enforced. We shall be assembled in one crowd, a mightier crowd than language can picture, or imagination grasp. The books shall be opened—books more terrible than this Book of Mercy. The Book of Life shall be unfolded and read, in which those washed in Jesus' blood, and so made clean, shall find their names recorded. They will be borne to Heaven! Listen to the music of the angels as they bear them up to God's right hand! Where will you be? Will you be with those who mount to Heaven, or with yonder trembling, shrieking, screaming souls, who, as Hell opens her mouth, descend alive into the pit of Hell? God help you if you are not on the right-hand side! It is not too late; Jesus Christ is still preached to you! The way of Salvation is very plain. It is this—believe in the Lord Jesus Christ, and you shall be saved. Believe in Jesus. Then make a profession of your faith in God's own ordained way, and method, and you have His Promise for it that you will be saved! God help you to believe, and you shall be saved through Jesus—and unto Him shall be the Glory forever and ever. Amen.

11

The Cleansing of the Leper

"And if a leprosy break out abroad in the skin and the leprosy cover all the skin of him that has the plague from his head even to his foot, wherever the priest looks; then the priest shall consider: and, behold, if the leprosy has covered all his flesh, he shall pronounce him clean that has the plague: it is all turned white: he is clean." (Leviticus 13:12-13)

THIS IS AN AMAZING PARADOX, but not a paradox to him who understands the Gospel. We have great reason to thank God that the terrible disease, leprosy, which was one of the demons of the East, is so little known in our own land; and even in the few cases where leprosy has broken out in our climate, it has always assumed a far more mild and mitigated shape than it did with the Jews in the land of Canaan. Yet, since they had so frightful a disease, God, in His infinite mercy, made use of it as a sort of sermon to the people. Leprosy is to be considered by us as being the type of sin; and as we read the Chapters in Leviticus, which concern the shutting up or putting apart, and the purification of a cleansed leper, we are to understand every sentence as having in it a Gospel sermon to us, teaching us what is the condition of a sinner in the sight of God, how that sinner is to be cured, and how he can be restored to the privileges from which the leprosy of sin had utterly shut him out.

I shall need no preface, for the subject is deeply interesting, and will be found especially so by many of us who can use the language of David in the Psalm which we have just read. If we have come up here conscious of guilt, and laden with iniquity, I am quite certain, and I speak positively and confidently, there will be something in the discourse of this morning to cheer our hearts, and to send us home rejoicing in the Lord our God. Carry in your thoughts the one key to our Text, namely, that leprosy is the great type of sin; and I shall want you, first of all, to see the leper, and to see in the leper the sinner. After we have well looked to him, we shall bring him before the priest and stand still while the priest examines him. This done and the sentence being pronounced, we shall listen attentively to the announcement of the rites and ceremonies which were necessary in order to cleanse this leper, which were but representations of the way whereby we, too, must be cleansed. And then, we shall have a little time to notice certain rites which follow after cleansing, which were not the cause of the cleansing, itself, but necessary before the man could actually enjoy the privileges which the cleansing gained for him.

I. First, then, let me ask you to turn your eyes *to the loathsome and ghastly spectacle of a leper.*

A leper was extremely loathsome in his person. The leprosy broke out at first almost imperceptibly in certain red spots which appeared in the skin. They were painless, but they gradually increased. Perhaps the man who was the subject of the complaint scarcely knew that he had it at all, but it increased, and further and further, and further it spread. The perspiration was unable to find a vent, and the skin became dry and pealed off in scales. The withering of the skin was too true an index of what was going on within, for in the very marrow of the bones there was a most frightful rottenness, which in due time would utterly consume the victim. The man would eat and drink; he would perform what is called by the physician, the naturalia—all the functions would be discharged as if in health. All things would go on as before, and he would be subject to very little pain; but by degrees the bones would rot, in many cases the fingers would drop off, and yet without any surgical operation, the rest of the body was healthy, so that there was no bleeding. When it came to its very worst phase, the body itself would drop altogether—all the strings being loosened, the whole house of manhood would become a horrible mass of animated rubbish, rather than the stately Temple which God originally made it. I could not in your presence this morning describe all the loathsomeness and ghastliness of the aggravated cases of Jewish leprosy; it would be too sickening, if not disgusting. But let me remind you that this, fearful as it seems to be, is a very poor portrait of the loathsomeness of sin.

If God could tell or, rather, if we could bear to hear what God could tell us of the exceeding wickedness and uncleanness of sin, I am sure we should die! God hides from all eyes but His own, the blackness of sin. There is no creature, not even an angel before the Throne of God that ever knew the intolerable wickedness of rebellion against God. Yet, that little of it which God the Holy Spirit taught you and me when we were under conviction of sin was enough to make us feel that we wished we had never been born. Ah, well must I confess, though my life was kept and preserved as a child from outward immorality, when I first saw myself as I was by nature, and in the thoughts and intents and imaginations of my heart, I thought that even devils in Hell could not be baser than myself! Certain I am that, whenever the Spirit of God comes into the soul, our good opinion of ourselves soon vanishes. We thought we were all that heart could wish—but when once taught of God the Holy Spirit—we think that we are vile and full of sin, that there is no good thing whatever in us. Loathsome, I say, as was the leper; it is not more so in the type than is sin in the estimation of every enlightened mind.

Think again. The leper was not only loathsome in his person, but was defiled in all his acts. If he drank out of a vessel, the vessel was defiled. If he lay upon a bed, the bed became unclean, and whoever sat upon the bed afterwards became unclean, too; if he touched but the wall of a house, the wall became unclean and must be purged. Wherever he went, he tainted the atmosphere; his breath was as dangerous as the pestilence. He shot baneful glances from his eyes. All that he did was full of the same loathsomeness as was himself. Now, this may seem to be a very humiliating truth, but faithfulness requires us to say it—all the actions of the natural man are tainted with sin! Whether he eats, or drinks, or whatever he does, he continues to sin against his God! No, if he should come up to God's House and sing and pray, there is sin in his songs for they are but hypocrisy—there is guilt in his prayers, for the prayers of the wicked are abominations unto the Lord. Let him attempt to perform holy actions, he is like Uzziah, who laid hold upon the censer of the priest while the leprosy was on his brow till he was glad enough to retire from the sacred place, lest he should be struck dead! Oh, when we saw or thought we saw the sinfulness of sin, this was one of the darkest parts of it that we discovered—all our actions were stained and tainted with evil! I know not whether I have any in this congregation who are prepared to deny what I assert. If there are, it is my duty to solemnly assure them that they are unclean and covered with an incurable leprosy; they are hopeless lepers who cannot be cleansed, for no man can be cleansed of sin till he is ready to confess that he is all unholy and unclean! Submission to this truth is absolutely necessary to Salvation! I am not to condemn any man, but still I must speak God's Word, and speak it in loving faithfulness—if you do not confess that all your actions before you were regenerate, were full of sin and abominable in the sight of God—

you have not yet learned what you are, and it is not likely that you will wish to know what a Savior is.

Think of the leper yet again. Being thus the medium of contagion and defilement wherever he went, the Lord demanded that he should be shut out from the society of Israel. There was a spot outside the camp, barren, solitary, where lepers were confined. They were commanded to wear a covering over the mouth, and upon the upper lip, and if any passed by, they were compelled to cry, "Unclean! Unclean! Unclean!" A sound which being muffled by reason of the covering which they wore, must have sounded more ghastly and deathlike than any other human cry. Some of the Rabbi translate the cry, "Avoid! Avoid! Avoid!" One of the American poets has put it, "Room for the leper! Room!" But certainly, the sense of it is generally understood to be, "Unclean! Unclean! Unclean!" Living apart from their dearest friends, shut out from all the pleasures of society, they were required never to drink from a running stream of water of which others might drink. Nor might they sit down on any stone by the roadside upon which it was probable any other person might rest. They were to all intents and purposes, dead to all the enjoyments of life—dead to all the endearments and society of their friends. Yes, and such is the case with the sinner with regard to the people of God. Do you not feel, poor convicted Sinner, that you are unfit to join Christ's Church? You can go and find such mirth as the company of your fellow lepers can afford. But where God's people are, you are out of place. You feel in yourself that you are shut out from the communion of saints. You cannot pray their prayer nor sing their hymns. You know not their joys. You have never tasted of their perfect peace. You have never entered into the rest which remains for them, but which remains not for you while you are such a one as you are now!

This, however, is the fearful part of the leprosy of sin—that many, who are shut out from goodness, become contented with the exclusion.

There are even some who pretend to despise the privileges which they cannot enjoy. Since they cannot be holy, they make holiness the theme of ridicule. Since they must not envy the delights of piety, they turn their heel upon them and say, "There is no joy in religion; nor bliss in love to Christ." This is perhaps one of the most fearful parts of this leprosy of sin—that it deceives the man, himself—makes him think himself to be healthy while he is full of disease, makes him imagine the healthy ones to be diseased, while he who is the true leper thinks himself to be the only sane person in the camp!

Once more, the leper was wholly unable to come up to the House of God. Other men might offer sacrifices, but not the leper; others had a share in the great High Priest's sacrifice, and when he went within the veil, he appeared for all others; but the leper had neither part nor lot in this matter. He was shut out from God, as well as shut out from man; he was no partaker of the sacred things of Israel, and all the ordinances of the Tabernacle were as nothing to him. Think of that, Sinner! As a sinner full of guilt, you are shut out from all communion with God! True, He gives you the mercies of this life as the leper had his bread and water, but you have none of the spiritual joys which God affords to His people. You can- not stand in His Presence, for He is a devouring fire and would consume you. Your prayers are shut out from Him, your words are unheard. You are a prodigal son, and your father is far from you! You have spent your substance in riotous living, and no man will give to you; you have become the companion of the swine, and you would gladly fill your belly with the husks which the swine eat. No father's eyes greets you; at no father's table do you sit; your father's hired servants have bread enough to spare, but you perish with hunger. Oh, Sinner! If you who do not feel yourself to be as I describe you now, you will one day find it to be a very awful thing to be denied all fellowship with God, for at last you may seek in vain to cross your father's threshold. After death you will long to enter within the pearly gates, and you shall be thrust back, for lepers and defiling ones can never stand in the sanctified Presence of the holy God! Where angels veil their faces, lepers shall not exhale their putrid breath! God drove Satan out of Paradise because he sinned, and will He always sin a second time to intrude into His Presence? No, you shall find that as long as you and your sins are one, God will always be at war with you; as long as you are at peace with your guilt, the Eternal God draws His sword and vows eternal warfare with you! Now, I wish I could more forcibly put the position of a sinner in God's sight this morning. Let me just recapitulate for a moment. Every man by nature is like a leper; loathsome in his person, infected in all his actions, and in all that he does; he is incapable of fellowship with God's people, and he is shut out utterly and entirely by his sin from the Presence and acceptance of God.

II. Having thus described the leper and the sinner, I shall now bring *the leper up to the high priest.*

There he stands; the priest has come out to meet him. Mark, whenever a leper was cleansed under the Jewish law—the leper did nothing—the priest did all. I invite you to read over this Chapter when you are at home, and you will see that, previous to his being pronounced clean, the leper was passive—the priest did everything! Well, the priest comes out from the sanctuary, comes to the place of the lepers, where no other man might go—but he in his priestly office. He calls up one leper before him; he looks at him, and there is a spot on that leper which is not leprous—quick, raw, healthy flesh; the priest puts him aside, he is an unclean leper. Here is another, and he has but one or two red spots appearing beneath the skin; all the rest of his body is perfectly sound, the priest puts him aside, he is an unclean leper. Here is another, he is from head to foot covered with a scaly whiteness of the filthy disease; the hair is all turned white, owing to the decay of the powers of Nature which are now unable to nourish the roots of the hair. There is not a single speck of health in him from the crown of his head to the sole of his foot—all is pollution and filth.

But listen! The high priest says to him, "You are clean." And after certain necessary ceremonies, he is admitted into the camp, and afterwards into the very sanctuary of God! My Text asserts that if there was found any sound place on him, he was unclean. But when the leprosy had covered him, wherever the priest looked, the man became by sacrificial rights a clean leper! who, as they come up here, are ready to confess that they have done many things which are wrong, but they say, "Though we have done much which we cannot justify, yet there have been many good actions which might almost counterbalance the sin. Have we not been charitable to the poor; have we not sought to instruct the ignorant; to help those who are out of the way? We have some sins, we do confess, but there is much at the bottom which is still right and good, and we therefore hope that we shall be delivered." I put you aside in God's name, this morning, as unclean lepers. For you, there is no hope and no promise of Salvation whatever! Here comes a second. He admits with candor that he has a very great measure of guilt—perhaps not open immorality—but he confesses that his thoughts, and the imaginations of his heart have been evil and evil frequently. "But, still," he says, "though I have neither one good work of which to boast, nor any righteousness in which to glory, yet I do hope that by repentance I may amend. I trust that by a resolute persistence in good works, I may yet blot out my past life, and so may enter into Heaven." I set him aside as being an unclean leper, for whom cleansing rites are not provided. He is one who must still be kept outside the camp; he has not arrived at that stage in which it is possible for him to be made clean.

But here comes another. Probably he is really a better man than either of the other two; but not in his own opinion. He stands before us and, with many a sigh and tears, confesses that he is utterly ruined and undone. "Sir, a month or two ago I would have claimed a righteousness with the very best of them. I, too, could have boasted of what I have done; but now, I see my righteousness to be as filthy rags, and all my goodness is as an unclean thing; I count all these things but dross and dung! I tread upon them and despise them; I have done no good thing; I have sinned and come short of the glory of God. If ever there was a sinner who deserved to be damned, Sir, I am that soul! If ever there was one who had not any excuse to make, but who must plead guilty, without any extenuating circumstances, I am that man! As for the future, I can make no promise! I have often promised and so often lied; I have so often trusted in myself to reform; often have I hoped the energy of my nature might yet heal my disease that I renounce, because I cannot help renouncing all such desires. Lord, if ever I am made whole, Your Grace must make me so. I do desire to be rid of sin, but I can no more rid myself of sin than I can pluck the sun from the firmament, or scoop the waters from the depth of the sea! I would be perfect, even as You are perfect, but I cannot change my heart. As well might the viper lose his will to poison, the Ethiopian change his skin, or the leopard his spots, as I cease to do evil! Lord, at Your feet I fall, full of leprosy from head to foot. Nothing have I to boast of, nothing to trust to except Your mercy."

My Brother, you are a clean leper! Your sins are forgiven you; your iniquities are put away. Through the blood of Jesus Christ, who died upon the Cross, you are saved. As soon as ever the leprosy had come right out, the man was clean, and as soon as ever your sin is fully manifest so that in your conscience you feel yourself to be really a sinner, there is a way of Salvation for you! Then, by the sprinkling of blood, and the washing of water, you may be made clean! As long as a man has anything to boast of, there is no Christ for him; but the moment he has nothing of his own, Christ is his! While you are anything, Christ is nothing to you—but when you are nothing, Christ is everything! All the warrant that a sinner needs in coming to Christ is to know that he is a sinner, for "Christ Jesus came into the world to save sinners." Do I know myself to be a sinner?

Then He came to save me, and there I rest, and there I trust. If I have any good feelings or good works which take away from me the power to call myself a sinner; or if they diminish the force and emphasis which I put upon the word when I use it, then may I fear that I have no right to come to Christ! Christ died, "The Just for the unjust, to bring us to God." Am I unjust? Do I honestly declare I am? "Christ died for the ungodly." Am I ungodly; is this my grief and sorrow that I am ungodly? Then, Christ died for me. "I do not know," said Martin Luther, "when men will ever believe that Text in which it is written, Christ died for our sins. They will think that Christ died for our righteousness, whereas He died for our sins! Christ had no eye to our goodness when He came to save us, but to our badness." A physician, when he comes to my house, has not an eye to my present health; he does not come there because I am healthy, but because I am sick; and the more sick I am, the more call for the physician's skill and the more argument does my sickness yield why he should exercise all his craft, and use his best medicines on my behalf. Your only plea with Christ is your guilt. Use it, Sinner, use it as David did when he said, "Lord have mercy upon my iniquity, for it is great!" If he had said "Have mercy upon my iniquity, for it is little," he would have been a legalist, and would have missed his mark. But when he said, "Have mercy, for it is great!" he understood the Gospel riddle—that strange paradox at which Pharisees always kick, and which worldlings always hate—the glorious fact that Jesus Christ came into the world, "not to call the righteous, but sinners, to repentance."

III. Having thus brought the man before the priest, we shall now briefly turn our attention to *the ceremonies which the priest used in the cleansing of the leper.* I will read the verses quickly, and expound them briefly. "And the priest shall go forth out of the camp, and the priest shall look and, behold, if the plague of leprosy is healed in the leper, then shall the priest command to take for him that is to be cleansed, two birds alive and clean, and cedar wood, and scarlet and hyssop: and the priest shall command that one of the birds be killed in an earthen vessel over running water: as for the living bird, he shall take it and the cedar wood, and the scarlet and the hyssop and shall dip them and the living bird in the blood of the bird that was killed over the running water: and he shall sprinkle upon him that is to be cleansed from the leprosy, seven times and shall pronounce him clean and shall let the dying bird loose into the open field." You will perceive, first, that the priest went to the leper, not the leper to the priest. We go not up to Heaven, first, till Christ comes down from His Father's Glory to the place where we, as lepers, are shut out from God. Oh, glorious High Priest, I thinks I see You this morning coming out from the Tabernacle of the Most High where You have offered Your complete Sacrifice and You come down to us loathsome and abhorred sinners! You take upon Yourself the form of Man; You do not disdain the Virgin's womb; You come to sinners; You eat and drink with them! But the coming of the priest was not enough, there must be a sacrifice, and on this occasion, in order to set out the two ways by which a sinner is saved, there was sacrifice mingled with resurrection.

First, there was sacrifice. One of the birds was taken, and his blood was shed in a vessel which was full, as the Hebrew has it, of "living water"—of water which had not been stagnant, but which was clean. Just as when Jesus Christ was put to death, blood and water flowed from His side to be "of sin, a double cure," so in the earthen vessel there was received, first, the "living water," and then the blood of the bird which had just been slain. If sin is put away, it must be by blood.

There is no way of putting sin from before the Presence of God except by the streams which flow from the open veins of Christ! It was nothing that the leper did. You notice he does nothing whatever in the whole affair, but stand still and humbly partake of the benefits which are given to him through the mission of the priest, and through the slaughter of the bird. And then, the second bird was dipped into the blood until all its feathers were red and dropping with gore. It was doubtless tied round the cedar stick at the end of which was the hyssop to make a kind of brush. The bird's wings were tied along the stick, and the whole was dipped in the blood of the bird that was slain. And when this had been done seven times, the strings were cut and the living bird allowed to fly away. This is a lively picture of Christ! As a living bird, He ascends on high after being slain for us—scattering the red drops of Atonement, He rises above the clouds which receive Him out of our sight, and there before His Father's Throne, He pleads the full merit of the Sacrifice which He offered for us once and for all!

The leper was made clean by sacrifice and by resurrection, but he was not clean till the blood was sprinkled on him. Christians, the Cross does not save us till Christ's blood is sprinkled on our conscience! Yet, the virtual Salvation was accomplished for all the Elect when Christ died for them upon the Cross. It is the joy of every Christian to stand here saved by Another! He knows that he is full of leprosy; that in himself there is no reason whatever why he should be cleansed. In fact, the reasons are all the other way—for there is every reason why he should continue to be shut out forever from the Presence of God. But there stands the High Priest, the great Melchizedek, the Son of the Virgin, and the Son of God. He has offered His own blood for us. He who offered it, applies it to the conscience and with this application—

"The Christian walks at large,
His Savior's blood, his full discharge!
At His dear feet his soul he'll lay,
A sinner saved and homage pay."

But the saving of your soul rests not with yourself, but with Christ Jesus, just as the cleansing of the leper was not with the leper, but with the priest. How many there are among God's people, who say, "I know that Christ died for sinners, but I don't get any comfort from it because I do not feel as if I were saved." That is self-righteousness in a very deceitful shape! You will not be saved by feeling that Christ died for you, but by His dying for you. If He died for you, you were saved when He died; if He took your sins, He took them in very deed, and they are not yours; if Christ was your Substitute at all, then God can never punish two for one offense—first, the Substitute and then, the sinner himself. If Christ really died for you, then your sins are pardoned, whether you feel that they are pardoned or not. "Yes," says one, "but I need to realize that." It is a very blessed thing to realize it, but it is not the realizing that saves—it is the death of Christ that saves—not your realizing the death! If there is a lifeboat and some poor man is ready to drown, and some strong hand rescues him—when he comes to himself, he realizes that he is in the boat, but it is not the realizing that he is in the boat that saves him—it is the lifeboat. So it is Christ who saves the sinner, not the sinner's feelings, or willings, or doings; and in Heaven the whole Glory of Salvation will be to the wounds of Jesus and nothing else.

"But," says one, "how am I to know Christ died for me?" You will never know it until you are willing to stand in the leper's place full of leprosy! If you know this day that you are full of sin; if you are conscious that in you, that is, in your flesh, there dwells no good thing, then it is written that Christ died for our sins, according to the Scriptures—not according to our feelings, but according to the Scriptures! How do I know that I am full of sin? Because I believe I am; because God tells me so—not merely because I feel it, but because God tells me so! How do I know that Christ died for me? Not because I feel it, but because God tells me so! He says Christ came into the world to save sinners. I am a sinner; I feel it; I know it; God forbid that I should be such a liar to myself as to deny it. Then He came to save me. "Come now, let us reason together; though your sins are as scarlet"—that is my case—"they shall be as wool; though they are red like crimson"—that is my case—"they shall be as snow." It is just this—if you are willing to stand today, condemned as a sinner, and nothing more than a sinner, then Christ died for you. Your business is to trust your soul on the fact that Christ did hang on the Cross for sinners; for mark—faith is trusting Christ and having done with self! Put your finger on any sound place in your flesh—you are a lost man! Point to any good thing that you can trust to, and there is no Heaven for you. Rely on anything that you have felt, or thought, or said, or done, and you rely on a broken reed! But trust in Christ, and Christ alone; cast your arms around His Cross, and cling to that—you are saved—yet it will not be the clinging, it will be the Cross that will save you! Do not trust your clinging! Trust the Cross! Still to the Cross flee away, you poor, lost, ruined ones, for under its shadow there is safety for the defenseless; there is hope even for the despairing!

IV. But pardon me while I keep you a minute or two longer to observe that *after the leper was cleansed, there were certain things which he had to do.* Until he is cleansed, he is to do nothing.

The sinner can do nothing towards his own Salvation; his place is the place of death. Christ must be his life. The sinner is so lost that Christ must begin, and carry on and finish all—but when the sinner is saved—then he begins to work in right good earnest! When once he is no more a leper, but a leper cleansed—then for the love he bears his Master's name, there is no trial too arduous, no service too hard—he spends his whole strength in magnifying and glorifying his Lord! I want to call your attention to the further cleansing of the leper. Mark, he was wholly cleansed by the priest, and what was done afterwards was done by a cleansed man. "He that is to be cleansed shall wash his clothes, and shave off all his hair, and wash himself in water." Blood first; water afterwards. No cleansing from evil habits until there has been cleansing from sin! There is no making the nature clean till the guilt is put away. "He shall wash his clothes, and shave off his hair, and wash himself in water that he may be clean; and after that he shall come into the camp, and shall tarry abroad out of his tent seven days." He did not tell him to wash, first; it would have been of no use to him whatever. He did not tell him to wash his clothes, and shave his hair first—

> "No outward forms could make him clean,
> The leprosy lay deep within."

No, the Priest must do all the work first. After that, the leper must be washed. So Sinner, if you are to be saved, Christ must do it all! But when once you have faith in Christ, you must be washed; then must you cease from sin and then, by the Holy Spirit's power, you shall be enabled to do so. What was ineffective before shall become mighty enough now through the life which God has put into you! The washing with water by the Word, and the cleansing of yourself from dead works shall become an effectual and mighty duty.

You shall be made holy and walk in white in the purity wherewith Christ has endowed you. The shaving off of his hair was fitly to represent how all the old things were to pass away, and everything was to become new. All the white hair was to be cut off, as you read in the 9th verse— "He shall shave all the hair off his head, and his beard and his eyebrows."

There was not a remnant or relic left of the old state in which the hair was white—all was to be given up. So it is with the sinner. When he is once pardoned, once cleansed—then, he begins to cut off the old habits, his old prides, his old joys. The beard on which the hoary Jew prided himself was to come off, and the eyebrows which seem to be necessary to make the countenance look decent, were all to be taken away!

So it is with the pardoned man. He did nothing before; he does everything now. He knew that good works were of no benefit to him in his carnal state, but now he becomes so strict that he will shave off every hair of his old state! Not one darling lust shall be left; not one iniquity shall be spared; all must be cut away. "He shall wash his clothes also; he shall wash his flesh in water, and he shall be clean." There is one thing I want you to notice in the 8th verse, namely, that he was not allowed to go into his own tent. He might go in with the people, but he might not go into his "tent." Now, though the sinner has to trust in Christ just as he is, yet that sinner will not at once be able to go into his own tent, that is, he will never be able to realize that Christ is personally his own until there has been something more than faith, namely, the cleansing purification of the Spirit's power.

As to full assurance, I do not think that is to be attained by immediate faith in Christ—full assurance is an after-result. Faith grows by the influence of the Spirit till it comes to assurance; yet mark that for seven days the man might not go into his own house! He was clean and so if you, as a sinner full of sin, trust Christ to be your All, though no joy may follow for seven days, yet you are a pardoned man! Though you may not be able to go into your house and say, "I know I am forgiven," yet you are forgiven! The very hour when sin abounds is the hour when Grace abounds. When sin has cut the throat of all your hopes, then Jesus Christ, the great Hope and Solace of His people, comes into your heart, and though you may scarcely be able to see Him, yet He is there, and you are a saved man! What a glorious Salvation is this, and its after-results, how pure and how heavenly!

I will not detain you further than to notice that this man, before he might further enjoy the privileges of his healed estate, was to bring an offering, and the priest was to take him to the very door of the Tabernacle. He never dare go there before, but he may come now. So the pardoned man may go right up to God's Mercy Seat, and may bring the offering of holiness and good works! He is a pardoned man now. You ask me how? Not by anything he did—but by what the priest did and that, alone. Read the 14th verse, "The priest shall take some of the blood of the trespass offering, and the priest shall put it upon the tip of the right ear of him who is to be cleansed." Here the Lord puts away the sins of the ear, which are very many; the sins of the ear—when you used to hear lascivious songs, malignant words and idle talk. "He shall put it upon the tip of the right ear of him who is to be cleansed, and upon the thumb of his right hand." Have you read that? How many times has the right hand sinned against God? How have your actions defiled you? "He shall put it upon the tip of the right ear of him who is to be cleansed, and upon the thumb of his right hand and upon the great toe of his right foot." How have your feet run after wickedness? How greatly you need to be cleansed! But mark—when this blood had been put on, the priest did more—for he anointed him. Read the 17th verse—"and of the rest of the oil that is in his hand, shall the priest put upon the tip of the right ear of him who is to be cleansed, and upon the thumb of his right hand, and upon the great toe of his right foot, upon the blood of the trespass offering." This was telling him again very plainly that which he might have seen already in the type of the two birds.

As soon as ever a man is pardoned, there elapses a time before he completely understands the plan of Salvation; when he does, he perceives that he is first cleansed with blood—all his sins, of ear, of hand, of foot, or whatever they may be—are all put away by blood! But next, that he may become God's servant, he is anointed by the influence of the Holy Spirit with the sanctifying oil; that oil is put on his ear, so that his ear hears his Master's voice, and listens to the Word of God. That oil is put upon his hand that he may be a consecrated man to serve his God. That oil is put upon his foot that his feet may run in the way of God's commands, even to the end. But, do mark, for I fear lest I should spoil that which I want to convey—all this was an after-piece, after the leper was cleansed! He could not have done any of this him- self until the first part had been done for him!

To sum up the whole sermon in one or two short sentences: Sinner, if you are this day unrenewed and unregenerate, you are loathsome to yourself; you are incapable of fellowship with God; you are preparing yourself for the pit of Hell. But the way of Salvation is simply this—if you are today full of sin, laden with iniquity; if you are ready to confess there is no good thing in you; if you are willing to take the place of a prisoner who has been tried, condemned, and cast, then, Christ has died for you! Christ has shed His blood; Christ has risen up on high, and your Salvation is finished. Say not in your heart, "I do not feel this; I do not feel that." It is not your feeling or doing; it is what Christ has done. He must do all for you, and all He asks of you is simply to stand in the place of the unjust, that He may come to you in the place of the Just, while He stands in your place. Is this too easy for you? Are you too proud to be saved by such a system as this?

Then, what can I say to you, but that you deserve to die if you neglect a plan of Salvation so simple and so admirably adapted to your case? But instead thereof, if you say, "That suits me, for I have nothing to trust to, I am lost." Why, Man, do you not see that inasmuch as it suits you, it is yours? For whom was the wedding garment made—for those who had fine robes of their own? No—for the naked! For whom was the bath open? For the clean? No—for the filthy! Step in filthy Man, your filth is your warrant! For whom is medicine provided? For the healthy? No, it were an insult. For the sick! Your sickness is your warrant—come to Mercy's hospital and be healed!

Whom do you think Christ came to carry on His shoulders to Heaven? Those who can walk there themselves? No, let them trudge their weary way; if they think they can go to Heaven with their good works, let them do so. One of two things—either you must be saved without deserving to be saved—saved by the works of Another—or else you must keep the whole Law, and so inherit Heaven of your own right and patent! If, then, you are willing to come to Christ—just as you are without any preparation, simply as a sinner—then Christ has made Atonement for you. Your guilt is put away—God accepts you—you are a pardoned man! You may go out at yonder door and say in your heart, "Therefore being justified by faith, we have peace with God through our Lord Jesus Christ. And not only so, but we also joy in God through our Lord Jesus Christ, by whom we now have received the Atonement." As for holiness and good works, these shall come afterwards! Having believed in Christ, His Spirit shall be given, and you shall be zealous for good works. While the legalist is talking about them, you shall do them! What you could not do before, you shall do now! When you have given up all trust in yourself, you shall become holy and pure, and the Spirit of God shall enter into you and shall renew you. You shall be kept by the power of God till, without spot, or wrinkle, or any such thing you shall be presented before your Father's face saved—eternally saved!

God add His blessing! I have sought to preach to you the Gospel as plainly as possible. I may still have been misunderstood. If so, I trust that it is not my fault. I have repeated myself over and over again that the sinner, near despairing, may now come and put his trust in Christ, and find life in Jesus' death, and healing in His wounds!

12

The Annual Atonement

"For on that day shall the priest make an atonement for you, to cleanse you, that you may be clean from all your sins before the Lord." (Leviticus 16:30)

B EFORE ADAM TRANSGRESSED, he lived in communion with God, but after he had broken the Covenant and grieved God's Spirit, he could have no more familiar fellowship with God. Under the Mosaic dispensation, in which God was pleased, in His Grace, to dwell among His people and walk with them in the wilderness, it was still under a reserve—there was a Holy Place wherein the symbol of God's Presence was hidden away from mortal gaze. No man might come near to it except in one way, only, and then only once in the year, "The Holy Spirit this signifying, that the way into the Holiest of All was not yet made manifest, while as the first Tabernacle was yet standing." Our subject today illustrates the appointed way of access to God. This chapter shows that the way of access to God is by Atonement and by no other method. We cannot draw near unto the Most High except along the blood-besprinkled way of sacrifice. Our Lord Jesus said, "No man comes unto the Father, but by Me." And this is true in many senses and in this, among them, that our way to God lies only through the Sacrifice of His Son.

The reason for this is that sin lies at the door. Brothers and Sisters, a pure and holy God cannot endure sin. He can- not have fellowship with it, or with those who are rendered unclean by it, for it would be inconsistent with His Nature to do so. On the other hand, sinful men cannot have fellowship with God—their evil nature could not endure the fire of His holiness! Who among us shall dwell with the devouring fire? Who among us shall dwell with everlasting burnings? What is that devouring fire and what are those everlasting burnings, but the Justice and Holiness of God? The Apostle says, "Even our God is a consuming fire." A guilty soul would perish if it were possible for it to draw near to God apart from the Mediator and His Atonement. The fire of God's Nature must consume the stubble of our nature so long as there is sin in us or about us. Hence the difficulty of access, a difficulty which only a Divine method can remove. God cannot commune with sinful men, for He is holy. Sinful men cannot commune with a holy God, because He must destroy them, even as He destroyed Nadab and Abihu when they intruded into His Holy Place. That terrible judgment is mentioned in the opening verses of the chapter before us as the reason why the ordinances herein contained were first of all made.

How, then, shall men come to God? Only in God's own way! He, Himself, devised the way and He has taught it to us by a parable in this chapter. It would be very wrong to prefer any one passage of Scripture beyond another, for all Scripture is given by Inspiration. But if we might do so, we should set this chapter in a very eminent and prominent place for its fullness of instruction—and its clear, yet deep doctrinal teaching. It treats upon a matter which is of the very highest importance to all of us. We are here taught the way by which the sin that blocks the door may be taken away, so that a seeking soul may be introduced into the Presence of

God—and stand in His Holy Place—and yet live. Here we learn how we may say, with the astonished Prophet, "I have seen God and my life is preserved!" Oh that we might, today, so learn the lesson that we may enter into the fullest fellowship with the Father and with His Son, Jesus Christ, in that safe way, that only way, which God has appointed for us! Oh for the power and guidance of the Holy Spirit, that we may know and use "the new and living way!"

Before I proceed to enlarge upon this chapter, I want to notice that, of course, this was only a type. This great Day of Atonement did not see an actual atonement made, nor sin really put away, but it was the figure of heavenly things—the shadow of good things to come. The substance is of Christ. If this Day of Atonement had been real and satisfactory, as touching God and the conscience of men, there would never have been another—for the worshippers once purged would have had no more conscience of sin! If they had lived 50 or a hundred years, they would never have needed another Day of Atonement—but because this was, in its nature, imperfect and shadowy, being only typical—therefore, every year, in the seventh month, on the 10th day of the month, a fast was proclaimed, sin was confessed, victims were slain and atonement was again presented.

In the Jewish year, so often as it came round, on one special day they were commanded to afflict their souls, even though it was a Sabbath of rest. In very deed a remembrance of sin was made every year, a painful remembrance for them, although sweetened by a new exhibition of the plan by which sin is cleansed. The Lord said, "This shall be an everlasting statute unto you." It lasted as long as the Mosaic economy in the letter, but its spirit and substance last on forever. They had that day to remember that their sin was not put away once and for all and forever by all their types and ceremonies and, therefore, they had again to humble themselves and come before God with sacrifices which could never truly put away sin! Israel had to do this constantly until Jesus, the true High Priest appeared—and now they have no sacrificing priest, nor altar, nor Holy of Holies. By Jesus Christ's one offering of Himself, sin was put away, once and for all, effectually and finally, so that Believers are really clean before God.

Now, if I should seem to run the type into the substance, you will just separate them in your own minds. It is not easy to speak as to keep shadow and substance quite clear of each other. We are apt to say, "This is so-and-so," when we mean, "this represents so-and-so," and we have our Lord's example for so doing, for He said, "this is My body and My blood," when He meant that the bread and wine represented His body and blood. We are not speaking to fools, nor to those who will wrench the letter from its obvious spiritual sense! I shall trust to your intelligence and the guidance of the Holy Spirit that you will, in this discourse, discern between the symbol and the substance! May the Divine Spirit help me and help you to a right understanding of this sacred type!

I. Now, then, let us come to the text and note, first, *what was done* on that particular day. The text tells us what was done symbolically—"On that day shall the priest make an atonement for you, to cleanse you, that you may be clean from all your sins before the Lord."

The persons, themselves, were cleansed. If any of them had become unclean so as to be denied communion with God and His people, they were made clean, so that they might go up to the Tabernacle and mingle with the congregation. All the host were, that morning, regarded as unclean—and all had to bow their heads in penitent sorrow because of their uncleanness. After the sacrifice and the sending away of the scapegoat, the whole congregation was clean and in a condition to rejoice. If it happened to be the Year of Jubilee, the joyful trumpets rang out as soon as the atonement was complete. Every year, within four days after the Day of Atonement, the people were so clean that they kept the joyful Feast of Tabernacles. Jewish Rabbis were known to say that no man had ever seen sorrow who had not seen the Day of Atonement and that no man had ever seen gladness who had not witnessed the hilarity and delight of the people during the Feast of Tabernacles!

The people, themselves, were made to be a clean people and I lay great stress on this, because unless you, yourself, are purged, everything that you do is defiled in the sight of God. When a man was unclean, if he went into a tent and sat upon anything, it was unclean. If a friend touched his garments, he was rendered unclean. The man, himself, needed, first, to be delivered from impurity and it is precisely the same in your case and mine! I have need to cry, "Purge me with hyssop, and I shall be clean! Wash me and I shall be whiter than snow." Your very person, by nature, is defiled and obnoxious to the justice of God. In body, soul and spirit you are, by nature, altogether as an unclean thing and all your righteousnesses are as filthy rags—you, yourself, need to be washed and renewed. It is a far simpler thing to remove outward stains than it is to purge the very substance and nature of man, yet this is what was done, typically, on the Day of Atonement—and this is what our redeeming Lord actually does for us! We are outlaws and His Atonement purges us of outlawry and makes us citizens. We are lepers and by His stripes we are so healed as to be received among the clean! By nature we are only fit to be flung into those fires which burn up corrupt and offensive things— but His Sacrifice makes us so precious in the sight of the Lord that all the forces of Heaven stand sentinel about us! Once black as night, we are so purged that we shall walk with Him in white, for we are worthy.

Their persons being made clean, they were also purged of all the sins confessed. I called attention, in the reading of the chapter, to its many, "alls." I think there are seven or eight of them. The work which was done on that day was comprehensive—a clean sweep was made of sin. I begin with that which was confessed, for it was that for which cleansing would be most desired. It is said that, "Aaron shall lay both his hands upon the head of the live goat and confess over him all the iniquities of the children of Israel." All sin that was confessed over the scapegoat was carried away into a land not inhabited. Sin that is confessed is evidently real sin and not a mere dream of a morbid conscience. There is a certain mythical cloud of sin which people talk about and pretend to deplore and yet they have no sense of the solid weight and heinousness of their actual iniquity. Certain grievous sins are comparable to cauldrons of foaming filth—no man will willingly acknowledge them, however clearly they may be his, but when he does admit them before God, let him remember that it is this real sin, this foul and essentially abominable transgression, which is put away by the Atonement of Christ!

Sin confessed with tears. Sin which causes the very heart to bleed—killing sin, damning sin—this is the kind of sin for which Jesus died! Sham sinners may be content with a sham Savior, but our Lord Jesus is the real Savior who did really die—and died for real sin. Oh, how this ought to comfort you, you that are sadly bearing the pressing burden of an execrable life! And you, too, who are crushed into the mire of despondency beneath the load of your guilt! Brothers and Sisters, sin which you are bound to admit to as most assuredly committed is the sort of pollution from which Jesus cleanses all Believers. Sin which you dare not confess to man, but acknowledge only as you lay your hand upon the Divine Sacrifice—such sin the Lord removes from you.

The passage is very particular to mention "all sins." "The goat shall bear upon him all their iniquities." This includes every form of sin of thought, of word, of deed, of pride, of falsehood, of lust, of malice, of blasphemy. This comprehends crimes against man and offenses against God of peculiar blackness. And it does not exclude sins of inadvertence, or carelessness, or of omission. Transgressions of the body, the intellect, the affections are all blotted out. The outrageous scandals which I dare not mention are yet pardonable—yes, such have been pardoned! There is not the same degree of virus in all sins, but whether or not, the Atonement is for all transgressions. The Lord Jesus Christ did not pour out His heart's blood to remove one set of stains and leave the rest—He takes away from the soul that puts its trust in Him every spot and trace of sin. "Wash me," said David, "and I shall be whiter than snow." He looked for the extreme of cleanness and such the Savior brings to the soul for whom He has made effectual Atonement. I desire to be so plain and broad that the chief of sinners may gather hope from my words. I speak in very simple language, but the theme is full of sublimity—especially to you that feel your need of it. The Atonement removed all sin. I must give you the exact expression. He says, "all the iniquities of the children of Israel, and all their transgressions in all their sins."

It seems that the Divine Atonement puts away the sin of sin—the essence and heart of sin. Sin has its core, its kernel, its mortal spot. Within a fruit there is a central stone, or pip—this may serve as the likeness of sin. Within each iniquity there seems to lie a something more essentially evil than the act itself—this is the kernel of intent, the core of obstinacy, the inner hate of the mind. Whatever may be the sin of the soul, or the soul of the sin, Atonement has been made for it all. Most sins are a conglomerate of sins. A sin may be compared to a honeycomb—there are as many sins within one sin as there are cells within a piece of comb. Sin is a swarming, hiving, teeming thing! You can never estimate its full vileness, nor perceive all its evil bearings. All sorts of sins may hide away in one sin.

It would puzzle all the theologians in the world to tell what sin was absent from Adam's first offense. I could take any point you choose and show that Adam sinned in that direction. All sin was within that first sin. Sin is a multitudinous evil, an aggregate of all manner of filthiness, a chain with a thousand deadly links! A sinner is like a man possessed with a devil who cries, "My name is Legion, for we are many!" It is one in evil and yet countless in forms. The Atonement is more than equal to sin—it takes away all our transgressions in all our sins. It is the fullest purgation that could be imagined. The Lord Jesus has not left upon those for whom He has made Atonement a single spot, or wrinkle, or any such thing, so far as their justification is concerned. He has not left an iniquity for which they can be condemned before the bar of judgment. "You are clean every whit," is His sure verdict and none can contradict it.

It appears from this chapter, too, that another thing was done. Not only were all the sins that they had committed put away, but also all their holy things were purged. There stood the altar upon which only holy things were offered, but because imperfect men ministered there, it needed to be sprinkled with blood before it could be clean. There was the Holy Place of the Tabernacle which was dedicated solely to God's service, wherein the holiest rites of God's ordaining were celebrated—but because the priests that served there were fallible and unholy thoughts might cross their minds even when they handled the holy vessels, therefore the blood was sprinkled seven times within the Holy Place! Inside, within the veil, the sanctuary was called the "Holy of Holiest." Yes, but standing, as it did at first, in the midst of the camp of an erring people and afterwards near to it, it needed to be purged! It is written, "the priest shall make an atonement for the Holy Place, because of the uncleanness of the children of Israel." Even the Mercy Seat and the ground whereon it rested were sprinkled with the blood of the sacrifice seven times!

O Brothers and Sisters, I feel so glad that our Lord has atoned for the sins of our holy things! I rejoice that Jesus forgives the sins of my sermons! I have preached my very soul out among you with purity of motive, seeking to win men for Christ, but I dare not hope to have them accepted in and of themselves, for I perceive that they are defiled with sin! I feel so glad that Jesus has purified our prayers! Many saints spend much time in hearty, earnest cries to God, but even on your knees, you sin—and herein is our comfort, that the precious blood has made Atonement for the shortcomings of our supplications. Sometimes when we get together, Beloved, we sing to the praise of our Lord with heart and will. I have felt in this place as if you and I and all of us were so many burning coals, all blazing within a censer and thus letting loose the odors of the sweet incense of our Lord's praise! How often has a pillar of fragrant smoke risen from this house to Heaven! Yes, but even then there was sin in our praises and iniquity in our doxologies. We need pardon for our Psalms and cleansing for our hymns! Blessed be God, Atonement is made for all our faults, excesses and shortcomings. Jesus puts away not only our unholy things, but also the sins of our holy things!

Once more, on that day, all the people were cleansed. All the congregation of the house of Israel were typically cleansed from all sin by the Day of Atonement—not only the priests, but all the people—not only the princes, but the poorest servants in the camp! The aged woman and the little child. The gray beard and the youth were, alike, purified. Men of business inclined to covetousness, they were cleansed. And younger men and maidens in their gaiety, too apt to descend into wantonness—they were all made clean that day! This gives great comfort to those of us who love the souls of the multitude. All who believe are justified from all things! It is written, "The blood of Jesus Christ, His Son, cleanses us from all sin." I have often heard the text quoted with the, "us," left out. Permit me to put it in at this moment—"cleanses us from all Sin." Now put yourself into the, "us." Dare to believe that Grace admits you there! By an act of faith, let all of us all round the galleries and in this great area say, "The blood of Jesus Christ, His Son, cleanses us." If you pull, "us," to pieces, it is made up of a great many "me's." A thousand, thousand times "me" will all pack away into a single "us!" Let each one say—"The blood of Jesus Christ, His Son, cleanses me, and cleanses me from all sin." Be glad and rejoice forever because of this gracious Truth of God! This was done on the *day of atonement* in the symbol—and it has really been done by the Lord Jesus through His atoning Sacrifice.

II. Now we notice, in the second place, *how it was done*. We have seen what was done and this is most cheering. But now we will see how it was done. I shall have to be brief in this description. The Atonement was made, first of all, by sacrifice. I see a bullock for a sin offering, a ram for a burnt offering and, again, a goat for a sin offering. Many victims were offered that day and thus the people were reminded of the instrumental cause of atonement, namely, the Blood of Sacrifice. We know that the blood of bulls and of goats could never take away sin, but very distinctly do these point to the sufferings of our dear Redeemer. The woes He bore are the Expiation for our guilt. "He was wounded for our transgressions, He was bruised for our iniquities: the chastisement of our peace was upon Him; and with His stripes we are healed."

If you want to know by what means sin is put away, think of Messiah's life of grief and shame and arduous service. Think of His agony and bloody sweat in the garden. Think of the betrayal and denial, the scourging and the spitting. Think of the false accusations and the reproaches and the jeers. Think of the Cross, the nailed hands and feet, the bruised soul and the broken spirit. Fierce were the fires which consumed our Sacrifice. "My God, My God, why have You forsaken Me?" is the quintessence of agony—and this came from the heart which was crushed for our sins! Atonement was made for your sins and mine by the shedding of blood—that is to say, by our Lord's suffering and especially by His laying down His life on our behalf. Jesus died—by that death He purged our sin, He who only has Immortality gave up the ghost—in the cold embrace of Death, the Lord of Glory slept! They wrapped Him in spices and linen cloths and laid Him in the tomb of

Joseph of Arimathaea. In that death lay the essential deed by which sin dies and Grace reigns through righteousness unto eternal life.

Notice, next, that the atonement was made not only by the blood of sacrifice, but by the presentation of the blood within the veil. With the smoke of incense and a bowl filled with blood, Aaron passed into the Most Holy Place. Let us never forget that our Lord has gone into the heavenly places with better sacrifices than Aaron could present. His merits are the sweet incense which burns before the Throne of the heavenly Grace. His death supplies that Blood of Sprinkling which we find even in Heaven. "For Christ is not entered into the holy places made with hands, which are the figures of the true; but into Heaven, itself, now to appear in the Presence of God for us." "Neither by the blood of goats and calves, but by His own blood He entered in once into the Holy Place, having obtained eternal redemption for us." The presenting of the blood before God effects the Atonement. The material of the Atonement is in the blood and merits of Jesus, but a main part of the atoning act lies in the presentation of these in the heavenly places by Jesus Christ, Himself.

Furthermore, atonement was made effectual by its application to the thing or person cleansed. The atonement was made for the Holy Place—it was sprinkled seven times with blood. The same was done to the altar—the horns thereof were smeared seven times. So to make the Atonement effectual between you and God, the blood of Jesus must be sprinkled upon you by a lively faith. Though this does not so plainly appear in the type before us as to the people on this occasion, yet it comes out in other types—the cleansing blood was always the Blood of Sprinkling. Before the blood of the Paschal lamb could cause the avenger to pass over the house, it must be marked with the crimson sign. This is that scarlet thread in the window which delivers the Lord's Rahabs in the day of destruction. Before any man can receive reconciliation with God, the Atonement must be applied to his own heart and conscience. Faith is that bunch of hyssop which we dip into the blood and, with it, sprinkle the lintel and two side posts of the house wherein we dwell—and so we are saved from destruction.

Further, my dear Brothers and Sisters, inasmuch as no one type was sufficient, the Lord set forth the method of the removal of sin, as far as we are concerned, by the scapegoat. One of two goats was chosen to live. It stood before the Lord and Aaron confessed all the sins of Israel upon its head. A fit man, selected for the purpose, led this goat away into a land not inhabited. What became of it? Why do you ask the question? It is not to edification. You may have seen the famous picture of the scapegoat, representing it as expiring in misery in a desert place. That is all very pretty and I do not wonder that imagination should picture the poor devoted scapegoat as a sort of cursed thing, left to perish amid accumulated horrors. But please observe that this is all fancy—mere groundless fancy! The Scripture is entirely silent as to anything of the kind and purposely so. All that the type teaches is this—in symbol the scapegoat has all the sin of the people laid upon it and when it is led away into the solitary wilderness, it has gone and the sin with it! We may not follow the scape- goat even in imagination! It is gone where it can never be found, for there is nobody to find it—it is gone into a land not inhabited—into "no man's land" in fact.

Stop where the Scripture stops! To go beyond what is written is unwise, if not presumptuous. Sin is carried away into the silent land, the unknown wilderness. By nature, sin is everywhere, but to Believers, in the Sacrifice of Christ, sin is nowhere! The sins of God's people have gone beyond recall. Where to? Do not ask anything about that. If they were sought for, they could not be found! They are so gone that they are blotted out. Into oblivion our sins have gone, even as the scapegoat went out of track of mortal man. The death of the scapegoat does not come into the type. In fact, it would mar the type to think of it. Of Melchizedek,

226

we read that he was without father, without mother, without descent and so on, because these things are not mentioned in Scripture and the omission is part of the teaching. So in this case, the fate of the scapegoat is not spoken of and the silence is a part of the instruction. The scapegoat is gone, we know not where, and so our sins have vanished quite away—nobody will ever find the scapegoat—and nobody will ever find the Believer's sins!

"Where are my sins? Oh where?" Echo answers, "Where?" Gone to the land of nobody, where Satan, himself, could not find them! Yes, where God Himself cannot find them. He says He has cast our sin behind His back where He cannot see. What part of the creation must that be which lies behind God's back, whereas He is everywhere present, beholding all things both by night and by day? There is no such place as, "behind His back"—and there is no place for our sins. They have gone into nowhere. "As far as the east is from the west, so far has He removed our transgressions from us." He has cast them into the depths of the sea—and even that is not so good a figure as the scapegoat, for things that are at the bottom of the sea are still there—but the scapegoat soon passed away altogether and, as far as Israel was concerned, it ceased to be. The sins of God's people are absolutely and irrevocably forgiven! Never, never, never can they be laid to our charge! They are extinct, buried, blotted out, forgotten. "Who shall lay anything to the charge of God's elect?"

Yet, dear Friends, the ceremony was not quite finished, for now everybody who had had a hand in it must be washed, so that everybody might be clean. There is Aaron—he takes off his garments and washes himself scrupulously clean! Yes, he does it a second time. Here is the man who took the scapegoat away and he washes himself. Here is a third person, who carried away the skin and the flesh of the sin offering and burnt them outside the camp—he also washes himself. Everybody becomes purged. The whole camp is clean right through. So, when Jesus completes His sacrifice, we sing—

"Now both the sinner and Surety are free."

No sin remains upon Him on whom the Lord once laid the iniquities of us all! The great Atonement is made and everything is cleansed, from beginning to end. Christ has put it all away forever by the water and the blood which flowed from His riven side. All is purified and the Lord looks down on a clean camp—and soon He will have them rejoicing before Him, each man in his home, feasting to the full! I am so glad, my joy overflows! O Lord, who is a pardoning God like You? Where can such forgiveness be found as You do freely give to sinners through Jesus, Your Son?

III. In the third place, I ask your attention, for a brief interval, to this special point—*who did it?* The answer is, Aaron did it all. Aaron was quite alone in the work of that day. It was heavy and even exhausting work, but he had no assistant. Aaron performed the work of priest and Levite that day and no one helped him, for it is written, "There shall be no man in the Tabernacle of the congregation when he goes in to make an atonement in the Holy Place until he comes out and has made an atonement for himself, and for his household, and for all the congregation of Israel." The Tabernacle seemed lonely that day. Aaron went into its courts and chambers and saw no sign of man. Of course there were lamps to be lighted, but Aaron had to light them himself—the showbread had to be changed—Aaron had to change it. All the offices of the tabernacle were left to his sole care for the day.

When it came to killing the victims, priests and Levites were there on other days, but now the High Priest must do it all. He must kill and receive the blood and sprinkle it himself. He must kindle the sacrificial fire and lay the burning coals upon the incense. He must carry both the incense and the basin of blood into the Holy Place with his own hands. I think I see him looking around in the solitude. He says, "I looked and there was no man." Of the people there was none with him. In the Holy Place there stood no priest to minister before the Lord except Aaron. It must have been with trembling that he lifted up the curtain and passed into the secret place of the Most High with the censer smoking in his hand. There he stood in that awful Presence quite alone with the Eternal—no man was with him when he sprinkled the blood again and again till the seven-fold rite was finished.

Three times he goes in and out and never a soul is there to so much as smile upon him. The tension of mind and heart which he endured, alone, that day, must have been trying, indeed. All that day he must have been conscious of a burden of responsibility and a weight of reverence enough to bow him to the dust and yet no one was present to cheer him. Now fix your eyes on the great Antitype of Aaron. There was none with our Lord—He trod the winepress alone. He bore our sins in His body on the tree. He alone went in where the thick darkness covered the Throne of God and none stood by to comfort Him. "All the disciples forsook Him and fled." It would have been a very natural thing, one would think, that Peter should have defended Him and even died with Him—but no one died with Jesus except thieves—and nobody could suspect that thieves aided Him in His Sacrifice! They showed the need of the Sacrifice, but they could do no more.

Worship our Lord as working salvation by His own single arm! Do not tolerate those who would share His work. Do not believe in priests of any church who pretend to offer sacrifice for the quick and the dead! They cannot help you and you do not need their help! Do not put your own merits, works, prayers, or anything else side by side with your one lone High Priest, who in His white garments of holy service performed the whole work of Expiation and then came forth in His garments of Glory and of beauty to gladden the eyes of His chosen! I say no more. Let that Truth of God abide in your hearts—our High Priest, alone, has made Reconciliation!

IV. Lastly, *what were the people to do* for whom this atonement was made? There were two things they had to do that day, only I must add that one of them was doing nothing. For the first thing, they had to afflict their souls that day. Brothers and Sisters, does it seem a strange thing to you that on a day of rest they were to afflict their souls? Think of it a little and you will see that there was cause for it. We most rightly sing—

> "Here let our hearts begin to melt,
> While we, His death record
> And with our joy for pardoned guilt
> Mourn that we pierced the Lord."

It was a day of confession of sin. And should not confession be made with sorrowful repentance? A dry-eyed confession is a hypocritical confession! To acknowledge sin without grieving over it is to aggravate sin. We cannot think of our sin without grieving—and the more sure we are that it is forgiven—the more sorry we are that ever it was committed! Sin seems all the greater because it was committed against a sin-forgiving God. If you do wrong to a person and he grows angry, you may be wicked enough to persist in the wrong. But if, instead of growing angry, he forgives and does you good in return, then you will deeply regret that ever you had an unkind thought towards him. The Lord's pardoning love makes us feel truly sorry to have offended Him.

Not only was it a day of confession, but it was a day of sacrifice. No tender-hearted Israelite could think of that bullock, ram and goat dying for him without saying, "That is what I deserve." If he heard the moans of the dying creature he would say, "My own heart groans and bleeds." When we think of our dying Lord, our emotions are mingled—we feel a pleasing grief and a mournful joy as we stand at Calvary. Thus it is we sing—

"Alas! And did my Savior bleed?
And did my Sovereign die?
Could He devote that sacred head
For such a worm as I?
Was it for crimes that I have done
He died upon the tree?

"Amazing pity, Grace unknown,
And love beyond degree!
Well might the sun in darkness hide
And shut his glories in,
When God the mighty Maker died
For man, the creature's sin!

"Well might I hide my blushing face
When His dear Cross appears,
Dissolve my heart in thankfulness,
And melt my eyes to tears."

It was a day of sacrifice and, therefore, a day of affliction of their souls and herein we are in sympathy with them.

Once more, it was a day of perfect cleansing and, therefore, by a strange logic, a day of the affliction of the soul, for, oh, when sin is forgiven, when we know it is forgiven, when, by Divine Assurance, we know that God has blotted out our sins like a cloud, then it is we mourn over our iniquities! "They shall look upon Me whom they have pierced"—that look gives life! "And they shall mourn for Him as one mourns for his only son and shall be in bitterness for Him, as one that is in bitterness for his first-born"—this bitterness is one of the truest signs of life! They were to afflict their souls. Brethren, we cannot talk of the Cross of Christ except in subdued tones. If you think you can laugh and sport yourself because your sin is forgiven, you know nothing of the matter. Sin has been pardoned at such a price that we cannot, from this day on, trifle with it. The sacrifice was so august that we must always speak of it with holy trembling.

I always feel a suspicion of those converts who get up and glibly boast that once they were drunks, thieves, blasphemers and so forth. Brothers and Sisters, if you tell the story of your sin, blush scarlet to think it should be true! I am ashamed to hear a man talk of his sins as an old Greenwich pensioner might talk of his sea-fights. I hate to hear a man exhibiting his old lusts as if they were scars of honor! Friend, these things are disgraceful to you, however much the putting of them away may be to the honor and Glory of God—and they are to be spoken of by you with shame and confusion of face. Afflict your soul when you remember what you once were!

On the Day of Atonement they were to afflict their souls and yet they were to rest. Can these things come together—mourning and resting? Oh yes, you and I know how they meet in one bosom. I never am so truly happy as when a sober sadness tinges my joy. When I am the fullest of joy I could weep my life away at Jesus' feet. Nothing is more really sweet than the bitterness of repentance. Nothing is more healthful than self-abhorrence mixed with the grateful love which hides itself in the wounds of Jesus! The purified people were to rest—they were to rest from all servile work. I will never do a hand's turn to save myself by my own merits, works, or feelings. I have done forever with all interference with my Lord's work. Salvation as to its meritorious cause is complete—

we will not think of beginning it over again, for that would be an insult to the Savior.

"It is finished," said our Lord Jesus, as He bowed His dear triumphant head and gave up the ghost. And if it is finished, we will not dream of adding to it. It is finished! We have no work to do with the view of self-salvation. But you say to me—"Have we not to work out our own salvation?" Certainly we have! We are to work out our own salvation because God works it in us. It is our own salvation and we show it forth in our lives—we work it out from within—we develop it from day to day and let men see what the Lord has done for us! It must first be worked for us and then in us, or we can never work it out!

They were assuredly to cease from all sinful work. How can the pardoned man continue in sin? We have done with toiling for the devil! We will no more waste our lives in his service. Many men are worn to rottenness in the service of their lusts, but the servant of God has been set free from that yoke of bondage. We are slaves no longer—we quit the hard bondage of Egypt and rest in the Lord.

We have also done with selfish work. We now seek first the Kingdom of Heaven and look that all other things shall be added unto us by the goodness of our heavenly Father. Henceforth we find rest by bearing the easy yoke of Christ. We joy to spend and be spent in His beloved service. He has made us free and, therefore, we are under bonds to His love forever. O Lord, I am Your servant, I am Your servant! You have loosed my bonds—from this day on I am bound to You. God grant that this may be a high day to you because you gladly realize the grand Truths of God which are shadowed forth in these delightful types! Amen.

13

The Day of Atonement

"This shall be an everlasting statute unto you, to make an atonement for the children of Israel for all their sins once a year." (Leviticus 16:34)

THE JEWS HAD MANY STRIKING ceremonies which marvelously set forth the death of Jesus Christ as the great expiation of our guilt and the salvation of our souls. one of the chief of these was the day of atonement, which I believe was pre-eminently intended to typify that great day of vengeance of our God, which was also the great day of acceptance of our souls, when Jesus Christ "died, the just for the unjust, to bring us to God." That day of atonement happened only once a year to teach us that only once should Jesus Christ die and, that though He would come a second time, yet it would be without a sin offering unto salvation. The lambs were perpetually slaughtered—morning and evening they offered sacrifice to God—to remind the people that they always needed a sacrifice. But the day of atonement, being the type of the one great propitiation, it was but once a year that the high priest entered within the veil with blood as the atonement for the sins of the people. And this was on a certain set and appointed time. It was not left to the choice of Moses, or to the convenience of Aaron, or to any other circumstance which might affect the date—it was appointed to be on a peculiar set day—as you find at the 29th verse—"In the seventh month, on the tenth day of the month." And at no other time was the day of atonement to be, to show us that God's great day of atonement was appointed and predestinated by Himself. Christ's expiation occurred but once and then not by any chance. God had settled it from before the foundation of the world and at that hour when God had predestinated, on that very day that God had decreed that Christ should die, was He led like a lamb to the slaughter and as a sheep before her shearers He was dumb! It was but once a year, because the sacrifice should be once. It was at an appointed time in the year, because in the fullness of time, Jesus Christ should come into the world to die for us.

Now, I shall invite your attention to the ceremonies of this solemn day, taking the different parts in detail. First, we shall consider the person who made the atonement; secondly, the sacrifice whereby the atonement was typically made; thirdly, the effects of the atonement; and fourthly, our behavior on the recollection of the atonement, as well set forth by the conduct prescribed to the Israelites on that day.

I. First, *the person who was to make the atonement.* And at the outset, we remark that Aaron, the high priest, did it. "Thus shall Aaron come into the holy place; with a young bullock for a sin offering and a ram for a burnt offering." Inferior priests slaughtered lambs. Other priests, at other times, did almost all the work of the sanctuary—but on this day, nothing was done by anyone, as a part of the business of the great day of atonement—except by the high priest. Old rabbinical traditions tell us that everything on that day was done by him, even the lighting of the candles and the fires and the incense and all the offices that were required. We are told that for a fortnight beforehand, the high priest was obliged to go into the tabernacle to slaughter the bullocks and assist in the work of the priests and Levites that he might be prepared to do the work which was unusual to him. All the labor was left to him.

So, beloved, Jesus Christ, the High Priest, and He, only, works the atonement. There are other priests, for, "He has made us priests and kings unto God." Every Christian is a priest to offer sacrifice of prayer and praise unto God, but none save the high priest must offer atonement. He and He alone, must go within the veil. He must slaughter the goat and sprinkle the blood—for though thanksgiving is shared in by all of Christ's elect body, atonement remains alone to Jesus Christ, the High Priest.

Then it is interesting to notice that the high priest on this day was a humbled priest. You read in the 4th verse, "He shall put on the holy linen coat and he shall have the linen breeches upon his flesh, and shall be girded with a linen belt and with the linen miter shall he be attired: these are holy garments." On other days he wore what the people were accustomed to call the golden garments. He had the miter with a plate of pure gold around his brow, tied with brilliant blue. The splendid breastplate, studded with gems, adorned with pure gold, and set with precious stones; the glorious ephod, the tinkling bells, and all the other ornaments wherewith he came before the people as the accepted high priest. But on this day he had none of them! The golden miter was laid aside, the embroidered vest was put away, the breast-plate was taken off and he came out simply with the holy linen coat, the linen breeches, the linen miter and girded with a linen belt. On that day he humbled himself, just as the people humbled themselves. Now that is a notable circumstance! You will see sundry other passages in the references which will bear this out—that the priest's dress on this day was different. As Mayer tells us, he wore garments and glorious ones, on other days, but on this day he wore four humble ones. Jesus Christ, then, when He made atonement, was a humbled priest. He did not make atonement arrayed in all the glories of His ancient throne in heaven.

Upon His brow there was no diadem, save the crown of thorns. Around Him was cast no purple robe, save that which He wore for a time in mockery. In His hand was no scepter, save the reed which they thrust in cruel contempt upon Him. He had no sandals of pure gold, neither was He dressed as king. He had none of those splendors about Him which would make Him mighty and distinguished among men! He came out in His simple body, yes, in His naked body, for they stripped off even the common robe from Him! And they made Him hang before God's sun, and God's universe, naked, to His shame and to the disgrace of those who chose to do so cruel and dastardly a deed! Oh, my soul, adore your Jesus, who when He made atonement, humbled Himself and wrapped around Him a garb of your inferior clay! Oh, angels, you can understand what were the glories that He laid aside! Oh, thrones, principalities, and powers, you can tell what was the diadem with which He dispensed and what the robes He laid aside to wrap Himself in earthly garbs. But, men, you can scarcely tell how glorious is your High Priest now! You can scarcely tell how glorious He was before! But oh, adore Him, for on that day it was the simple clean linen of His own body, of His own humanity in which He made atonement for your sins!

In the next place, the high priest who offered the atonement must be a spotless high priest—and because there were none such to be found, Aaron, being a sinner, himself, as well as the people—had to sanctify himself and make atonement for his own sin before he could go in to make an atonement for the sins of the people. In the 3rd verse you read, "Thus shall Aaron come into the holy place: with a young bullock for a sin offering, and a ram for a burnt offering." These were for him. In the 6th verse it is said, "And Aaron shall offer his bullock of the sin offering, which is for him, and make an atonement for himself and for his house." Yes, more—before he went within the veil with the blood of the goat which was the atonement for the people, he had to go within the veil to make atonement there for him. In the 11th, 12th and 13th verses, it is said, "And Aaron shall bring the bullock of the sin offering, which is for him, and shall make an atonement for himself, and for his house, and shall kill the bullock of the sin offering, which is for himself. And he shall take a censer full of burning coals of fire from off the altar before the Lord and his hands full of sweet incense beaten small, and bring it within the veil. And he shall put the incense upon the fire before the Lord, that the cloud of the incense may cover the mercy seat that is upon the testimony, that he die not. And he shall take of the blood of the bullock (that is, the bullock that he killed for himself) and sprinkle it with his finger upon the mercy seat eastward; and before the mercy seat shall he sprinkle of the blood with his finger seven times." This was before he killed the goat, for it says, "Then shall he kill the goat." Before he took the blood which was a type of Christ within the veil, he took the blood (which was a type of Christ in another sense), wherewith he purified himself. Aaron must not go within the veil until by the bullock his sins had been typically expiated, nor even then without the burning smoking incense before his face, lest God should look on him and he should die, being an impure mortal. Moreover, the Jews tell us that Aaron had to wash himself, I think, five times in the day and it is said in this chapter that he had to wash himself many times. We read in the 4th verse, "These are holy garments; therefore shall he wash his flesh in water and so put them on."

And at the 24th verse, "He shall wash his flesh with water in the holy place and put on his garments." So you see it was strictly provided for that Aaron, on that day, should be a spotless priest. He could not be so as to nature, but, ceremonially, care was taken that he should be clean. He was washed over and over again in the sacred bath. And besides that, there was the blood of the bullock and the smoke of the incense, that he might be acceptable before God. Ah, beloved, we have a spotless High

Priest! We have one who needed no washing, for He had no filth to wash away!

We have one who needed no atonement for Himself for He, forever, might have sat down at the right hand of God and never have come on earth at all! He was pure and spotless. He needed no incense to wave before the mercy seat to hide the angry face of justice. He needed nothing to hide and shelter Him, He was all pure and clean! Oh, bow down and adore Him, for if He had not been a holy High Priest, He could never have taken your sins upon Himself and never have made intercession for you! Oh, reverence Him, that spotless as He was, He should come into this world and say, "For this cause I sanctify Myself, that they also may be sanctified through the truth." Adore and love Him, the spotless High Priest, who, on the day of atonement took away your guilt!

Again, the atonement was made by a solitary high priest—alone and unassisted. You read in the 17th verse, "And there shall be no man in the tabernacle of the congregation when he goes in to make an atonement in the holy place, until he comes out and has made an atonement for himself and for his household, and for all the congregation of Israel." No other man was to be present, so that the people might be quite certain that everything was done by the high priest, alone. It is remarkable, as Matthew Henry observes, that no disciple died with Christ. When He was put to death, His disciples forsook Him and fled. They crucified none of His followers with Him, lest any should suppose that the disciple shared the honor of atonement. Thieves were crucified with Him because none would suspect that they could assist Him—but if a disciple had died, it might have been imagined that he had shared the atonement. God kept that holy circle of Calvary select to Christ, and none of His disciples must go to die therewith Him. O glorious High Priest, You have done it all alone! O, glorious antitype of Aaron, no son of Yours stood with You—no Eliezer, no Phineas burned incense—there was no priest, no Levite save, Himself. "I have trodden the winepress alone, and of the people there was none with Me." Then give all the glory unto His holy name, for alone and unassisted He made atonement for your guilt! The bath of His blood is your only washing. The stream of water from His side is your perfect purification! None but Jesus, none but Jesus, has worked out the work of our salvation!

Again it was a laborious high priest who did the work on that day. It is astonishing how, after comparative rest, he should be so accustomed to his work as to be able to perform all that he had to do on that day. I have endeavored to count up how many creatures he had to kill and I find that there were 15 beasts which he slaughtered at different times, besides the other offices, which were all left to him. In the first place, there were the two lambs, one offered in the morning, and the other in the evening— they were never omitted, being a perpetual ordinance. On this day the high priest killed those two lambs.

Further, if you will turn to Numbers 29:7-11, "And you shall have on the tenth day of this seventh month an holy convocation; and you shall afflict your souls: you shall not do any work therein: But you shall offer a burnt offering unto the Lord for a sweet savor; one young bullock, one ram, and seven lambs of the first year; they shall be unto you without blemish: And their meat offering shall be of flour mingled with oil, three tenth deals to a bullock, and two tenth deals to one ram. A several tenth deal for one lamb throughout the seven lambs: one kid of the goats for a sin offering: besides the sin offering of atonement, and the continual burnt offering, and the meat offering of it, and their drink offerings." Here, then, was one bullock, a ram, seven lambs, and a kid of the goats, making ten. The two lambs made twelve. And in the chapter we have been studying, it is said in the 3rd verse: "Thus shall Aaron come into the holy place: with a young bullock for a sin offering and a ram for a burnt offering," which makes the number fourteen. Then after that, we find there were two goats but only one of them was killed, the other being allowed to go away. Thus, there were 15 beasts to be slaughtered, besides the burnt offerings of thanksgiving which were offered by way of showing that the people now desired to dedicate themselves to the Lord from gratitude, that the atonement of sin offering had been accepted.

He who was ordained priest in Jeshurun, for that day, toiled like a common Levite, worked as laboriously as priest could do and far more so than on any ordinary day! Just so with our Lord Jesus Christ! Oh, what a labor the atonement was to Him! It was a work that all the hands of the universe could not have accomplished—yet He completed it alone! It was a work more laborious than the treading of the winepress and His frame, unless sustained by the divinity within, could scarcely have borne such stupendous labor. There was the bloody sweat in Gethsemane. There was the watching all night—just as the high priest did—for fear that uncleanness might touch Him. There was the hooting and the scorn which He suffered every day before—something like the continual offering of the Lamb. Then there came the shame, the spitting, and the cruel flagellations in Pilate's Hall; then there was the Via Dolorosa through Jerusalem's sad streets; then came the hanging on the cross, with the weight of His people's sins on His shoulders. Yes, it was a Divine labor that our great High Priest did on that day—a labor mightier than the making of the world—it was the making new of a world, the taking of its sins upon His Almighty shoulders, and casting them into the depths of the sea! The atonement was made by a toilsome laborious High Priest who worked, indeed, that day; and Jesus, though He had toiled before, yet never worked as He did on that wondrous day of atonement!

II. Thus have I led you to consider the person who made the atonement; let us now consider for a moment or two, *the means whereby this atonement was made.* You read at the 5th verse, "And he shall take of the congregation of the children of Israel, two kids of the goats for a sin offering and one ram for a burnt offering;" and at the 7th, 8th, 9th and 10th verses, "And he shall take the two goats and present them before the Lord at the door of the tabernacle of the congregation. And Aaron shall cast lots upon the two goats, one lot for the Lord, and the other lot for the scapegoat. And Aaron shall bring the goat upon which the Lord's lot fell, and offer him for a sin offering. But the goat, on which the lot fell to be the scapegoat, shall be presented alive before the Lord, to make an atonement with him and to let him go for a scapegoat into the wilderness." The first goat I considered to be the great type of Jesus Christ the atonement—such as I do not consider the scapegoat to be. The first is the type of the means whereby the atonement was made, and we shall keep to that first.

Notice that this goat, of course, answered all the prerequisites of every other thing that was sacrificed—it must be a perfect, unblemished goat of the first year. Even so was our Lord, a perfect man, in the prime and vigor of His manhood. And further, this goat was an eminent type of Christ from the fact that it was taken of the congregation of the children of Israel, as we are told at the 5th verse. The public treasury furnished the goat. So, beloved, Jesus Christ was, first of all, purchased by the public treasury of the Jewish people before He died—thirty pieces of silver they had valued Him—a goodly price. And as they had been accustomed to bring the goat, so they brought Him to be offered—not, indeed, with the intention that He should be their sacrifice—but unwittingly they fulfilled this when they brought Him to Pilate and cried, "Crucify Him, crucify Him!" Oh, beloved! Indeed, Jesus Christ came out from the midst of the people, and the people brought Him! Strange that it should be so. "He came unto His own, and His own received Him not." His own led Him forth to slaughter! His own dragged Him before the mercy seat!

Note, again, that though this goat, like the scapegoat, was brought by the people, God's decision was still in it. Mark, it is said, "Aaron shall cast lots upon the two goats; one lot for the Lord and the other lot for the scapegoat." I conceive this mention of lots is to teach that although the Jews brought Jesus Christ of their own will to die, yet, Christ had been appointed to die—and even the very man who sold Him was appointed to it—so says the Scripture. Christ's death was foreordained, and there was not only man's hand in it, but God's. "The lot is cast into the lap but the whole disposing thereof is of the Lord." So it is true that man put Christ to death, but it was of the Lord's disposal that Jesus Christ was slaughtered, "the just for the unjust, to bring us to God."

Next, behold the goat that destiny has marked out to make the atonement. Come and see it die. The priest stabs it. Mark it in its agonies. Behold it struggling for a moment. Observe the blood as it gushes forth. Christians, you have here your Savior! See His Father's vengeful sword sheathed in His heart? Behold His death agonies. See the clammy sweat upon His brow? Mark His tongue cleaving to the roof of His mouth! Hear His sighs and groans upon the cross. Listen to His shriek, "Eli, Eli, lama sabachthani." And you have more, now, to think of than you could have if you only stood to see the death of a goat for your atonement. Mark the blood as from His wounded hands it flows and from His feet it finds a channel to the earth. From His open side in one great river see it gush! As the blood of the goat made the atonement typically, so, Christian, your Savior dying for you made the great atonement for your sins and you may go free!

But mark, this goat's blood was not only shed for many for the remission of sins as a type of Christ, but that blood was taken within the veil and there it was sprinkled. So with Jesus' blood: "Sprinkled now with blood, the throne." The blood of other beasts (save only of the bullock) was offered before the Lord and was not brought into the most holy place. But this goat's blood was sprinkled on the mercy seat and before the mercy seat, to make an atonement. So, O child of God, your Savior's blood has made atonement within the veil. He has taken it there Himself; His own merits and His own agonies are now within the veil of glory, sprinkled now before the throne of God! O glorious sacrifice, as well as High Priest, we would adore You, for by Your one offering, You have made atonement forever, even as this one slaughtered goat made atonement once in a year for the sins of all the people!

III. We now come to the *effects*. One of the first effects of the death of this goat was the sanctification of the holy things which had been made unholy. You read at the end of the 15th verse, "He shall sprinkle it upon the mercy seat: and he shall make an atonement for the holy place because of the uncleanness of the children of Israel and because of their transgressions in all their sins: and so shall he do for the tabernacle of the congregation that remains among them in the midst of their uncleanness." The holy place was made unholy by the people. Where God dwelt should be holy—but where man comes, there must be some degree of unholiness. This blood of the goat made the unholy place holy. It was a sweet reflection to me as I came here, this morning. I thought, "I am going to the House of God and that house is a holy place."

But when I thought how many sinners had trodden its floors, how many unholy ones had joined in its songs, I thought, "Ah, it has been made defiled, but oh, there is no fear, for the blood of Jesus has made it holy again!" "Ah," I thought, "there is our poor prayer that we shall offer—it is a holy prayer—for God the Holy Spirit dictates it. But then it is an unholy prayer, for we have uttered it and that which comes out of unholy lips like ours, must be tainted." "But ah," I thought again, "it is a prayer that has been sprinkled with blood and therefore it must be a holy prayer."

And as I looked on all the harps of this sanctuary, typical of your praises and on all the censers of this tabernacle, typical of your prayers, I thought within myself, "There is blood on them all, our holy service this day has been sprinkled with the blood of the great Jesus and as such it will be accepted through Him." Oh, beloved, is it not sweet to reflect that our holy things are now really holy—that though sin is mixed with them all and we think them defiled—yet they are not, for the blood has washed out every stain? And the service this day is as holy in God's sight as the service of the cherubim and is acceptable as the psalms of the glorified. We have washed our worship in the blood of the Lamb and it is accepted through Him!

But observe, the second great fact was that their sins were taken away. This was set forth by the scapegoat. You read at the 20th verse, "And when he has made an end of reconciling the holy place and the tabernacle of the congregation and the altar, he shall bring the live goat: And Aaron shall lay both his hands upon the head of the live goat and confess over him all the iniquities of the children of Israel and all their transgressions in all their sins, putting them upon the head of the goat and shall send him away by the hand of a fit man into the wilderness: And the goat shall bear upon him all their iniquities unto a land not inhabited and he shall let go the goat in the wilderness." When that was done, you see, the great and wonderful atonement was finished and the effects of it were set forth to the people. Now, I do not know how many opinions there are about this scapegoat. One of the strangest opinions to me is that which is held by a very large portion of learned men and I see it is put in the margin of my Bible.

Many learned men think that this word, scapegoat, Azazel, was the name of the devil who was worshipped by the heathen in the form of a goat. And they tell us that the first goat was offered to God as an atonement for sin and the other went away to be tormented by the devil and was called Azazel, just as Jesus was tormented by Satan in the wilderness. To this opinion, it is enough to object that it is difficult to conceive when the other goat was offered to God, this should be sent

245

among demons. Indeed, the opinion is too gross for belief! It needs only to be mentioned to be refuted! Now the first goat is the Lord Jesus Christ making atonement by His death for the sins of the people. The second is sent away into the wilderness and nothing is heard of it any more, forever—and here a difficulty suggests itself—"Did Jesus Christ go where He was never heard of any more, forever?" That is what we have not to consider at all! The first goat was a type of the atonement—the second is the type of the effect of the atonement. The second goat went away, after the first was slaughtered, carrying the sins of the people on its head. And so it sets forth, as a scapegoat, how our sins are carried away into the depth of the wilderness. There was this year exhibited in the Art Union, a fine picture of the scapegoat dying in the wilderness. It was represented with a burning sky above it, its feet sticking in the mire, surrounded by hundreds of skeletons and there dying a doleful and miserable death.

Now, that was just a piece of gratuitous nonsense, for there is nothing in the Scripture that warrants it in the least degree! The rabbis tell us that this goat was taken by a man into the wilderness and there tumbled down a high rock to die, but, as an excellent commentator says, if the man did push it down the rock he did more than God ever told him to do! God told him to take a goat and let it go. As to what became of it, neither you nor I know anything—that is purposely left out. Our Lord Jesus Christ has taken away our sins upon His head, just as the scapegoat, and it is gone from us—that is all—the goat was not a type in its dying, or in regard to its subsequent fate.

God has only told us that it should be taken by the hand of a fit man into the wilderness. The most correct account seems to be that of one Rabbi Jarchi who says that they generally took the goat twelve miles out of Jerusalem and at each mile there was a booth provided where the man who took it, might refresh himself till he came to the tenth mile. Then there was no more rest for him till he had seen the goat go. When he had come to the last mile, he stood and looked at the goat till it was gone and he could see it no more. Then the people's sins were all gone, too.

Now, what a fine type that is if you do not inquire any further! But if you will get to meddling where God intended you to be in ignorance, you will get nothing by it. This scapegoat was not designed to show us the victim or the sacrifice, but simply what became of the sins. The sins of the people are confessed upon that head. The goat is going. The people lose sight of it. A fit man goes with it. The sins are going from them and now the man has arrived at his destination. The man sees the goat in the distance skipping here and there over the mountains, glad of its liberty. It is not quite gone—a little farther—and now it is lost to sight. The man returns and says he can no longer see it—then the people clap their hands, for their sins are all gone, too!

Oh, soul, can you see your sins all gone? We may have to take a long journey and carry our sins with us. But oh, how we watch and watch till they are utterly cast into the wilderness of forgetfulness where they shall never be found any more against us! But mark, this goat did not sacrificially make the atonement—it was a type of the sins going away—and so it was a type of the atonement. For you know, since our sins are thereby lost, it is the fruit of the atonement—but the sacrifice is the means of making it. So we have this great and glorious thought before us—that by the death of Christ, there was full, free, perfect remission for all those whose sins are laid upon His head, for I would have you notice that on this day all sins were laid on the scapegoat's head—sins of presumption, sins of ignorance, sins of uncleanness, little sins and great sins, few sins and many sins, sins against the law, sins against morality, sins against ceremonies, sins of all kinds were taken away on that great day of atonement. Sinner, oh, that you had a share in my Master's atonement! Oh, that you could see Him slaughtered on the cross! Then might you see Him go away leading captivity captive, and taking your sins where they might never be found!

I have now an interesting fact to tell you, and I am sure you will think it worth mentioning. Turn to Leviticus 25:9, and you will read—"Then shall you cause the trumpet of the jubilee to sound on the tenth day of the seventh month, in the day of atonement shall you make the trumpet sound throughout all your land." So we see that one of the effects of the atonement was set forth to us in the fact that when the year of jubilee came, it was not on the first day of the year that it was proclaimed, but "on the tenth day of the seventh month." Yes, I think that was the best part of it! The scapegoat is gone, and the sins are gone—and no sooner are they gone than the silver trumpet sounds—

"The year of jubilee is come!
Return, you ransomed sinners, home."

On that day sinners go free; on that day our poor mortgaged lands are liberated, and our poor estates which have been forfeited by our spiritual bankruptcy are all returned to us! So when Jesus dies, slaves win their liberty, and lost ones receive spiritual life again! When He dies, heaven, the long lost inheritance is ours! Blessed day! Atonement and jubilee ought to go together. Have you ever had a jubilee, my friends, in your hearts? If you have not, I can tell you it is because you have not had a day of atonement!

One more thought concerning the effects of this great day of atonement and you will observe that it runs throughout the whole of the chapter—entrance within the veil. Only on one day in the year might the high priest enter within the veil and then it must be for the great purposes of the atonement. Now, beloved, the atonement is finished and you may enter within the veil—"Having boldness, therefore, to enter into the holiest, let us come with boldness unto the throne of the heavenly grace." The veil of the temple is rent by the atonement of Christ, and access to the throne of God is now ours! O child of God, I know not of any privilege which you have, save fellowship with Christ, which is more valuable than access to the throne! Access to the mercy seat is one of the greatest blessings mortals can enjoy. Precious throne of grace! I never would have had any right to come there if it had not been for the day of atonement! I never would have been able to come there if the throne had not been sprinkled with the blood!

IV. Now we come to notice, in the fourth place, what is our *proper behavior when we consider the day of atonement?* You read at the 29th verse, "And this shall be a statute forever unto you: that in the seventh month, on the tenth day of the month, you shall afflict your souls." That is one thing that we ought to do when we remember the atonement. Surely, sinner, there is nothing that should move you to repentance like the thought of that great sacrifice of Christ which is necessary to wash away your guilt. "Law and terrors do but harden," but I think the thought that Jesus died is enough to make us melt. It is well, when we hear the name of Calvary, always to shed a tear, for there is nothing that ought to make a sinner weep like the mention of the death of Jesus. On that day "you shall afflict your souls." And even you, you Christians, when you think that your Savior died, should afflict your souls—you should say,

"Alas! And did my Savior bleed?
And did my Sovereign die?
Would He devote that sacred head
For such a worm as I?"

Drops of grief ought to flow—yes, streams of sympathy with Him—to show our grief for what we did to pierce the Savior. "Afflict your souls," O you children of Israel, for the day of atonement is come! Weep over your Jesus! Weep for Him who died; weep for Him who was murdered by your sins! "Afflict your souls."

Then, better still, we are to "do no work at all," as you find in the same verse, the 29th. When we consider the atonement, we should rest, and "do no work at all." Rest from your works as God did from His on the great Sabbath of the world! Rest from your own righteousness, rest from your toilsome duties—rest in Him. "We that believe do enter into rest." As soon as you see the atonement finished, say, "It is done, it is done! Now will I serve my God with zeal; now I will no longer seek to save myself—it is done, it is done forever!"

Then there was another thing which always happened. When the priest had made the atonement, it was usual for him, after he had washed himself, to come out, again, in his glorious garments. When the people saw him, they attended him to his house with joy and they offered burnt offerings of praise on that day—he being thankful that his life was spared, (having been allowed to go into the holy place and to come out of it)— and they being thankful that the atonement was accepted. Both of them offering burnt offerings as a type that they now desired to be "a living sacrifice, holy and acceptable unto God." beloved, let us go into our houses with joy; let us go into our gates with praise. The atonement is finished! The High Priest is gone within the veil—salvation is now complete! He has laid aside the linen garments, and He stands before you with His breastplate, and His miter, and His embroidered vest, in all His glory! Hear how He rejoices over us, for He has redeemed His people, and ransomed them out of the hands of His enemies! Come, let us go home with the High Priest—let us clap our hands with joy, for He lives, He lives! The atonement is accepted and we are accepted, too! The scapegoat is gone; our sins are gone with it! Let us then go to our houses with thankfulness, and let us come up to His gates with praise, for He has loved His people, He has blessed His children and given unto us a day of atonement, and a day of acceptance, and a year of jubilee! Praise the Lord! Praise the Lord!

14

The Day of Atonement

"And this shall be an everlasting statute unto you, to make an atonement for the children of Israel, for all their sins, once a year." (Leviticus 16:34)

W E HAVE TAKEN THESE words for our text. The whole Chapter, however, will have our attention. I must be allowed to say at this time, though I seldom say anything in the way of an apology, that this is not the place, nor would time serve us to go into a full exposition of the very wonderful teaching of this Chapter. If we may ever set any portion of Scripture before another, this is one of the most precious Chapters in the whole compass of Revelation and, in some respects, the most remarkable of all. It is so full of wonderfully deep teaching that, instead of a sermon, it might require a volume! And then, perhaps, we would scarcely have done more than skimmed the surface. And there are difficulties, I may also add, connected with the interpretation—very great difficulties—which have puzzled the most learned of the Reformed and of the Puritan divines. I do not at all attempt to solve those difficulties, nor profess that all I say might be able to support and carry out. I desire to give, instead of any attempt at criticism or deep explanation, a simple exposition of this Chapter, bringing out of it, I hope, some Truths of God which, if they do not belong to the Chapter, are, nevertheless, exceedingly precious ones and will, I hope, be useful to us all.

In a remarkable way God dealt with Israel in the wilderness. There were special tokens of His peculiar Presence, as in the cloudy and fiery pillars which were the emblems of His Presence, and in the bright light called the Shekinah, which shone between the wings of the cherubim which overshadowed the Ark. But God cannot dwell where there is sin. He is a holy Being. "Holy, holy, holy, Lord God of Hosts," is the song which continually rises into His ears. In order, then, that He might dwell in the midst of Israel without compromising His Character, He was pleased to appoint one day in the year which was called "the Day of Atonement," which should be considered to purify the camp and make it fit to be the dwelling place of Jehovah.

Now, God has promised that He will dwell among men, and He does dwell among His own people at this very time. He dwells with them in a remarkable way. "The Lord is my portion," says my soul. God is the heritage, the Friend, the Companion of all His people, but because of their sin He cannot dwell with these believing men unless an Atonement is made. The annual atonement among the Jews was the picture of the great Atonement—but the real Atonement, the effectual Expiation which, not once a year, but once and for all, the Lord Jesus Christ has offered— now renders it possible for God to walk with men and dwell among them!

In the ceremony of the atonement, in the Chapter before us, there are four things that struck me.

The first is—I. *The way in which that remarkable ceremony set forth the sacrifice made to God's honor.*

My Brothers and Sisters, the offense of man against God was, so to speak, a stain upon God's honor. Man set himself up in rebellion against the Most High! He stood out, therefore, against Divine Sovereignty! He impugned the Divine Love. His offense blasphemed the Divine Wisdom. Every human sin is an attack upon the whole Character and life of God—and sin, itself, is a dishonor done to the glorious attributes of Jehovah. Before God can be reconciled to man and deal with Him at all, except by way of retribution, there must be something done to restore the Divine Honor. Now, we have it declared in this Revelation which comes to us from Heaven, that Christ has fully restored the Divine Glory and that since He suffered on the tree, the Just for the unjust, God can be gracious without a violation of His Justice and He can dwell with us—with us poor fallen creatures—without the marring of the luster of any single one of His attributes! The model man has honored God more fully than sinful man ever dishonored Him! And if God was angry with the race for our sins, He is now towards the race full of tenderness and pity because of the transcendent goodness of the new Head of the race, Christ Jesus our Lord, who has magnified God's Law and made it honorable!

Now, this is the Truth of God that was taught in the first part of the ceremony on the Day of Atonement. It was taught thus. Two goats were brought to the door of the Tabernacle. Lots were cast and the first goat was selected to teach this lesson. The goat was brought by the people. It was their common property. It would not have sufficed—it would not have been of any use at all if it had not been so. Read the Chapter and you will see. Learn from this that the compensation to God's honor for man's sin must come from men. It was a man in the Garden who dared to rebel—it must be a man, another man, who shall honor God's Law so as to set the race in a fresh relationship towards God.

The goat is given by all Israel—the Atonement to God's honor must come out of our race, and hence it is that our Lord is the son of Mary, bone of our bone, flesh of our flesh—qualified, being a Man, to perform the obedience required of man and to right, as a Man for men, the wrongs which man had done to God. Note that first. The goat which was brought was given up to the appointed priest. God will have everything done according to order. The sacrifice must not be left to the whims and fancies of men. So the man who shall offer up the sacrifice to the Divine Honor must be appointed of God, as Aaron was. And so our Lord Jesus Christ was God's chosen One, appointed by God to stand in the gap, and for us to vindicate the Divine Glory which we had tarnished by our iniquities.

This goat, being thus offered, must be presented to God, but there must be something with it. Sweet perfume must be cast upon the live coals and the sweet smell must go up before the Mercy Seat. So before God can ever be satisfied for the wrong done to Him by the Fall and by our common sin, there must be an offering of sweet merits unto Him which, let me say, Jesus Christ has most abundantly offered. He took His hands full of the, most blessed compound of all the graces and all the virtues beaten small, for there was an exact obedience to every jot and tittle of the Divine Law. Christ's obedience was perfect in its kind in the most minute respects—and this merit has been brought before our God, who is a consuming fire, and burns up every evil work. And as He lays hold upon this work of Christ, He makes a sweet smell of it—which is poured out throughout Heaven and earth—"the savor of a sweet odor" in the nostrils of the Most High.

Do not let me cover up, however, what I mean, under the cloak of allegory. I mean this—that if God is to accept our race of men and all that we have done against Him and still deal with us on the footing of mercy—somebody must be found who can be so obedient, so delighting in God's will, that there shall be a sweet offering made, as morally and spiritually acceptable to God's Spirit as sweet perfume is to the nostril of man. And that has been done. When they talk in Heaven of man's sin—if they ever there speak of it and wonder how God can bear with man, some bright seraph speaks of man's perfect obedience, even unto death, and they say to one another, "What man, what man is this?" and they clap their hands with joy as they say, It's He that sat at the right hand of the Father, Jesus Christ, the Son of God, the Son of David."

One man threw down the race, but another Man has lifted us up! One man brought ruin by the Fall—another Man restored it and made the race acceptable to God. If man dishonored God, yet man has more honored Him than he dishonored Him, now that Christ has become the great representative Man!

All the glory of Redemption is greater than ever there could have been of dishonor to God by sin! I believe that God is more honored by the world having sinned, and having been restored by Christ, than He could have been if there had never been sin upon this planet and if a perfectly sinless race had tenanted its bounds!

After this burning of perfume, the goat must die. Nothing could permit the Justice of God to look upon man at all until there had been something more than merit. There must be a penalty. "Die he, or Justice must." Man must die, or God's Justice must die. There must be blood—life poured out for sin. Now, when that goat was put to death and the blood flowed forth into the golden bowl, then, Brothers and Sisters, you saw before your eyes of faith, Jesus Christ put to death upon Calvary. He who needed not to have died, the Perfect One, voluntarily offered Himself up as the Victim to Justice, suffering in His own Person, so as to compensate the Justice of God. Do not imagine that Christ died to placate Divine Vengeance—not at all—but that it is sternly necessary if God is to govern this universe at all, that sin must be punished. The very pillars and the foundations of moral government would, not to say, be shaken, but actually be torn up if sin should be permitted to go unpunished! Now, to vindicate the Justice of God, the sword is drawn and who suffers?

Not the human race. Behold, myriads of the race go streaming up to everlasting felicity. Who suffers, then? Why, a Man so marvelously perfect, and withal, so majestically glorious, that His sufferings are a recompense to God for all that sin had done—and so made an effectual Atonement for all the transgressions that had dishonored God! You will observe that I am speaking in very popular, comprehensive and general terms—and designedly so because I believe I am speaking the Infallible Truth of the mind of God! So far as God is concerned, the Atonement that Christ made was universal in its worth and efficacy!

So far as the vindication of the Justice of God and all His other attributes are to be considered, that vindication was absolutely complete. And whether one man had been saved, or 50 men saved, or all saved, or none saved, it would have made no difference. The work was done! God's honor was clear! God's attributes were glorified—and this was perfectly done by the putting away of Christ.

Once more. The blood was sprinkled on the Mercy Seat seven times. That was typical of Christ, who goes up into Heaven in His own proper Person and there displays before God, the holy angels and elect spirits, the tokens of His passion, the ensign of His suffering, taking the blood up to God that henceforth when the Eternal Mind thinks of sin and the dishonor done to God by sin, it might think of the sufferings of the blessed Man, Christ Jesus, and see how all dishonor is forever put away! You know, when you are reading Scripture, dear Friends, you find a great many passages which speak about Christ's dying for all men, and about God's having reconciled the world unto Himself.

And I know you are apt to say to me, "You teach us Particular Redemption—that Christ only died as a Substitute for some men." That I always say, and stand to—and believe to be a Biblical Doctrine! But do I, therefore, clip away other texts? No, not in any degree! I believe them as they stand. I count it treason to try and clip a text, or to make it say the contrary of what it does say! So far as God's honor was concerned, the death of Christ for men so obliterated human sin as such that God could, without dishonor to Himself, deal with mankind. Hence it is that the wicked live! Hence it is that they enjoy innumerable mercies! Hence it is that there is a good, strong, substantial ground for offering the Gospel to every man—and a righteous reason for commanding every man to believe in Jesus Christ that he may be saved!

This was the first teaching of the day of atonement and every Jew, when he saw, ought to have understood the presentation of that blood within the veil, that now God no longer looked on the race as being a race that He must curse and must destroy, but looked upon it with mercy and was prepared to treat it on the footing of tenderness. And that now there was a Gospel presented to the sons of men. Oh, I do so love this thought, that my sin, which did dishonor to God, which did as much as say that He was not a good God, that it was better for me to hate Him than to love Him, better for me to be His enemy than to be His friend, made out as though His Commandments were grievous and that it gave me pleasure to break them—all the mischief towards God that my sin could ever do is all put away by the holy life and the blessed death of Christ Jesus my Lord—and put away forever, forever, forever—so that God can now deal with me on the terms of Divine Grace!

But my time flies and, therefore, I come to the next point—

II. *Sin is now utterly driven away.*

There was another goat—and this goat was to live and not to die—which set forth quite another Truth of God. I do not think the common explanation of this is at all correct. And all the expositors I have met with are clear that it is not correct. Some have said that the scapegoat typifies our Lord Jesus bearing our sins away in His Resurrection and ascending into Heaven. The incongruity of the metaphor has always struck me, but there are reasons in the Hebrew text which prevent our believing that

that could have been the meaning of it. The living goat was taken by a fit man right away into the wilderness and there it was left. What became of it afterwards, we do not know. Painters have depicted it as expiring in the midst of desolation, in the agonies of famine—a mere fancy picture! The scapegoat did not, very probably, die sooner than any other goat—and it is not at all necessary that it should. We never need enlarge a topic beyond what Scripture says. Indeed, there is often as much teaching in a type's stopping short as there is in its going on!

These two goats had each its name. One was said to be for Jehovah—that represents Christ, I say, as making recompense to God's honor! The other is said to be for Azazel, which, if I understand it at all, means, "for evil." What? Then was that other goat offered to the Devil? By no means! He is not evil, but one of the ministering spirits in the service of evil. Evil made Satan what he is. He is its slave, its chief plotter and schemer, but still not evil, itself! Did you ever notice—you must have noticed—that the wrong of evil, the sinfulness of sin, even if it were forgiven, works nothing but evil, so that if God were to forgive us all, but leave the evil in us, we should be in Hell for all that because evil of itself holds Hell and works towards its being realized by us. Evil is, in itself, essentially misery—it has only to work itself out and it will be so.

Now, how am I to get rid of this sin that is in me as to the evil consequences inherent in the evil? Suppose God to be perfectly reconciled to me so far, yet still there is an evil that mischief brings upon me in itself, apart from God—and how do I get rid of that? Why, through the scapegoat! The sin of the people was, first of all, transferred to this scapegoat—all confessed and all laid on the scapegoat. Then, by Divine appointment, the scapegoat, being chosen by lot and the lot being guided by God, it was accepted as being the substitute for the people. The scapegoat was then taken away. And what was done with it? Why, nothing was done with it but this—it was relinquished—it was given up!

259

Now, can I get out what I mean? I am very much afraid I cannot. Our Lord Jesus Christ took upon Himself the sin of His people. And He was given up to evil, that is to say, to all the power that evil could put out against Him—first in the wilderness, tempted from all quarters, tempted by the temptations of Satan. And then in the Garden, tempted in such a way as you and I never were—the powers of evil let loose upon Him as they never were upon us! Did He not say, "This is your hour, and the power of darkness?" And so dreadful was the assault of evil upon Him, the devil going forth as the type and incarnation of evil, that He sweat, as it were, great drops of blood falling to the ground! And while especially on the tree, where the conflict reached its climax, was He given up.

That cry, "My God! My God! Why have You forsaken Me?" is like the cry of the goat when it is given up, quite given up, and led away. Evil was permitted to work out in Him all its own dread and havoc, to which it must bring our spirits, unless God interposes to stop evil from making the soul become unutterably wretched, even unto death. I do not know how to get out the thought which seems to be in my soul, but I do rejoice to think that all the evil I have ever done shall not go on to plague and vex me because it has vexed and plagued Him. That all the essential misery that lies in my past sin—which must, even if God forgave it, still come back to sting and torment me throughout all my existence—was so laid on Him and so spent all its force and venom on Him who was given up to it, that it will never touch me again!

You know, Brothers and Sisters, there was no other man who could have borne all that power of evil but our Lord. And it all fell on Him and yet it never stained His matchless purity and perfection of Character. The misery of it came to Him, but the guilt of it could never defile Him! The misery of sin spent itself on the lonely One who was given up to its awful force, but it could do no more. The type says nothing about the scapegoat, whether it died or not, and Christ did not die because of the misery of His spirit—He died for quite another reason and in another sense—laying down His life for His people!

There is something, I think, interesting in this if we can carry it out, but there is this to be said—by that scapegoat being thus given up, the sin of the congregation was taken away—all taken away and all gone. And so, through Jesus Christ having borne our sicknesses and carried our sorrows, the whole force and power of evil to do damning mischief against a saint has been taken away forever from everyone of us who have laid our hands, by faith, upon His dear and blessed head. It is gone! The sin is gone, gone into the wilderness, where it shall never be found against us any more forever.

I must hasten on, however, for time flies. There was yet a third part of this expiation. Did you notice it? It is a grand thing when we can see God's honor clear. It is a grand thing, next, when we can see ourselves clear as to the effects of evil by Christ's taking evil quite away. The third grand thing is to see—

III. *Sin, itself, made the subject of contempt.*

God cannot dwell with us if sin is petted and loved. Sin must be detested and loathed. Now, read on in the Chapter and you will find that the bullock and the goat which were there, and whose blood was taken into the Holy Place, were afterwards burned outside the camp—see the 27th verse. They were burned, and burned with ignominy, burned outside the camp in the common sewer, the kennel of the camp—and burned, too, under circumstances that imply disgust. "They shall burn in the fire, their skins and their flesh, and their dung"—put in purposely to show what a contempt was to be put upon the beasts that had been, for a while, made to take and to typify sin!

That burning outside the camp looked to a stranger like the burning of a heap of rubbish. There was a foul smell of the burning flesh and refuse. Persons, as they passed turned their heads away to avoid the terrible odor. They would say, "What is all this?" "Why, this was a sin-offering, and when the blood, which God accepted, had gone, this was what was left—the filth of sin—and the people were just being taught how they should hate, loathe and destroy it! Every man that touched it washed himself! And no man could touch any of these things that day without bathing again and again, the thing was so detestable!

Now, in the Person of our blessed Lord, sin is made most detestable. Did you ever really hate sin until you learned to love Christ? I will ask you when do you hate sin the most? Why, when you love Christ the most! I believe you shall always find that in proportion as you understand and see the work of Christ, you will see in that work, as in a glass, that Christ has made sin to be the most loathsome and disgusting thing that was ever heard of, for what do the angels say—"Man sinned, did he? Oh, foolish man, to sin against his God and his Maker!" "Ah," says one of the angels, "but he did worse than that—he sinned against the God that loved him so, that He would sooner let His Only-Begotten Son die than poor man should perish!" "Oh," they say, "what a shameful thing to sin against so dear and kind a God!" If God were a ty- rant, it might not seem atrocious to rebel against Him. But when He becomes so dear and tender a Father as to give His Only-Begotten Son—away with you, Sin! Talk of the Devil! He is not black compared with you, O Sin— you are the Devil's tempter, the Devil's ruin! You make him black. It is sin, sin that is so foul a thing that I can liken it unto nothing! There is nothing on earth, there is nothing anywhere in Hell that can be likened unto it! Sin is made to appear exceedingly sinful and loathsome to the uttermost degree through the Expiatory Sacrifice of Jesus Christ!

Now, these are three grand things for God to have done in this world—after man sinned to have made His name as glorious as ever. After man's sin, to have set pardoned man straight, as straight as ever from his sin. And after that, to have made sin which came with the apple in its hand and which comes every day, now, with painted face, and with the cup in its hand, filled to the brim with sweet wine, seem hateful and to be really so! Oh, it is a grand work, that which Christ has done! Blessed be His name!

Now, the last point—and I shall need your earnest consideration for a minute or two—is this. I must call your attention to—

IV. *The behavior of the people during the whole of that day* in which this wonderful panorama was made to pass before them.

During that day they were to afflict their souls. Do you want to have your sin forgiven? Put away your jollity and your mirth. A repenting sinner had need to be a mourner and, Brothers and Sisters, when sin is put away, how the forgiven sinner afflicts his soul! He is happy! He was never more happy! Never so happy, but how grieved he is to think he ever sinned!—

"My sins, my sins my Savior!
How sad on You they fall!
Seen through your gentle patience,
I tenfold feel them all.

"I know they are forgiven,
But still their pain to me,
Is all the grief and anguish,
They laid, my Lord, on Thee.

"My sins, my sins, my Savior!
Their guilt I never knew,
Till, with You, in the desert,
I near Your passion drew.

"Till with You, in the Garden,
I heard Your pleading prayer,

263

And saw the bloody sweat drops,
That told Your sorrow there."

Oh, there is never, never such affliction of soul for sin as when you see the great Atonement! Let me invite you to hate sin, tonight, you pardoned ones. Take care to do it. And you unpardoned ones, rend your hearts, but not your garments! And turn unto God with afflicted spirits and say, "Lord, through the precious Atonement of which I have heard so much tonight, blot out my sins!"

The next thing concerning the people that day was that they were to do no servile work on that day. There was to be no hewing of wood, no drawing of water—nothing was to be done throughout all the camp by way of labor. So, when a soul comes to the Atonement of Christ, it has done with all its works of righteousness and all its deeds of human merit! You can never have the Atonement of Christ while you are working out your own works and trying to be saved by them. And the Believer that has once come to take Christ to be his Savior will never try to get any merits of his own. Oh, he has thrown away forever the fooleries of self-righteousness! He sees the absurdity of hoping that foul, black hands can ever present a fair, white sacrifice to God. He takes his lord and he has done with his own doings!

Once more—it was to be to the people a Sabbath unto the Lord. That day was not the seventh day of the week, but still it was to be a kind of Sabbath. And what a glorious Sabbath the Atonement always makes! Why, I feel a Sabbath, tonight, apart from the Sabbath Day. I have a Sabbath in my soul, to think that the sin of man has not, after all, done lasting damage to the Throne of God. I feel so happy to think, next, that there is a special sacrifice made for the elect, by the scapegoat's having taken away their sin, so that the evil of their sin will never come on them. I feel so thankful, tonight, to think that God has made sin to appear to be exceedingly sinful. These three grand things ring a peal of bells in my soul, for now I feel content—for God is satisfied to come to God—and I can see why He should let me come to Him.

I can understand now how it is that He should let a fallen creature hold converse with His thrice holy Self after His great work is done! And it is better for me, and better for you, that we should come to God by so good and reasonable, and proper, and glorious a way—rather than that we should have been permitted, had it been possible, to come by any breach of the Law, or by any setting aside of the Divine Command.

I do not think I would have been happy had it been possible for me to go to Heaven, and God's honor had thereby been sullied, for God's honor is the very happiness of a reconciled creature! And if that had suffered any loss through me, I would have been miserable. But it shall suffer no loss or stain! Christ has completely undone the mischief of the Fall! Glory be to His blessed name for this!

And now, Beloved in the Lord, I wish that I could speak in the name of you all and accept the Man, Christ Jesus, tonight, as our representative. Remember, though He has done this much for us all, that God can dwell with us, yet He has not taken the sin of us all upon Himself, but only of so many as stand and confess their sin and trust it with Him. Come, will you do it? Poor Sinner, will you do it for the first time tonight? Backslider, will you do it again? You Believers that have lost some of your evidences, will you do it anew tonight? Oh, I wish I could now say these words and you could all say, "Amen," from your hearts—

> "My faith does lay her hand
>   On that dear head of Thine,
> While, like a penitent I stand,
>   And here confess my sin."

265

Well, if you won't have Christ for your Savior, I will have Him for mine! And there are thousands of you here who will say, "Yes, and He shall be mine, too!" The longer I live, the more I love to rest upon Him. I did try to rest somewhere else, once, but the dream is over and now the more I think of my Lord, the more firm I feel the conviction that He is a rock that will bear the weight of my salvation! The more I think of what that glorious Man, that blessed Son of God, who is as much God as He is Man, has done for me, the more do I feel that if I had fifty thousand times the sin I have, I would rest on Him! And if I were as wicked as all men put together, I would rest on Him, still, believing that no amount of sin could outweigh His merit and that no extent of iniquity could ever surpass the infinite bounds of His eternal Grace. He is able to save to the uttermost them that come to God by Him! Come to God by Him, poor Sinner, and may God the Holy Spirit lead you, and He shall have the glory! Amen, and Amen.

15

A Plain Man's Sermon

"It must be perfect to be accepted; there shall be no defect in it." (Leviticus 22:21)

THE CEREMONIAL LAW, as ordained by the hand of Moses and Aaron, called the worshippers of God to great carefulness before Him. Before their minds that solemn Truth was always made visible, "I the Lord your God am a jealous God." Nothing might be done thoughtlessly. Due heed was the first requisite in a man who would draw near unto the Thrice-Holy God, whose perfections demand lowly and considerate reverence from all those who are round about Him. The spirit must be awake and on the stretch if it would please the great Father of Spirits. There were little points—I may truthfully call them minute—upon which everything would depend as to right worship and its acceptance with the Lord. No Israelite could come to the tabernacle door aright without thinking of what he had to do and thinking it over with an anxious fear lest he should, by omission or error, make his offering into a vain oblation. He must draw near unto the Lord with great carefulness, or else he might miss his aim, spend his money upon a sacrifice, cause labor to the priest and go home unaccepted. He might duly perform a large portion of a ceremony and yet no good might come to him through it because he had omitted a point of detail—for the Lord would be sought according to the due order—or He would not be found by the worshipper. Of every ceremony it might be said, "It must be perfect to be accepted." There was the rule and the rule must be followed with the most careful exactness. God must have the minds and thoughts of men, or He counts that they are no worshippers!

This is no easy lesson to learn, dear Friends for I am afraid that in our usual worship we are not always as thoughtful as we ought to be. Mark well our singing. Do we join in it with the heartiness, the solemnity and the correctness which are due to Him who hears our Psalms and hymns? I may not judge, but I have my suspicions. Look at the way we pray. Is it not to be feared that at times we rush into God's Presence and utter the first words that come to hand? Are not liturgies repeated with minds half asleep? Are not extempore prayers uttered in the most formal manner? I refer both to public and private prayer. Moreover, look at the style in which some will even preach. With facility of language they will deliver themselves of their own thoughts, without seeking the anointing from on high and the power of the Spirit of God! I do not say that any of you ever go into your Sunday school classes without thought. I do not say that any of you ever take your tract district and go from door to door without seeking a blessing. I will not say that any of you ever come to the Communion Table without examining yourselves and discerning the Lord's body. But if I do not say it, I may think it and possibly that thought may be true!

O, my Brothers and Sisters, let conscience sit in judgment and decide this matter! We need to think a great deal more about how we come before the Most High! And if we thought more and prayed more, we would become more certain of our inability to do anything as we ought to do it—and we Would be driven to a more entire dependence upon the Spirit of God in every act of worship! This in itself would be a great blessing.

I do not know, however, that the Ceremonial Law did make men thoughtful since, for the most part, it failed of its designed effect through the hardness of men's hearts. Earnest heed was the design of it, but superstition and a spirit of bondage were the more usual results. Brethren, without a multitude of ceremonies which might become a yoke to us, let us, by other means, arrive at the same and even a better thoughtfulness of heart! Let love to God so influence us that, in the least and most ordinary matters, we shall behave ourselves as in the immediate Presence of the Lord and so shall strive with the utmost watchfulness of holy care to please the Lord our God.

The Ceremonial Law also engendered in men who did think, a great respect for the holiness of God. They could not help seeing that God required everything in His service to be of the very best.

The priest who stood for them before God must be, himself, in bodily presence, the perfection of manhood. When old age crept upon him, he must give place to one who showed no such sign of decay. His garments must be perfectly white and clean in his daily service. And when once a year there was a joy day, then for glory and beauty he shone in all the radiance that the purest gold and the most precious stones could put upon him!

The victims that were offered must all be without blemish. You are constantly meeting with that demand and it was carried out with rigid care. You meet with a stringent instance in the text, "It must be perfect to be accepted."

Under the Law of Moses, the guilt of sin and the need of atonement were always most vividly brought before the mind of the worshipping Israelite. If you stepped within the Holy Place, everywhere you saw the marks of blood. Our very delicate-minded friends who raise the silly objection that they cannot bear the sound of the word, "blood"—what would they have done if they had gone into the Jewish tabernacle and had seen the floor, the curtain and every article stained like a shambles? How would they have endured to worship where the blood was poured in bowlfuls upon the floor and sprinkled on almost every holy thing? How would they have borne with the continual spattering of blood—all indicating that without shedding of blood there is no remission of sin?

Truly, there can be no approach to a Thrice-Holy God without the remission of sin and that remission of sin must be obtained through the atoning blood! The Israelite, if he thought rightly, must have been deeply aware that he served a God who was terrible out of His holy places, a God who hated sin and would by no means spare the guilty, or pardon man without atonement! All the more would this be sealed home upon the mind of the Israelite by the knowledge that in every case the sacrifice must be unblemished. As he looked on the blood of the victim, he would remember the sacred rule, "It must be perfect to be accepted." He saw in the necessity for a perfect sacrifice, a declaration of the holiness of God. He must have felt that sin was not a trifle—not a thing to be committed, winked at and blotted out—but a thing for which there must be life given and blood shed before it could be removed. And that life and blood must be the life and blood of a perfect and unblemished offering!

Under the Jewish Ceremonial Law, one of the most prominent thoughts, next to a great respect for the holiness of God, would be a deep regard for the Law of God. Everywhere that the Israelite went, he was surrounded by the Law of God. He must not do this and he must do that—the Law was continually before him. Now, Brothers and Sisters, it is a blessed thing to declare the Gospel, but I do not believe that any man can preach the Gospel who does not preach the Law. The book of Leviticus and all the other typical books are valuable as Gospel-teaching to us because there is always in them most clearly the Law of God. The

Law is the needle and you cannot draw the silken thread of the Gospel through a man's heart unless you first send the needle of the Law through the center, to make way for it. If men do not understand the Law of God, they will not feel that they are sinners! And if they are not consciously sinners, they will never value the Sin Offering. If the Ten Commandments are never read in their hearing, they will not know why they are guilty. And how shall they make confession? If they are not assured that the Law is holy, just, good and that God has never demanded of any man more than He has a right to demand, how shall they feel the filthiness of sin, or see the need of flying to Christ for cleansing? There is no healing a man till the Law of God has wounded him! No making him alive till the Law has slain him!

I do pray, dear Friends, that God, the Holy Spirit, may lay the Law of God, like an axe, at the root of all our self-righteousness, for nothing else will ever hew down that Upas tree. I pray that He may take the Law and use it as a mirror, that we may see ourselves in it and discover our spots, blots and all the foulness of our lives—for then we shall be driven to wash until we are clean in the sight of the Lord. The Law is our teacher to bring us to Christ and there is no coming to Christ unless the stern teacher shall lead us there with many a stripe and many a tear.

In this text we have Law and Gospel, too. There is the Law which tells us that the sacrifice must be perfect to be accepted. And behind it there is the blessed hint that there is such an unblemished Sacrifice which is accepted which we may, by faith, bring to God without fear of being rejected. Oh, for Grace to learn both Law and Gospel at this time!

This is the text for our present meditation, "It must be perfect to be accepted." I want to preach this Truth of God right home into every heart by the power of the Spirit of God! If I could be an orator, I would not be. The game of eloquence, with the souls of men for the counters and eternity for the table, is the most wicked sport in the world! I have often wished that there were no such things as rhetoric and oratory left among ministers—and that we were all forced to speak in the pulpit as plainly as children do in their simplicity. Oh, that all would proclaim the Gospel with plain words! I long that all may understand what I have to say.

I would be more simple if I knew how. The way of salvation is far too important a matter to be the theme of oratorical displays. The Cross is far too sacred to be made a pole on which to hoist the flags of our fine language! I want to tell you just things that will make for your peace—things which will save your souls. At least I would declare Truths which, if they do not save you, will leave you without excuse in that dread day when He, whose ambassador I am, shall come to judge both you and me!

I. First, then, *the rule of our text, "it must be perfect to be accepted," may be used to shut out all those faulty offerings on which so many place their confidence.*

It most effectually judges and casts forth as vile, all self-righteousness, although this is the great deceit by which thousands are buoyed up with false hopes! Alas, this is the destroyer of myriads and, therefore, I must speak as with a voice of thunder and with words of lightning! Hearken unto me, you that hope to be accepted of God by your own doings! Look to what will be demanded of you if you are to be accepted on your own merits! "It must be perfect to be accepted; there shall be no defect in it." If you can come up to this rule, you shall be saved by your own righteousness! But if you cannot reach this mark. If you come short in any degree whatever, you will not be accepted! It is not said, "It must be partially good to be accepted." Or, "It must be hopefully good."

No! "It must be perfect to be accepted." It is not written, "It must have no great and grievous blemish," but, "There shall be no defect in it." See you not the height of the standard, the absolute completeness of the model set before you? Let the plummet hang straight and see whether you can build according to it, or, whether, after all, your building is but as a bowing wall and as a tottering fence, altogether out of the perpendicular as tested by this uncompromising text—"It must be perfect to be accepted; there shall be no defect in it."

Why, look, Sirs, you that hope to be saved by your own doings, your nature, at the very first, is tainted! God's Word assures you that it is so! There is evil in your heart from the very beginning, so that you are not perfect and are not without defect! This sad fact spoils all at the very beginning. You are blemished and imperfect! Who can bring a clean thing out of an unclean? Not one!

If the fountain is tainted, shall the streams be pure? Do you think it possible that you, who are a fallen man in your very parentage—in whom there is a bias towards evil—can possibly render perfect service unto God? Your hands are foul! How can your work be clean? How can it possibly be that you should produce sweet fruit when you, as a tree, are of sour stock and of bitter nature? O my Friend, it cannot be that darkness should produce light, nor death bring forth life!

How can your thoughts, words and ways be perfect? And yet all must be perfect to be accepted. Look again for I feel sure that there must have been a blemish somewhere, as matter of fact. As yet you are not conscious of a blemish, or of a fault and, possibly there is some justification for this unconsciousness. Looking upon you, I feel inclined to love you, as Jesus loved that young man who could say of the Commandments, "All these have I kept from my youth up." But I must beg you to answer this question—has there not been a blemish in your motives? What have you been doing all these good things for? "Why, that I might be saved!" Precisely so! Therefore, selfishness has been the motive which has ruled your life. Every self-righteous man is a selfish man! I am sure he is. At the bottom, that is the motive of the best life that is ever lived which is not actuated by faith in Jesus Christ. The Law is,

"You shall love the Lord your God with all your heart, and with all your soul, and with all your mind." But you have loved yourself, and lived for yourself—how, then, can you have kept the first precept of the Law? What has been done by you has been done either out of a servile fear of Hell, or else out of a proud and selfish hope that you would win Heaven by your own merits. These are not love, nor even akin to it! The absence of love is a flaw and a very serious one—it taints and spoils the whole of your life. "It must be perfect to be accepted" and, if the motive is imperfect, then the life is altogether imperfect.

Moreover, it is not only your nature and your motive which are imperfect. My dear Friend, you certainly must have erred somewhere or other, in some act of your life. If you can say that you have served God and man without fault throughout all your days, you can say much more than I would venture to do! The Scripture also is dead against you when it says, "there is none righteous; no, not one." If you can say that in not one action of your life, select what you may, was there anything blameworthy, anything that fell short, anything that could be censured— you say very much more than the best of men have ever claimed for themselves! As for the poor faulty being who now addresses you, I dare not claim that the best deed I have ever done, or the most fervent prayer I have ever prayed could have been accepted in and of itself before God. I know that I have no perfection in my best things, much less in my worst.

Tell me, my Friend, was there not something wrong in your spirit? Was there not a shortcoming in the humility with which you worshipped? Or in the zeal with which you served? Or in the faith with which you prayed? Was there not something of omission, even if nothing of commission? Could not the work have been better done? If so, it is clear that it was not perfect, for had it been perfect it could have been no better. Might you not have lived better than you have lived? Might you not have been more pure, more generous, more upright, more loving, more gentle, more firm, more heavenly- minded than you have been? Then this confession shows that, to some extent, you must have fallen short and, remember, "It must be perfect to be accepted; there shall be no defect in it."

Ah, I am talking very smoothly now, for I am only touching the surface and dealing with guess-work. But I fear there are greater evils underneath, if all were known. I think if I could read all hearts, there is not one here, however self-righteous he may be, who would not have to confess distinct acts of sin. Still, I will keep to the smooth strain and believe that you are as good as you seem to be. Indeed, I have a high opinion of many of you! I know how some of you have lived. You were amiable girls and excellent young women and have grown up to be careful, loving wives and, therefore, you say, "I never did anybody any harm. Surely I may be accepted." Or, perhaps you are quiet young men, blessed with excellent parents and screened from temptation—and so you have never gone into open vice, but have gained a most respectable character. I wish that there were more like you! I am not condemning you—far from it—but I know that your tendency is to think that because of all this, you must, in yourselves, be accepted of God.

Give me your hand and let me say to you, with tears—"It is not so, my Sister! It is not so, my Brother! It must be perfect to be accepted; there must be no defect in it." This is a deathblow to your self-confidence, for there was a time, some day or other in your life, in which you did wrong. What? Have you no hasty temper? Have no quick words escaped from you which you would wish to recall? What? Have you never murmured against God, or complained of His Providence? Have you never been slothful when you ought to have been diligent? Have you never been careless when you ought to have been prayerful? Have you always spoken the truth? Has a lie never fallen from your lips? Can you say that your heart has never desired evil—never imagined impurity?

Remember, the thought of evil is sin! Even a wanton desire is a blemish in the life and an unchaste imagination is a stain upon the character in the sight of God, though not in the sight of man! "It must be perfect to be accepted."

I verily used to think concerning myself that I was a quiet, good, hopeful lad, addicted much to reading, seldom in brawls and doing nobody any harm. Oh, it was the outside of the cup and the platter I had seen! And when I was led by Grace to look inside, I was astonished to see what filthiness was there! When I heard in my heart that sentence of the Law of God, "It must be perfect to be accepted," I gave up all hope of self-righteousness! And now I hate myself for having doted upon such a lie that I could be acceptable with God in myself!

Have you never gone to live in an old house which looked like new? You had fresh paint, varnish and paper in superabundance—and you thought yourself dwelling in one of the sweetest of places—until, one day, it happened that a board was taken up and you saw under the floor. What a gathering of every foul thing! You could not have lived in that house at peace for a minute had you known what had been covered up! Rottenness had been hidden, decay had been doctored, death had been decorated! That is just like our humanity. We put on fresh paper, varnish and paint—and we look very respectable. But from below an abomination of the sewer gas of sin comes steaming up, enough to kill everything that is like goodness within us—while all manner of creeping lusts and venomous passions swarm in the secret corners of our nature! When lusts are quiet, they are still there. The best man in this place, who is not a believer in Christ, would go mad if he were to see himself as God sees him! No eyes could bear the horrible sight of the Hell within the human breast! Yes, I mean you good people—you very nice, amiable, lovable sort of people! You will have to be born again and you will have to give up all trust in yourselves, as much as even the worst of men must do! As surely as the chief of sinners are unaccepted, so surely are you—for a righteousness must be perfect to be accepted, there must be no defect in it—and that is not the case with your righteousness. You know it is not.

"Well," says one, "this is very hard doctrine." I mean it to be so, for I love you too well to deceive you! When a door has to be shut to save a life, there is no use in half-shutting it! If a person may be killed by going through it, you had better board it up, or brick it up. I want to brick up the dangerous opening of self-confidence, for it leads to deception, disappointment and despair! The way to Heaven by works is only possible to a man who is absolutely perfect—and none of you are in that condition. Do not pretend to it, or you will be arrant liars! I put no fine face upon it—you are not perfect, no, not one of you, for, "all have sinned and come short of the Glory of God."

Thus, then, our text shuts out all self-righteousness. It also shuts out all priestly performances. There is a notion among some people that the priest is to save them, alias the minister, for men easily, in these charitable days, make even Dissenting ministers into priests! I have heard people say, "Just as I employ a lawyer to attend to my temporal business and I do not bother my head any more about it, so I employ my priest or my clergyman to attend to my spiritual business and there is the end of it." This is evil talk and ruinous to the man who indulges in it! I will speak of this priest craft very plainly. Remember, "It must be perfect to be accepted," therefore all that this gentleman does for you must be perfect. I do not know what it is that he does, I am sure. I never could make out what a priest of the Roman or Anglican order can be supposed to do in his highest function of the "mass." I have seen him walk this way and I have seen him walk that way—and I have seen him turn his back—and it has been decorated with crosses and other embellishments! And I have seen him turn his face and I have seen him bow—and I have seen him drink wine and water—and I have seen him munch wafers. I have seen him perform many genuflections and prostrations, but what the performance meant, I have not been able to gather! To me it seemed a meaningless display.

I would not like to risk my soul on it, for, suppose that during that service he should think of something that he ought not to think upon? And suppose he should have no intention whatever of performing the "mass"—what, then, becomes of those who trust in him and it? Everything, you know, depends upon the intention of the priest. If a good intention is not there, according to the dictates of his own church, it is all good for nothing, so that your souls all hang upon the intention of a poor mortal in a certain dress! Perhaps he has not, after all, been rightly anointed and is not in the apostolic succession? Perhaps there is no apostolic succession! Perhaps the man, himself, is living in mortal sin! Ah, me, there are many dangers about your confidence! Are you going to hang your soul on that man's orders or disorders? Mine is too heavy to hang upon so slender a nail, driven into such rotten wood! If you have a soul big enough to think, you will feel, "No, no, there cannot be sufficient ground of dependence in the best pontiff that ever officiated at an altar. God requires of me, myself, that I bring to Him a perfect Sacrifice, and it is all a device of my folly that I should try and get a sponsor and lay this burden on him. It cannot be done. I have to stand before the judgment bar of God in my own person, to be tried for the sins that I have done in the body—and I must not deceive myself with the idea that another man's performance of ceremonies can clear me at the Judgment Seat of Christ. This man cannot bring a perfect sacrifice for me and—"it must be perfect to be accepted." O Sirs, do not be deluded by priest craft and sacramentarianism, whether the priest is of the school of Rome or of Oxford—you must believe in the Lord Jesus for yourselves, or you will be lost forever!

This text makes a clean sweep of all other kinds of human confidences. Some are deceived in this way—"Well," they say, "I do not trust in my works, but I am a religious person and I attend the sacrament. And I go to my place of worship pretty regularly. I feel that I must certainly be right. I have faith in Jesus Christ and in myself." In various ways men thus compose an image whose feet are part of iron and part of clay. With that kind of mingle-mangle, many are unconsciously contenting themselves. But hear this Word of God—"It must be perfect to be accepted; there shall be no defect in it." If we trust Christ and nothing else, that will be perfect! But if you are trusting Christ up to 15 ounces in the pound and yourself for the last ounce of the 16, you will be a lost man, for that last ounce is an ounce of imperfection and, therefore, you cannot be accepted of God!

There are some others who say, "I have suffered a great deal and that will make amends." There is a current idea among men that all will go well with poor people and hard-working people because they have had their bad times here on earth. When a man has had a long illness and suffered a great deal in the hospital, his friends say, "Poor soul, he has gone where he is better off!" They feel sure of it because he has suffered so much! Ah, me, but, "It must be perfect to be accepted"—and what is there perfect in a human life, even if it is checkered with suffering, poverty and need? Ah, no! Poverty does not work perfection! Sickness does not make perfection! My text stands like a cherub, waving a fiery sword before the gates of Paradise, shutting out all fancies and notions, of which I will not now speak particularly, by this dread sentence—"It must be perfect to be accepted; there shall be no defect in it."

II. This brings me to note, with great delight of heart, that as this rule shuts out all other confidences, *so this rule shuts us up to the sacrifice of Jesus Christ.* O Beloved, if I had the tongues of men and of angels, I could never fitly tell you of Him who offered Himself without spot unto God, for He is absolutely perfect—there is no defect in Him!

He is perfect in His Nature as God and Man. No stain defiled His birth, no pollution touched His body or His soul. The Prince of this world, himself, with keenest eyes, came and searched the Savior, but he found nothing in Him. "In all points tempted like as we are, yet without sin." There was not the possibility of sinning about the Savior—no tendency that way, no desire that way. Nothing that could be construed into evil ever came upon His Character. Our perfect Sacrifice is without spot, or wrinkle, or any such thing!

As He was perfect in His Nature, so was He in His motive. What brought Him from above but love to God and man? You can find no trace of ambition in Christ Jesus. In Him there is no thought of self. No sinister or sordid motive ever lingered in His breast, or even crossed His mind. He was purity and holiness in the highest degree. Even His enemies have nothing to allege against the purity of the motive of Jesus of Nazareth!

As His Nature was perfect, so was His spirit. He was never sinfully angry, nor harsh, nor untrue, nor idle. The air of His soul was the atmosphere of Heaven rather than of earth. Look at His life of obedience and see how perfect that was. Which Commandment did He ever break? Which duty of relationship did He ever forget? He honored the Law of God and loved the souls of men. He gave the Character of God perfect reflection in His human life. You can see what God is as you see what Christ is. He is perfect, even as His Father who is in Heaven is perfect. There is no redundancy, or excess, or superfluity in His Character, even as there is no coming short in any point.

Look at the perfection of His Sacrifice. He gave His body to be tortured and His mind to be crushed and broken, even unto the agony of death. He gave Himself for us, a perfect Sacrifice. All that the Law could ask was in Him. Stretch the measure to its utmost length and still Christ goes beyond, rather than falls short of the measure of the requirements of justice. He has given to His Father double for all our sins! He has given Him suffering for sin committed and yet a perfect obedience to the Law. The Lord God is well pleased with Him. He rests in the Son of His love and, for His sake He smiles upon multitudes of sinners who are represented in Him. My heart rejoices as I think of Gethsemane, Calvary and of Him who by one offering has perfectly sanctified all who put their trust in Him! "It is finished," He said, and finished it is forever! Our Lord has presented a perfect Sacrifice! "It must be perfect to be accepted"— and it is perfect. "There shall be no defect in it"—and there is no defect in it. Glory be to God Most High!

Now, I want you just to let me stop preaching, as it were, while every man among you brings this Sacrifice to God. By faith take it to be yours. You may. Christ belongs to every Believer. If you trust Him, He is yours! Poor guilty Soul as you are, whether you have been a Christian 50 years or 10 years, or whether you are just now converted, if you believe, you may now come with Christ in your hands and say to the Father, "O my Lord, You have provided for me what Your Law requires—a perfect Sacrifice! There is no defect in it. Behold, I bring it to You as mine!" God is satisfied. What joy! God is satisfied! The Father is well pleased! He has raised Christ from the dead and set Him at His own right hand in the heavenly places in token of that satisfaction!

Let us be satisfied, too! That which contents God may well content me. My Soul, when your eyes are full of tears on account of your sin and your heart is disquieted on account of your infirmities and imperfections, look right away from yourself "to the full Atonement made, to the utmost ransom paid." The offering of Jesus is perfect and accepted! The righteousness of your Lord Jesus is without blemish and you are, "accepted in the Beloved."

That delightful passage in Exodus came flashing up to my mind just now, where the Israelite sprinkled the blood on the lintel and the two side posts. Then he shut the door. He was inside: he did not see the blood any more. The blood was outside upon the posts and he could not see it—but was he safe? Yes, because it is written, "When I see the blood, I will pass over you." It is God's sight of the blood of His dear Son that is the everlasting safeguard of all who are in Christ! Though it is most precious and sweet to me to look at that blood once shed for many for the remission of sins—and I do look at it—yet if ever there should come a dark night to me in which I cannot see it, still, God will see it, and I am safe! I am save because it is written, not, "when you see it," but, "when I see the blood I will pass over you." It is the perfection of the Sacrifice, not your perfection of sight, which is your safeguard! It is the absence of all blemish from the Sacrifice—not the absence of blemish from your faith—that makes you "accepted in the Beloved."

Well, now, as is too often the case, I have run on so much upon the first points that I have not time enough for much more! But I was going to finish up by saying that I address myself, for a minute or two, to Christians, only. Listen, you that follow after righteousness, you that know the Lord! You are saved. You have not, therefore, to bring any sacrifice by way of a sin offering, but you have to bring sacrifices of thanksgiving. It is your reasonable service that you offer your bodies a living sacrifice unto God. If you do this, you cannot bring an absolutely perfect sacrifice, but you must labor to let it be perfect in what is often the Biblical sense of perfection.

Beloved Brothers and Sisters, you must take care that what you bring is not blind, for the blind were not to be offered. You must serve God with a single eye to the Glory of God. If you attend a Prayer Meeting, or teach a class, or preach a sermon, you must not do it with a view to your own selves in any way, or it cannot be accepted! The sacrifice must see—it must be intelligent, reasonable service—having for its objective the Glory of God. It must in that sense be perfect to be accepted.

And as it must not be blind, so it must not be broken. Whenever we serve God, we must do it with the whole of our being, for if we try to serve God with a bit of our nature and leave the rest unconsecrated, we shall not be accepted. Certain professors prefer one class of Christian duties and they neglect others—this must not be. Christ gave "Himself" for you and you must give your whole self to Him. To be acceptable, the life must be entire—there must be complete consecration of every faculty. How is it with you? Have you brought to the Lord a divided sacrifice? If so, He claims the whole.

Next, they were not to bring a maimed sacrifice, that is, one without its limbs. Some people give grudgingly, that is to say they come up to the collection box with a limp. Many serve Christ with a broken arm. The holy work is done, but it is painfully and slowly done. Among the heathen, I believe, they never offered, in sacrifice to the gods, a calf that had to be carried. The reason was that they considered that the sacrifice ought to be willing to be offered and so it must be able to walk up to the altar. Notice in the Old Testament, though there were many creatures both birds and beasts, that were offered to God, they never offered any fish on the holy altar. The reason probably is that a fish could not come there alive. Its life would be spent before it came to the altar and, therefore, it could not render a life unto God. Take care that you bring your bodies a living sacrifice.

I notice that many men are all alive when they are in the shop. The way they talk, the way they call out to the men and the way they bustle everybody about are conclusive evidence that their life is abundant. But when they get into the Church of God, what a difference! There may be life, somewhere or other, but nobody knows where it is! You have to look for it with a microscope. You see no activity, no energy! Oh, that these people would remember, "It must be perfect to be accepted!" That is to say, there must be energy put into it, soul put into it, heart put into it or God will not accept it. We must not bring Him the mere chrysalis of a man, out of which the life has gone, but we must bring before Him our living, worshipping selves if we would be acceptable before Him.

It is then added, "or having a scab." It does not look as though it would hurt the sacrifice much to have a scab, yet there must not be a scab, or spot, or wrinkle, or any such thing. Above all, avoid that big scab of pride. When we feel that we are doing a grand thing and are acting in a most satisfactory manner, we may know that we are not accepted! A sermon wept over is more acceptable with God than one gloried over. That which is given to God with a sigh because you cannot do more—and with the humble hope that he may accept it for Christ's sake, is infinitely superior to that which is bestowed with the proud consciousness that you deserve well of your fellow men, if not of your God.

The sacrifice was not to be scabbed, or to have the scurvy. That is to say, it was to be without any sort of outward fault. I have heard men say, "It is true I did not do that thing well, but my heart was right." That may be, my dear Brother, but you must try and make the whole matter as good as it can be! What a deal of scabbed service our Lord gets! Men try to be benevolent to their fellow creatures with an irritable temper. Certain people try to serve God and write stinging letters to promote brotherly love—and dogmatic epistles in favor of large-mindedness! Too many render to the Lord hurried, thoughtless worship and many more give for offerings their smallest coins and such things as they will never miss! God has many a scurvy sheep brought before Him.

Did you never bring any, my Brother? Did I never bring any? Ah, me! Ah, me! But still, let us mend our ways and, since the Lord Jesus offered Himself without spot, let us try to serve Him with our utmost care. The best of the best should be given to the Best of the best! We sometimes sing—

"All that I am, and all I have."

Oh, that we practiced it as well as sang it! Would God that the best of our lives, the best hours of the morning, the best skill of our hands, the best thoughts of our minds, the very cream of our being were given to our God! But, alas, Christ's cause is sent round to the back door to get the broken meat and, "Mind you do not leave too much meat on the bone," is the kind of instruction that is given to her who hands it out! Christ Jesus is sent to the dung heap for the odds and ends! Cheese parings and candle ends are given to the Missionary Society. Perhaps the statement is too liberal—it would be well if they were! Three-pennies and four-pennies are gracious gifts from struggling tradesmen and poor work people, but they are hardly decent when sent in by folk who spend hundreds of pounds upon their own pleasure! To God's altar we ought to bring the best bullock from the stall and the best sheep from the fold!

I leave you to yourselves to judge whether it is not so. If you are not overhead and ears in debt to the mercy of God in Christ, then it is not so. But if you are debtors to Divine Mercy beyond all compute, you shall, each one, reckon up for himself—"How much owe you unto my Lord?" If it is a debt you can never calculate—then give the Lord, from this day forth—the fullness of your being! May God grant that you and your offerings may be accepted in Christ Jesus! Amen and amen.

Made in the USA
San Bernardino, CA
27 March 2015